*Acclaim for Bryce Ca...*
*and Vanesa R. Del R...*

"A violent piece of 1950s noir…comics' next big *HIT*"

**— USA Today**

"Loved *HIT*…dark, twisted noir"

**— Scott Snyder**

"…a fresh approach to the detective genre…"

**— IGN**

"You may think you've had your fill of L.A. cop stories…But trust me; you haven't heard this one before. Not in the way Bryce and Vanesa tell it."

**— Duane Swierczynski**

"…a captivating crime comic…"

**— The A.V. Club**

"Suspenseful and quirky without being hard to read or impenetrable."

**— Mark Waid**

"…one complicated slice of nasty noir during the golden age of Los Angeles…"

**— Newsarama**

**2014 Harvey Award Nominee**
Best Continuing or Limited Series
*HIT*

**2014 Harvey Award Nominee**
Best Inker
Vanesa R. Del Rey, *HIT*

**2014 Russ Manning Promising Newcomer Award Nominee**
Vanesa R. Del Rey, *HIT*

**2015 Harvey Award Nominee**
Best Graphic Album Previously Published
*HIT: 1955*

**2015 Russ Manning Promising Newcomer Award Nominee**
Vanesa R. Del Rey, *HIT*

# BOOM! STUDIOS

**HIT: 1957, March 2016.** Published by BOOM! Studios, a division of Boom Entertainment, Inc. Hit is ™ & © 2016 Boom Entertainment, Inc. Originally published in single magazine form as HIT: 1957 No. 1-4. ™ & © 2015 Boom Entertainment, Inc. All rights reserved. BOOM! Studios™ and the BOOM! Studios logo are trademarks of Boom Entertainment, Inc., registered in various countries and categories. All characters, events, and institutions depicted herein are fictional. Any similarity between any of the names, characters, persons, events, and/or institutions in this publication to actual names, characters, and persons, whether living or dead, events, and/or institutions is unintended and purely coincidental. BOOM! Studios does not read or accept unsolicited submissions of ideas, stories, or artwork.

A catalog record of this book is available from OCLC and from the BOOM! Studios website, www.boom-studios.com, on the Librarians Page.

BOOM! Studios, 5670 Wilshire Boulevard, Suite 450, Los Angeles, CA 90036-5679. Printed in China. First Printing.

ISBN: 978-1-60886-817-9
eISBN: 978-1-61398-488-8

WRITTEN BY
# BRYCE CARLSON

ILLUSTRATED BY
# VANESA R. DEL REY

COLORS BY
## NIKO GUARDIA

LETTERS BY
## ED DUKESHIRE

COVER & COLLECTION DESIGN BY
## KELSEY DIETERICH
WITH ART BY **VANESA R. DEL REY**

EDITOR
## ERIC HARBURN

**HIT**™ CREATED BY
## BRYCE CARLSON

SPECIAL THANKS TO **P.**

# CHAPTER **ONE**
# SOME THINGS
# **NEVER CHANGE**

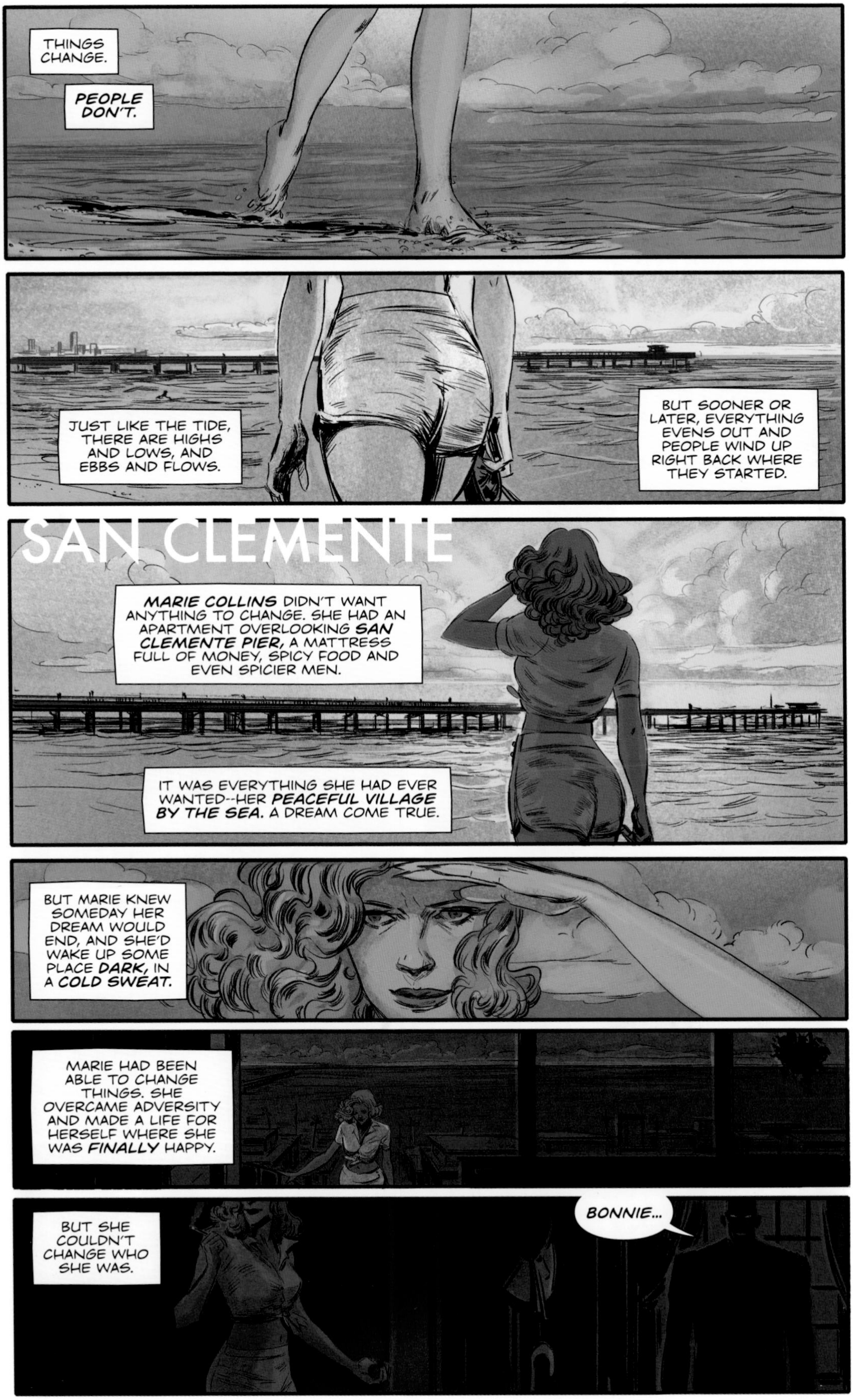
THINGS CHANGE.
PEOPLE DON'T.
JUST LIKE THE TIDE, THERE ARE HIGHS AND LOWS, AND EBBS AND FLOWS.
BUT SOONER OR LATER, EVERYTHING EVENS OUT AND PEOPLE WIND UP RIGHT BACK WHERE THEY STARTED.
SAN CLEMENTE
MARIE COLLINS DIDN'T WANT ANYTHING TO CHANGE. SHE HAD AN APARTMENT OVERLOOKING SAN CLEMENTE PIER, A MATTRESS FULL OF MONEY, SPICY FOOD AND EVEN SPICIER MEN.
IT WAS EVERYTHING SHE HAD EVER WANTED--HER PEACEFUL VILLAGE BY THE SEA. A DREAM COME TRUE.
BUT MARIE KNEW SOMEDAY HER DREAM WOULD END, AND SHE'D WAKE UP SOME PLACE DARK, IN A COLD SWEAT.
MARIE HAD BEEN ABLE TO CHANGE THINGS. SHE OVERCAME ADVERSITY AND MADE A LIFE FOR HERSELF WHERE SHE WAS FINALLY HAPPY.
BUT SHE COULDN'T CHANGE WHO SHE WAS.
BONNIE...

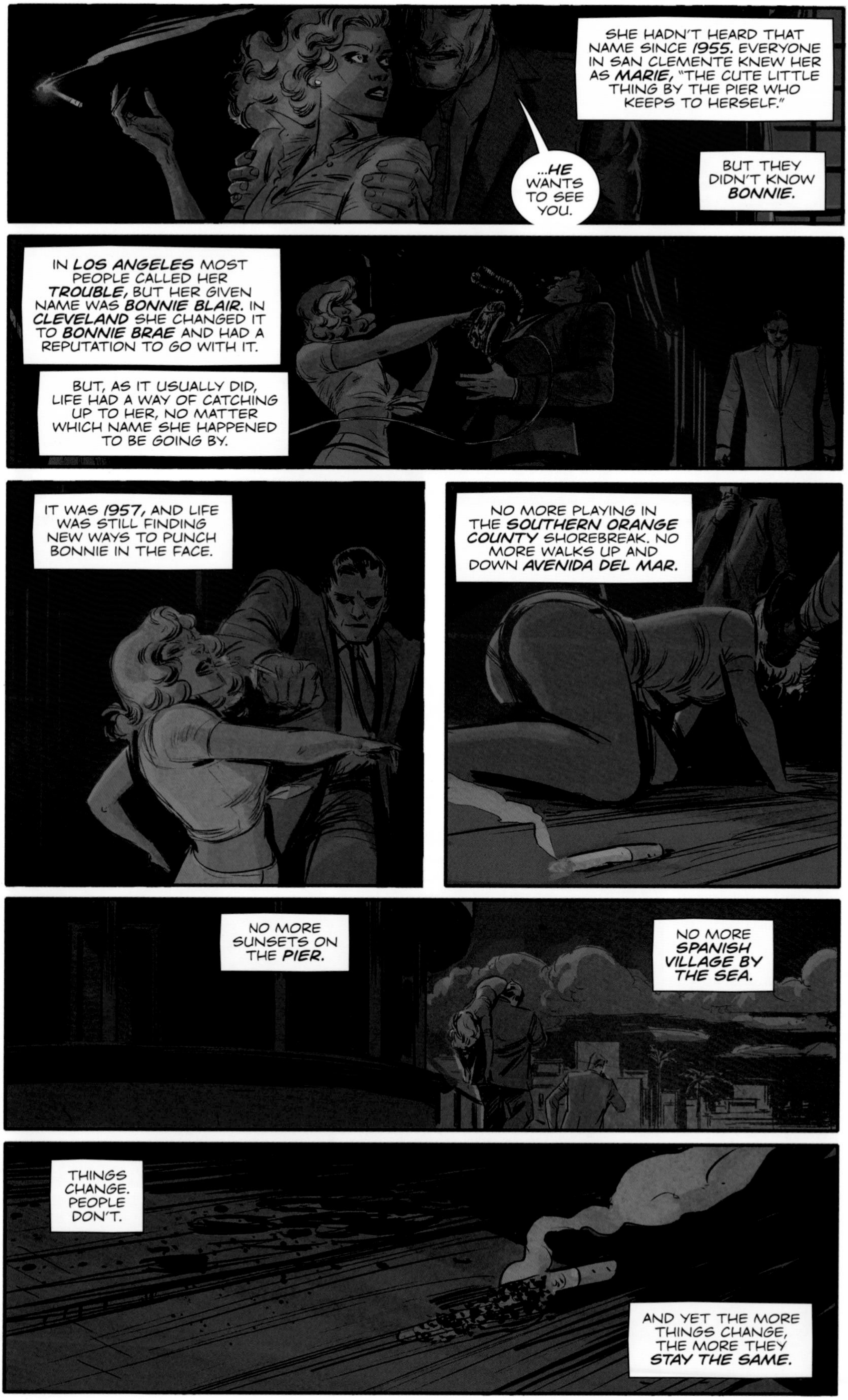
SHE HADN'T HEARD THAT NAME SINCE 1955. EVERYONE IN SAN CLEMENTE KNEW HER AS MARIE, "THE CUTE LITTLE THING BY THE PIER WHO KEEPS TO HERSELF."
...HE WANTS TO SEE YOU.
BUT THEY DIDN'T KNOW BONNIE.
IN LOS ANGELES MOST PEOPLE CALLED HER TROUBLE, BUT HER GIVEN NAME WAS BONNIE BLAIR. IN CLEVELAND SHE CHANGED IT TO BONNIE BRAE AND HAD A REPUTATION TO GO WITH IT.
BUT, AS IT USUALLY DID, LIFE HAD A WAY OF CATCHING UP TO HER, NO MATTER WHICH NAME SHE HAPPENED TO BE GOING BY.
IT WAS 1957, AND LIFE WAS STILL FINDING NEW WAYS TO PUNCH BONNIE IN THE FACE.
NO MORE PLAYING IN THE SOUTHERN ORANGE COUNTY SHOREBREAK. NO MORE WALKS UP AND DOWN AVENIDA DEL MAR.
NO MORE SUNSETS ON THE PIER.
NO MORE SPANISH VILLAGE BY THE SEA.
THINGS CHANGE. PEOPLE DON'T.
AND YET THE MORE THINGS CHANGE, THE MORE THEY STAY THE SAME.

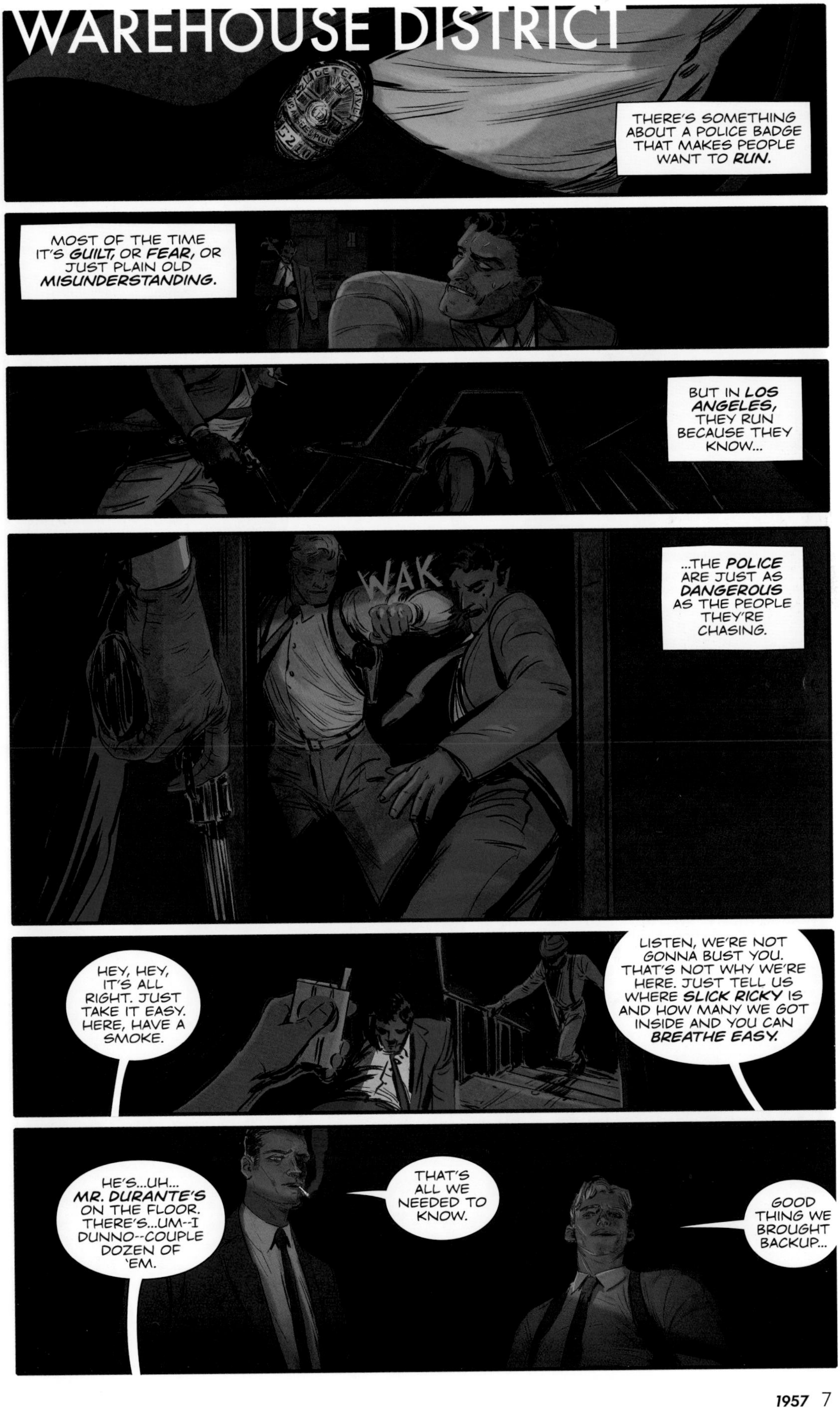
WAREHOUSE DISTRICT
THERE'S SOMETHING ABOUT A POLICE BADGE THAT MAKES PEOPLE WANT TO RUN.
MOST OF THE TIME IT'S GUILT, OR FEAR, OR JUST PLAIN OLD MISUNDERSTANDING.
BUT IN LOS ANGELES, THEY RUN BECAUSE THEY KNOW...
WAK
...THE POLICE ARE JUST AS DANGEROUS AS THE PEOPLE THEY'RE CHASING.
HEY, HEY, IT'S ALL RIGHT. JUST TAKE IT EASY. HERE, HAVE A SMOKE.
LISTEN, WE'RE NOT GONNA BUST YOU. THAT'S NOT WHY WE'RE HERE. JUST TELL US WHERE SLICK RICKY IS AND HOW MANY WE GOT INSIDE AND YOU CAN BREATHE EASY.
HE'S...UH... MR. DURANTE'S ON THE FLOOR. THERE'S...UM--I DUNNO--COUPLE DOZEN OF 'EM.
THAT'S ALL WE NEEDED TO KNOW.
GOOD THING WE BROUGHT BACKUP...

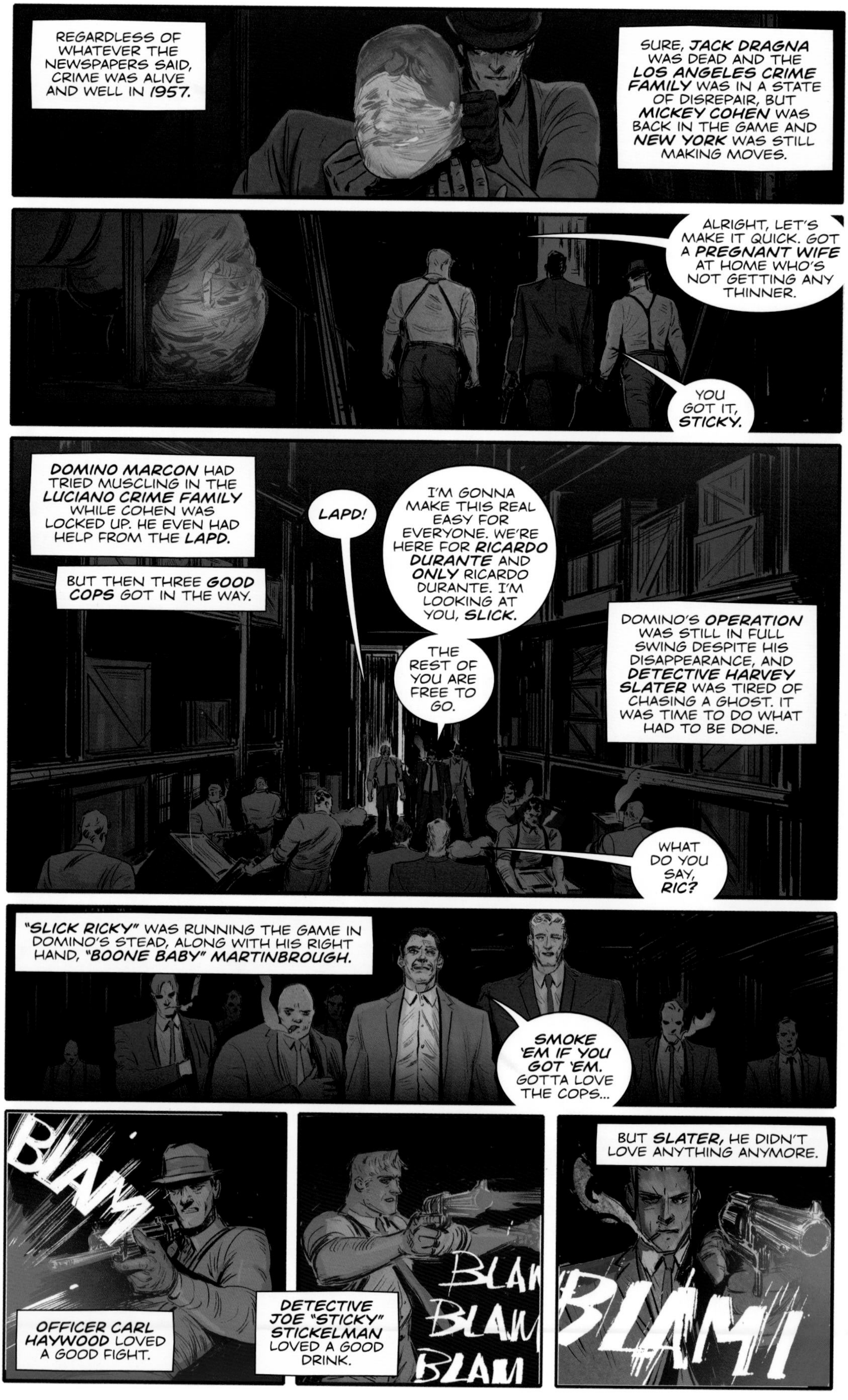
REGARDLESS OF WHATEVER THE NEWSPAPERS SAID, CRIME WAS ALIVE AND WELL IN 1957.
SURE, JACK DRAGNA WAS DEAD AND THE LOS ANGELES CRIME FAMILY WAS IN A STATE OF DISREPAIR, BUT MICKEY COHEN WAS BACK IN THE GAME AND NEW YORK WAS STILL MAKING MOVES.
ALRIGHT, LET'S MAKE IT QUICK. GOT A PREGNANT WIFE AT HOME WHO'S NOT GETTING ANY THINNER.
YOU GOT IT, STICKY.
DOMINO MARCON HAD TRIED MUSCLING IN THE LUCIANO CRIME FAMILY WHILE COHEN WAS LOCKED UP. HE EVEN HAD HELP FROM THE LAPD.
BUT THEN THREE GOOD COPS GOT IN THE WAY.
LAPD!
I'M GONNA MAKE THIS REAL EASY FOR EVERYONE. WE'RE HERE FOR RICARDO DURANTE AND ONLY RICARDO DURANTE. I'M LOOKING AT YOU, SLICK.
THE REST OF YOU ARE FREE TO GO.
DOMINO'S OPERATION WAS STILL IN FULL SWING DESPITE HIS DISAPPEARANCE, AND DETECTIVE HARVEY SLATER WAS TIRED OF CHASING A GHOST. IT WAS TIME TO DO WHAT HAD TO BE DONE.
WHAT DO YOU SAY, RIC?
"SLICK RICKY" WAS RUNNING THE GAME IN DOMINO'S STEAD, ALONG WITH HIS RIGHT HAND, "BOONE BABY" MARTINBROUGH.
SMOKE 'EM IF YOU GOT 'EM. GOTTA LOVE THE COPS...
BLAM
OFFICER CARL HAYWOOD LOVED A GOOD FIGHT.
BLAM
BLAM
BLAM
DETECTIVE JOE "STICKY" STICKELMAN LOVED A GOOD DRINK.
BUT SLATER, HE DIDN'T LOVE ANYTHING ANYMORE.
BLAM!

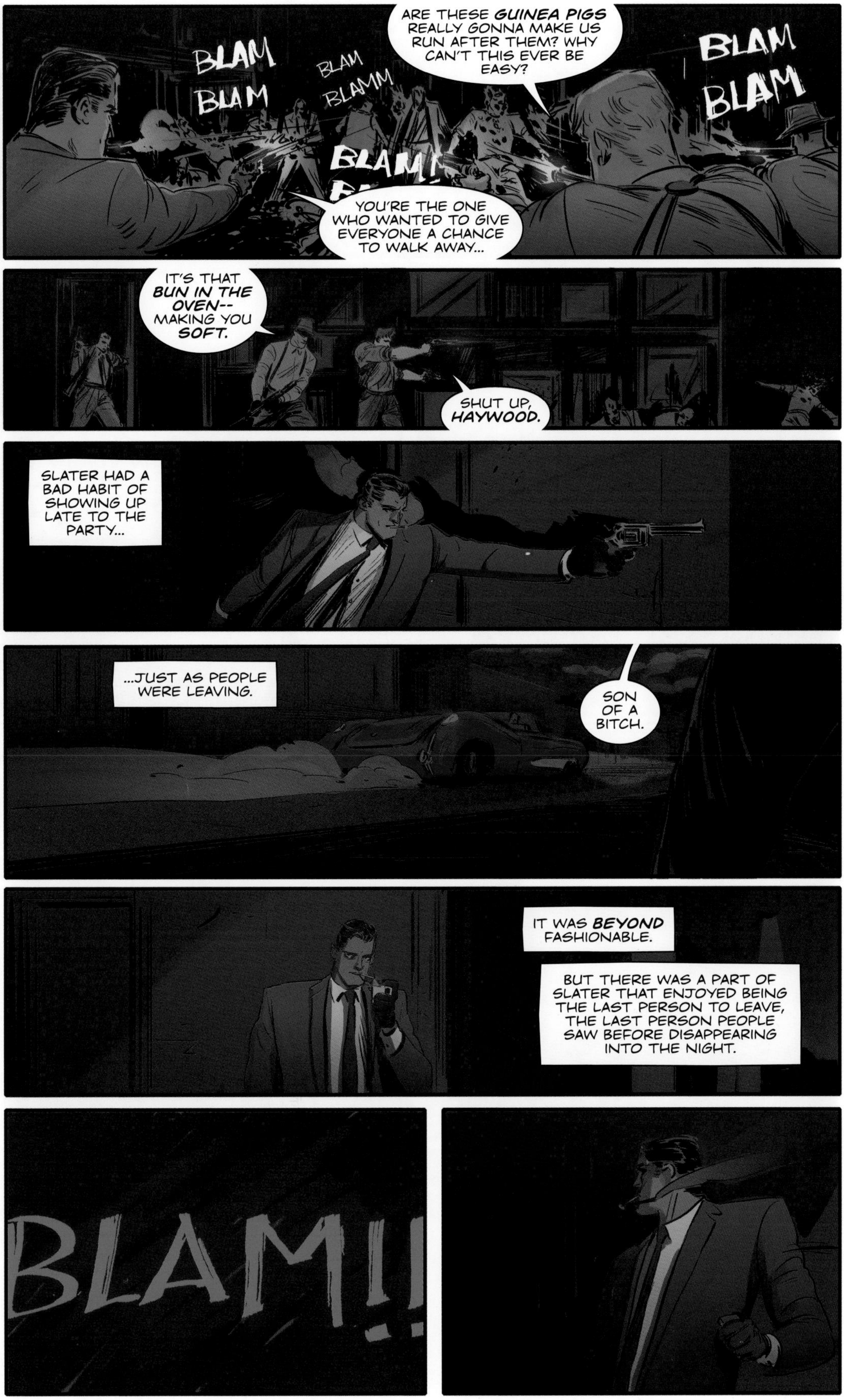
BLAM
BLAM
BLAM
BLAMM
ARE THESE GUINEA PIGS REALLY GONNA MAKE US RUN AFTER THEM? WHY CAN'T THIS EVER BE EASY?
BLAM
BLAM
BLAM
YOU'RE THE ONE WHO WANTED TO GIVE EVERYONE A CHANCE TO WALK AWAY...
IT'S THAT BUN IN THE OVEN-- MAKING YOU SOFT.
SHUT UP, HAYWOOD.
SLATER HAD A BAD HABIT OF SHOWING UP LATE TO THE PARTY...
...JUST AS PEOPLE WERE LEAVING.
SON OF A BITCH.
IT WAS BEYOND FASHIONABLE.
BUT THERE WAS A PART OF SLATER THAT ENJOYED BEING THE LAST PERSON TO LEAVE, THE LAST PERSON PEOPLE SAW BEFORE DISAPPEARING INTO THE NIGHT.
BLAM!!

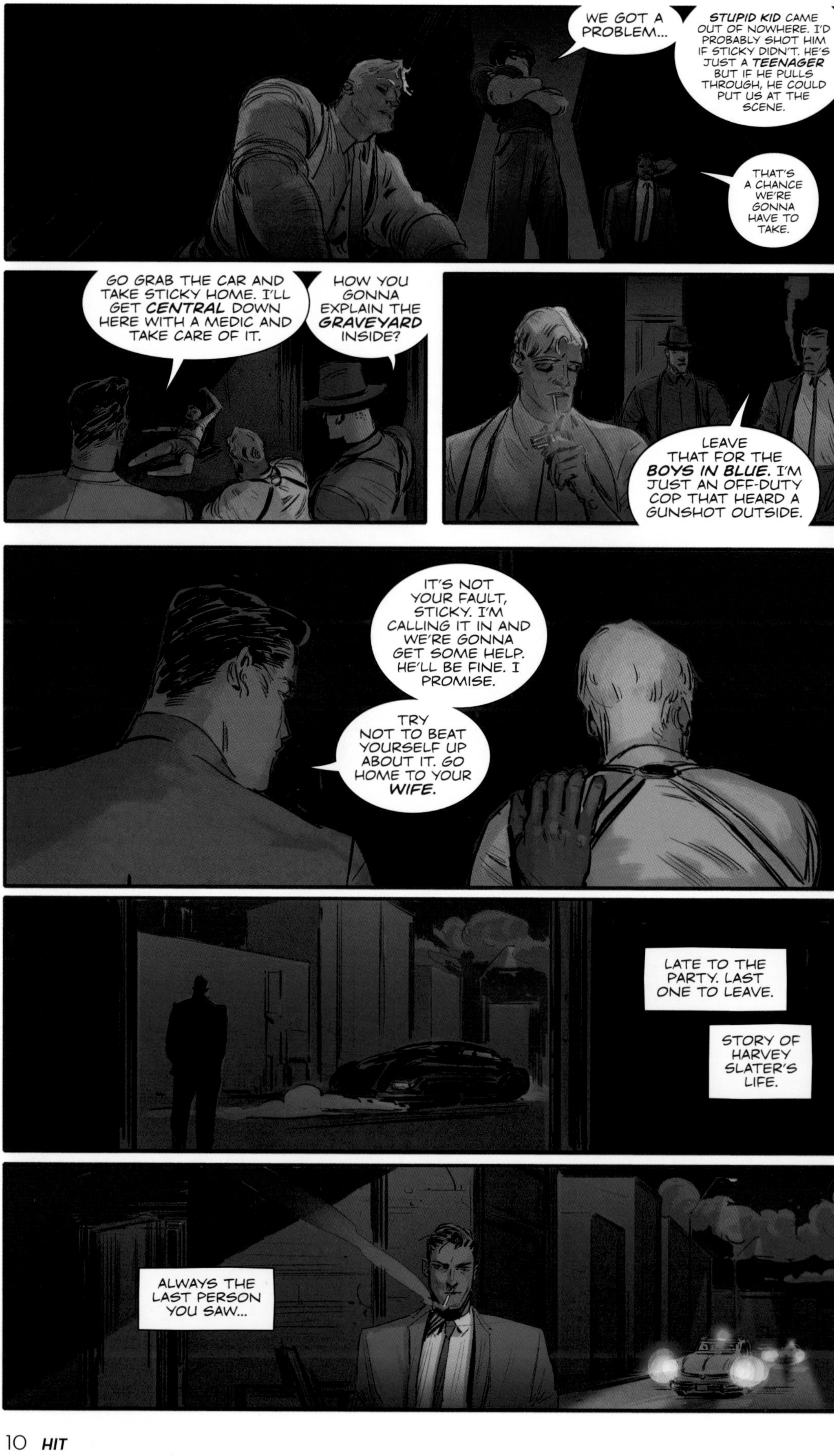

WE GOT A PROBLEM...
STUPID KID CAME OUT OF NOWHERE. I'D PROBABLY SHOT HIM IF STICKY DIDN'T. HE'S JUST A TEENAGER BUT IF HE PULLS THROUGH, HE COULD PUT US AT THE SCENE.
THAT'S A CHANCE WE'RE GONNA HAVE TO TAKE.
GO GRAB THE CAR AND TAKE STICKY HOME. I'LL GET CENTRAL DOWN HERE WITH A MEDIC AND TAKE CARE OF IT.
HOW YOU GONNA EXPLAIN THE GRAVEYARD INSIDE?
LEAVE THAT FOR THE BOYS IN BLUE. I'M JUST AN OFF-DUTY COP THAT HEARD A GUNSHOT OUTSIDE.
IT'S NOT YOUR FAULT, STICKY. I'M CALLING IT IN AND WE'RE GONNA GET SOME HELP. HE'LL BE FINE. I PROMISE.
TRY NOT TO BEAT YOURSELF UP ABOUT IT. GO HOME TO YOUR WIFE.
LATE TO THE PARTY. LAST ONE TO LEAVE.
STORY OF HARVEY SLATER'S LIFE.
ALWAYS THE LAST PERSON YOU SAW...

...BEFORE DISAPPEARING INTO THE NIGHT.

JUST AS BONNIE HAD EXPECTED.

DARK. COLD SWEAT.

NNNGGHHH...

USUALLY WHEN SHE WAS TIED UP IT WAS *CONSENSUAL* AND WITH SOMETHING A LITTLE EASIER ON THE WRISTS THAN *ROPE.*

RIP

RIP

LUCKILY, BONNIE KNEW WHAT SHE WAS DOING WHEN THE LIGHTS WERE OFF.

BUT THEN SHE HAD TO DO SOMETHING SHE WASN'T USED TO.

SIT TIGHT AND WAIT.

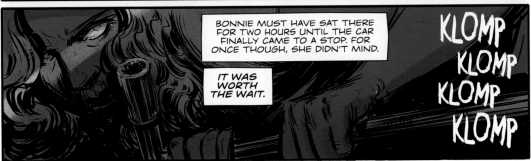

BONNIE MUST HAVE SAT THERE FOR TWO HOURS UNTIL THE CAR FINALLY CAME TO A STOP. FOR ONCE THOUGH, SHE DIDN'T MIND.

IT WAS WORTH THE WAIT.

KLOMP

KLOMP

KLOMP

KLOMP

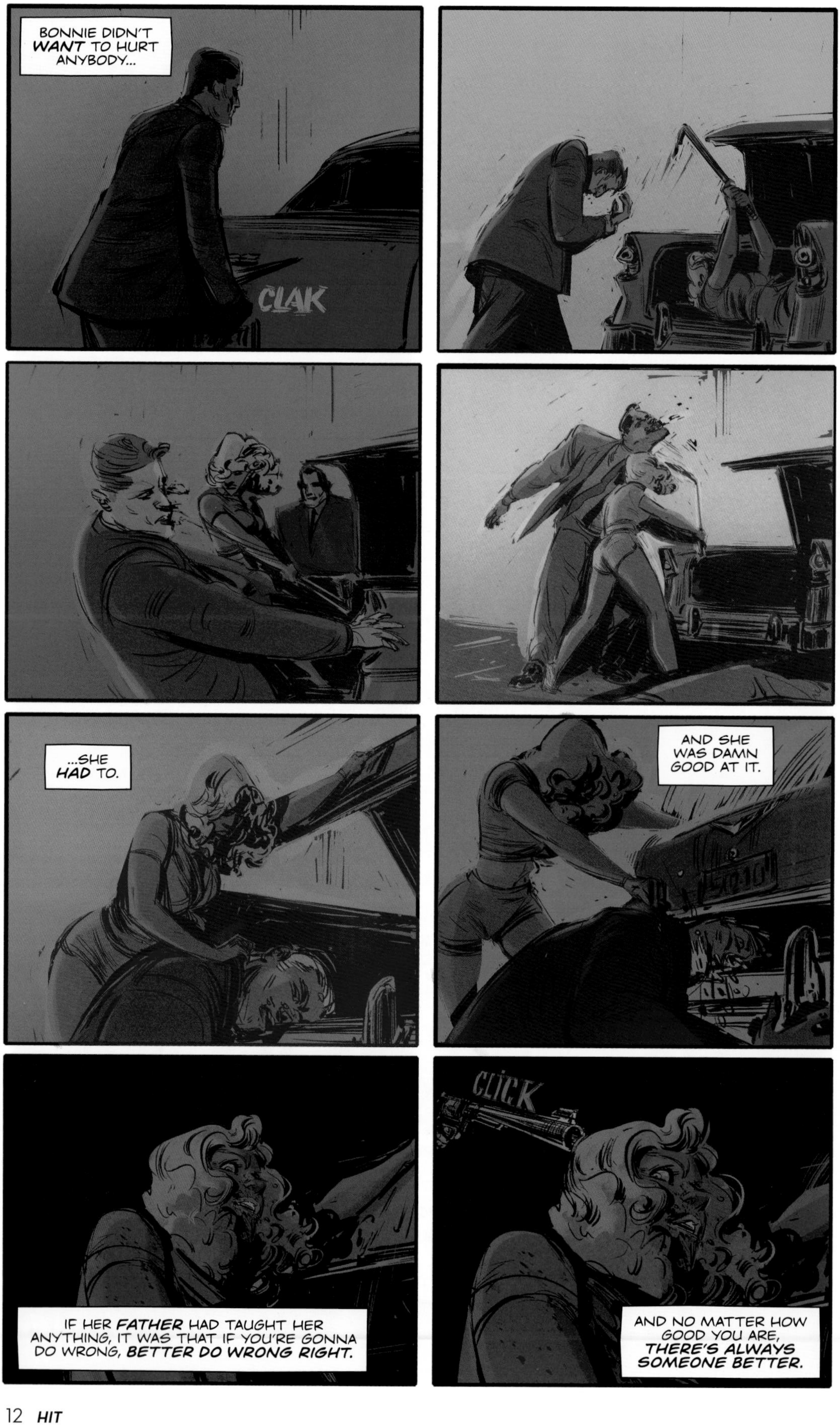
BONNIE DIDN'T WANT TO HURT ANYBODY...
CLAK
...SHE HAD TO.
AND SHE WAS DAMN GOOD AT IT.
IF HER FATHER HAD TAUGHT HER ANYTHING, IT WAS THAT IF YOU'RE GONNA DO WRONG, BETTER DO WRONG RIGHT.
CLICK
AND NO MATTER HOW GOOD YOU ARE, THERE'S ALWAYS SOMEONE BETTER.

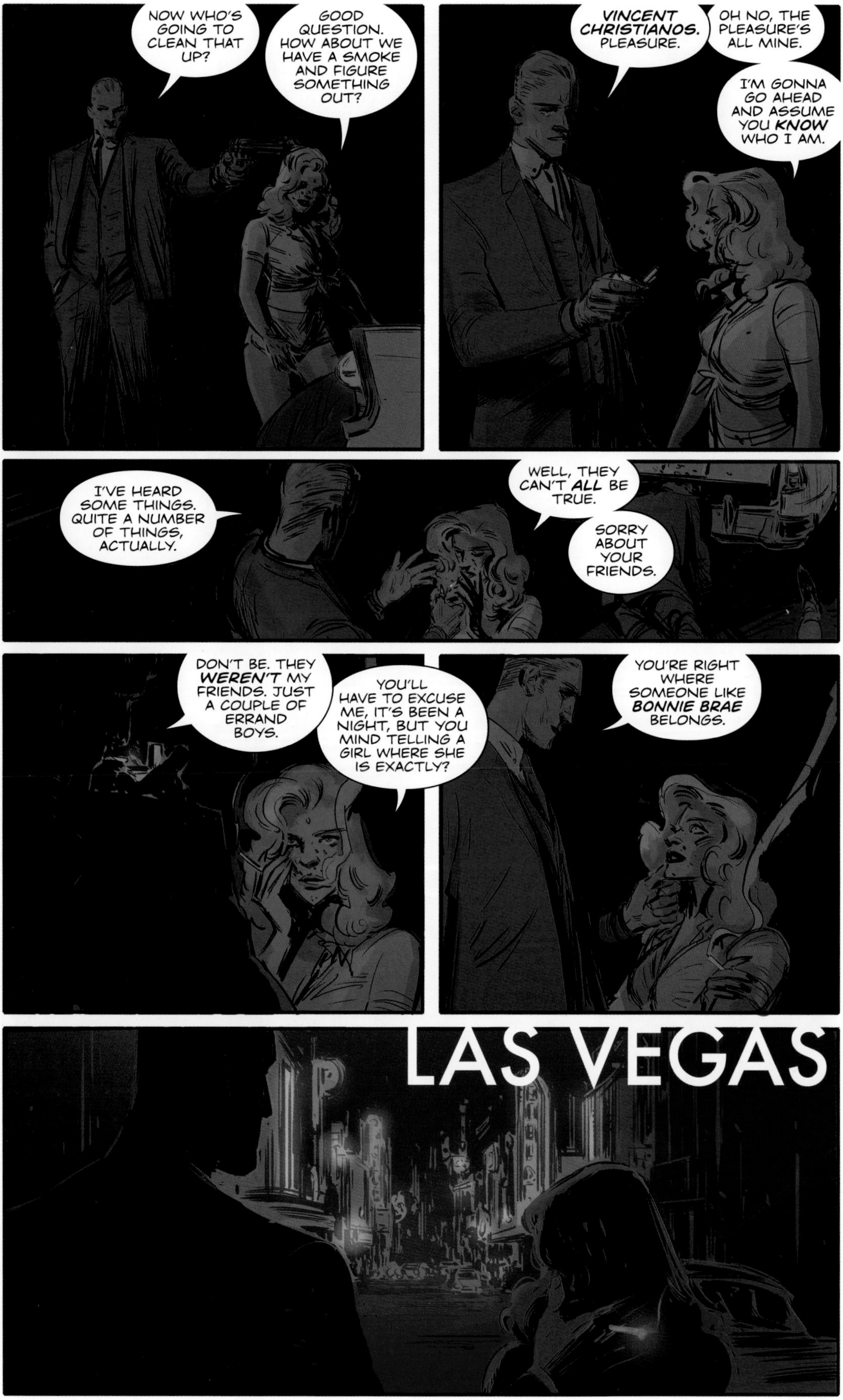
NOW WHO'S GOING TO CLEAN THAT UP?
GOOD QUESTION. HOW ABOUT WE HAVE A SMOKE AND FIGURE SOMETHING OUT?
VINCENT CHRISTIANOS. PLEASURE.
OH NO, THE PLEASURE'S ALL MINE.
I'M GONNA GO AHEAD AND ASSUME YOU KNOW WHO I AM.
I'VE HEARD SOME THINGS. QUITE A NUMBER OF THINGS, ACTUALLY.
WELL, THEY CAN'T ALL BE TRUE.
SORRY ABOUT YOUR FRIENDS.
DON'T BE. THEY WEREN'T MY FRIENDS. JUST A COUPLE OF ERRAND BOYS.
YOU'LL HAVE TO EXCUSE ME, IT'S BEEN A NIGHT, BUT YOU MIND TELLING A GIRL WHERE SHE IS EXACTLY?
YOU'RE RIGHT WHERE SOMEONE LIKE BONNIE BRAE BELONGS.
LAS VEGAS

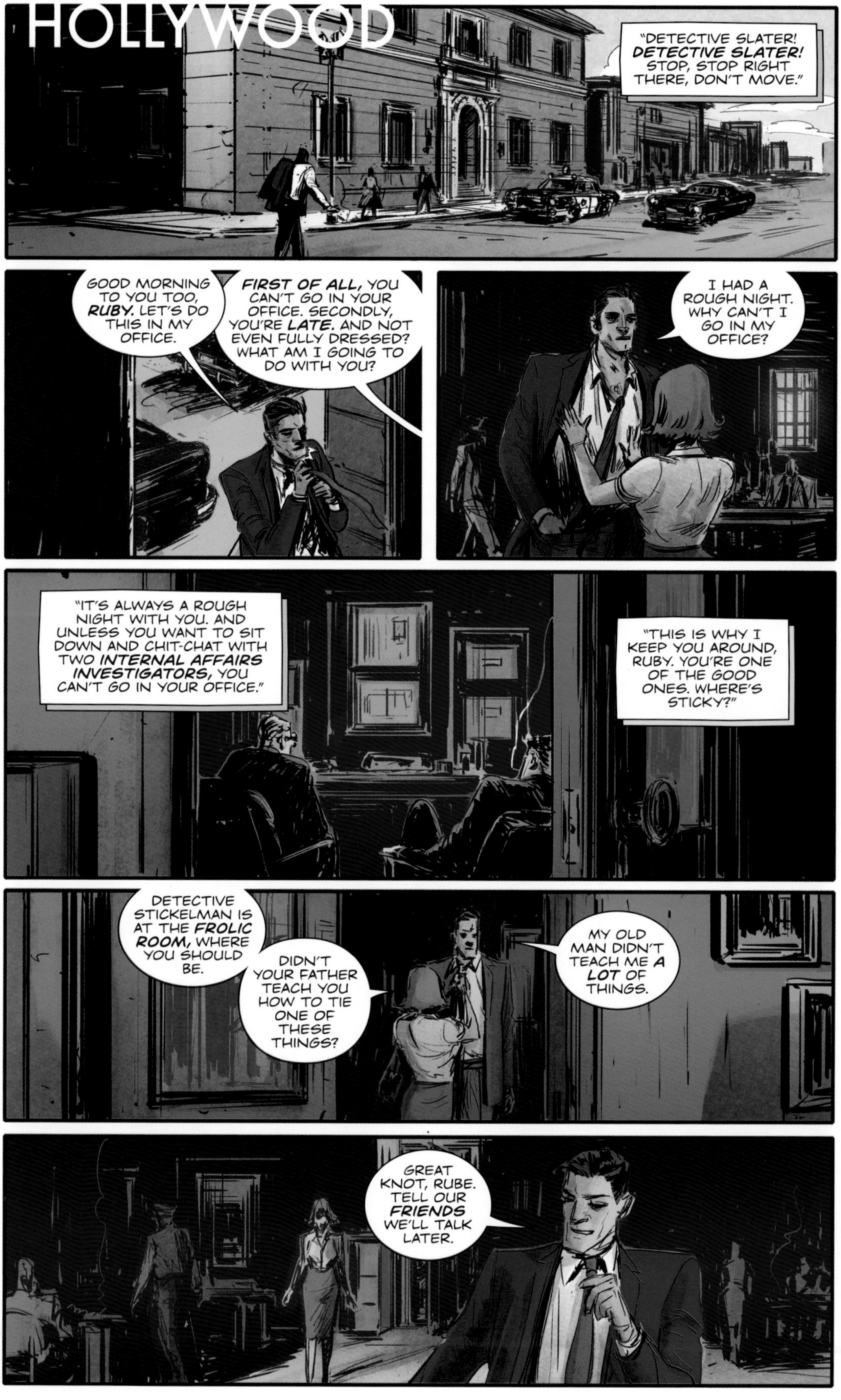
HOLLYWOOD
"DETECTIVE SLATER! DETECTIVE SLATER! STOP, STOP RIGHT THERE, DON'T MOVE."
GOOD MORNING TO YOU TOO, RUBY. LET'S DO THIS IN MY OFFICE.
FIRST OF ALL, YOU CAN'T GO IN YOUR OFFICE. SECONDLY, YOU'RE LATE. AND NOT EVEN FULLY DRESSED? WHAT AM I GOING TO DO WITH YOU?
I HAD A ROUGH NIGHT. WHY CAN'T I GO IN MY OFFICE?
"IT'S ALWAYS A ROUGH NIGHT WITH YOU. AND UNLESS YOU WANT TO SIT DOWN AND CHIT-CHAT WITH TWO INTERNAL AFFAIRS INVESTIGATORS, YOU CAN'T GO IN YOUR OFFICE."
"THIS IS WHY I KEEP YOU AROUND, RUBY. YOU'RE ONE OF THE GOOD ONES. WHERE'S STICKY?"
DETECTIVE STICKELMAN IS AT THE FROLIC ROOM, WHERE YOU SHOULD BE.
DIDN'T YOUR FATHER TEACH YOU HOW TO TIE ONE OF THESE THINGS?
MY OLD MAN DIDN'T TEACH ME A LOT OF THINGS.
GREAT KNOT, RUBE. TELL OUR FRIENDS WE'LL TALK LATER.

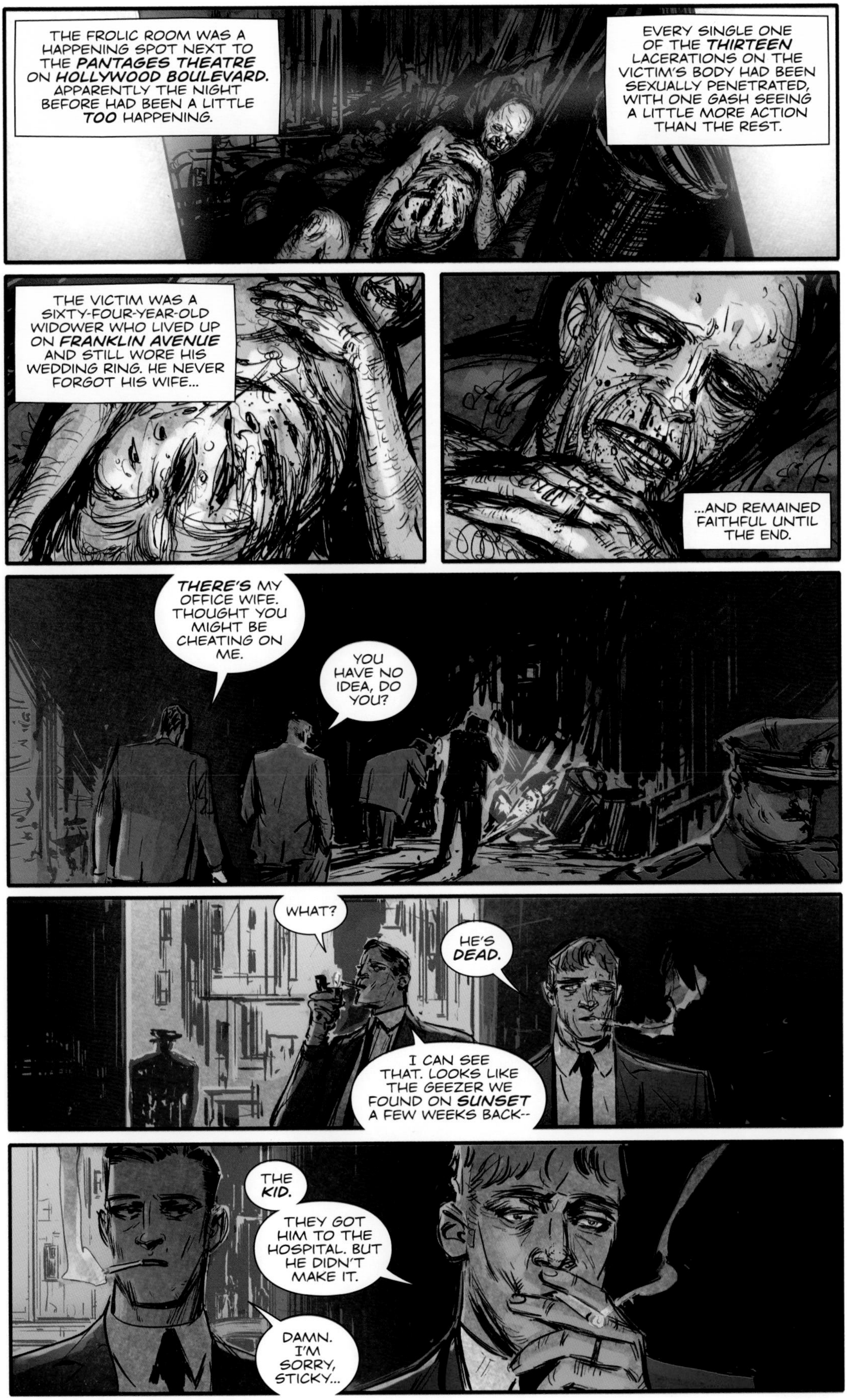
THE FROLIC ROOM WAS A HAPPENING SPOT NEXT TO THE **PANTAGES THEATRE** ON **HOLLYWOOD BOULEVARD.** APPARENTLY THE NIGHT BEFORE HAD BEEN A LITTLE **TOO** HAPPENING.
EVERY SINGLE ONE OF THE **THIRTEEN** LACERATIONS ON THE VICTIM'S BODY HAD BEEN SEXUALLY PENETRATED, WITH ONE GASH SEEING A LITTLE MORE ACTION THAN THE REST.
THE VICTIM WAS A SIXTY-FOUR-YEAR-OLD WIDOWER WHO LIVED UP ON **FRANKLIN AVENUE** AND STILL WORE HIS WEDDING RING. HE NEVER FORGOT HIS WIFE...
...AND REMAINED FAITHFUL UNTIL THE END.
**THERE'S** MY OFFICE WIFE. THOUGHT YOU MIGHT BE CHEATING ON ME.
YOU HAVE NO IDEA, DO YOU?
WHAT?
HE'S **DEAD.**
I CAN SEE THAT. LOOKS LIKE THE GEEZER WE FOUND ON **SUNSET** A FEW WEEKS BACK--
THE **KID.**
THEY GOT HIM TO THE HOSPITAL. BUT HE DIDN'T MAKE IT.
DAMN. I'M SORRY, STICKY...

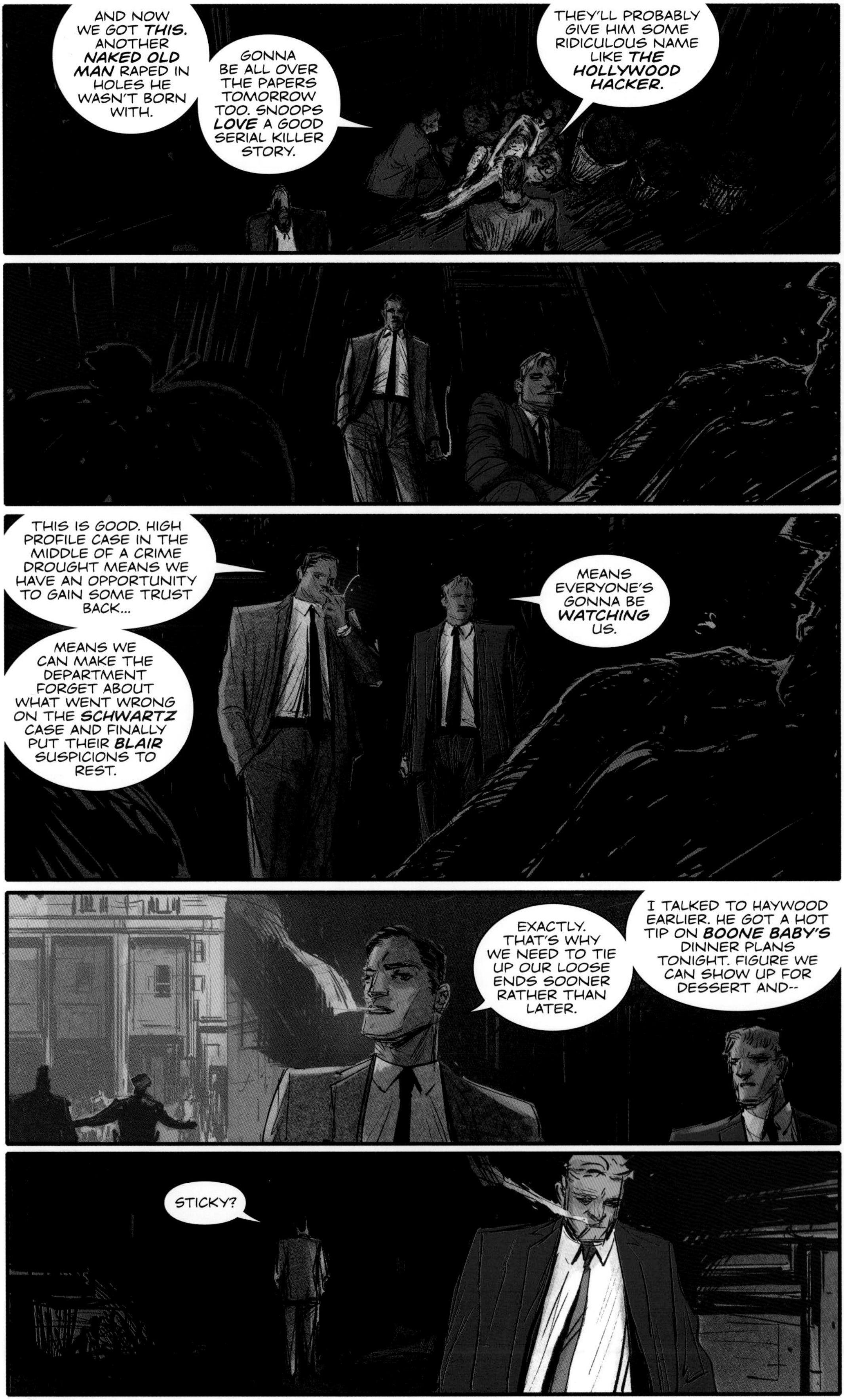
AND NOW WE GOT THIS. ANOTHER NAKED OLD MAN RAPED IN HOLES HE WASN'T BORN WITH.
GONNA BE ALL OVER THE PAPERS TOMORROW TOO. SNOOPS LOVE A GOOD SERIAL KILLER STORY.
THEY'LL PROBABLY GIVE HIM SOME RIDICULOUS NAME LIKE THE HOLLYWOOD HACKER.
THIS IS GOOD. HIGH PROFILE CASE IN THE MIDDLE OF A CRIME DROUGHT MEANS WE HAVE AN OPPORTUNITY TO GAIN SOME TRUST BACK...
MEANS WE CAN MAKE THE DEPARTMENT FORGET ABOUT WHAT WENT WRONG ON THE SCHWARTZ CASE AND FINALLY PUT THEIR BLAIR SUSPICIONS TO REST.
MEANS EVERYONE'S GONNA BE WATCHING US.
EXACTLY. THAT'S WHY WE NEED TO TIE UP OUR LOOSE ENDS SOONER RATHER THAN LATER.
I TALKED TO HAYWOOD EARLIER. HE GOT A HOT TIP ON BOONE BABY'S DINNER PLANS TONIGHT. FIGURE WE CAN SHOW UP FOR DESSERT AND--
STICKY?

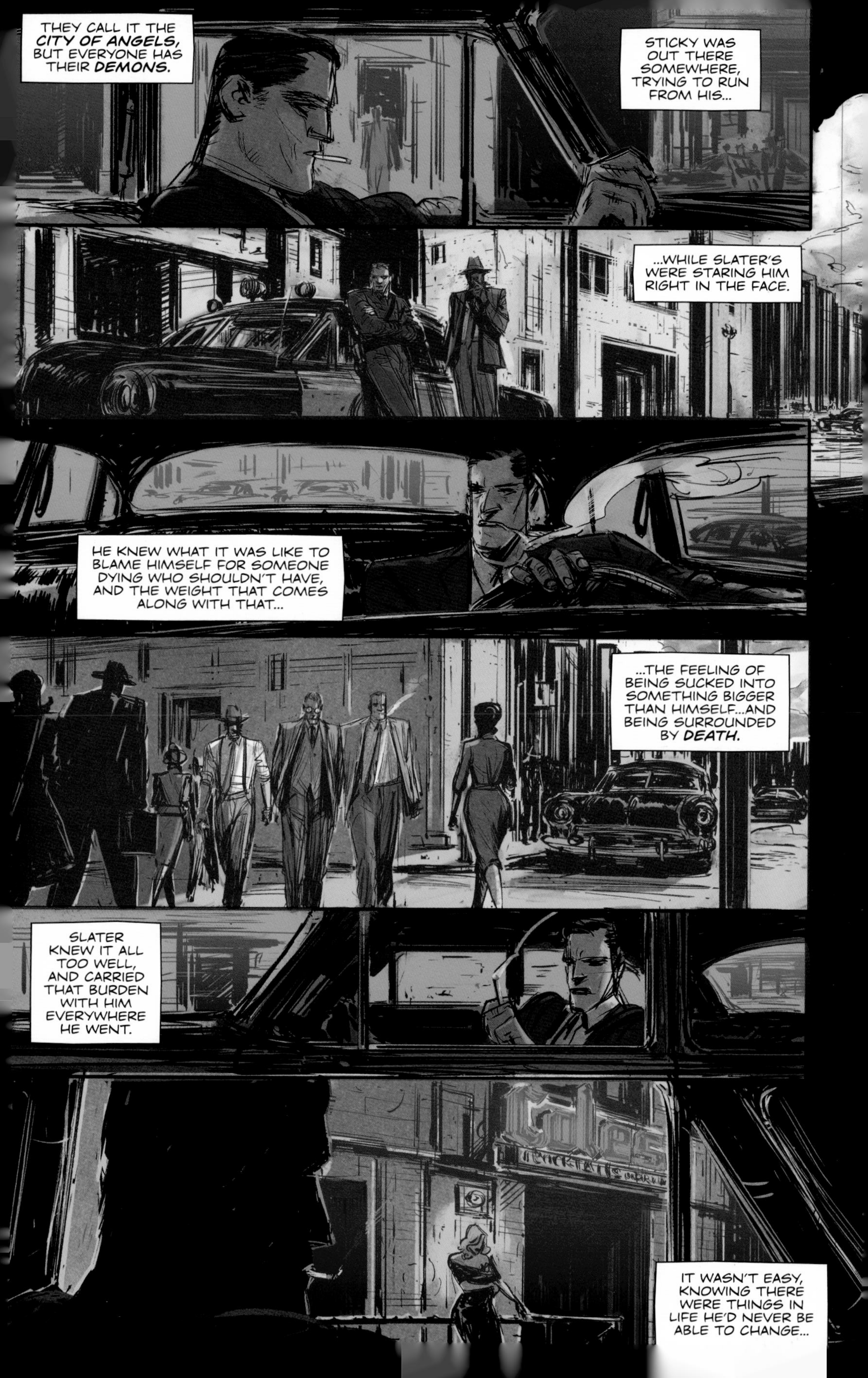
THEY CALL IT THE CITY OF ANGELS, BUT EVERYONE HAS THEIR DEMONS.
STICKY WAS OUT THERE SOMEWHERE, TRYING TO RUN FROM HIS...
...WHILE SLATER'S WERE STARING HIM RIGHT IN THE FACE.
HE KNEW WHAT IT WAS LIKE TO BLAME HIMSELF FOR SOMEONE DYING WHO SHOULDN'T HAVE, AND THE WEIGHT THAT COMES ALONG WITH THAT...
...THE FEELING OF BEING SUCKED INTO SOMETHING BIGGER THAN HIMSELF...AND BEING SURROUNDED BY DEATH.
SLATER KNEW IT ALL TOO WELL, AND CARRIED THAT BURDEN WITH HIM EVERYWHERE HE WENT.
IT WASN'T EASY, KNOWING THERE WERE THINGS IN LIFE HE'D NEVER BE ABLE TO CHANGE...

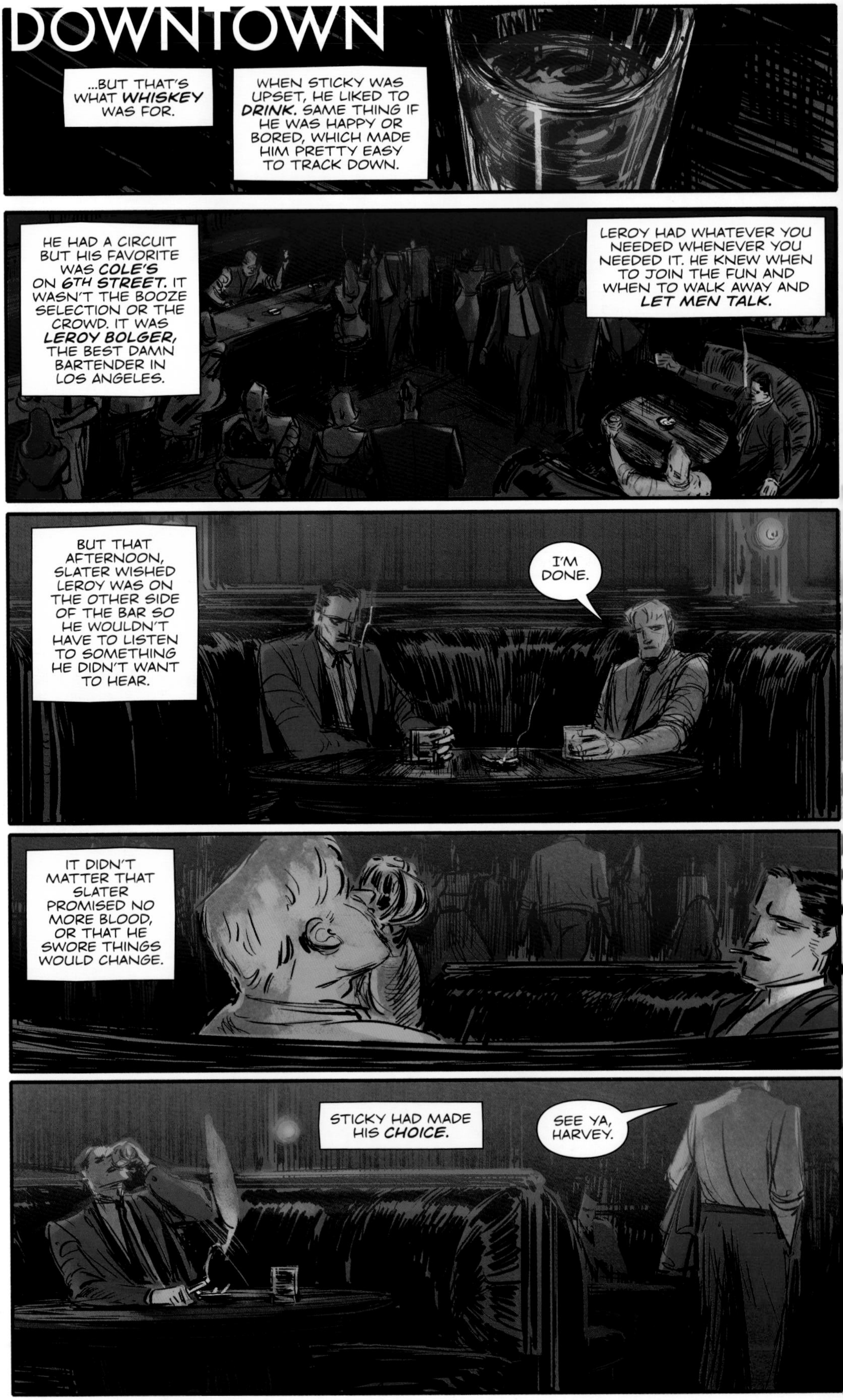
DOWNTOWN
...BUT THAT'S WHAT WHISKEY WAS FOR.
WHEN STICKY WAS UPSET, HE LIKED TO DRINK. SAME THING IF HE WAS HAPPY OR BORED, WHICH MADE HIM PRETTY EASY TO TRACK DOWN.
HE HAD A CIRCUIT BUT HIS FAVORITE WAS COLE'S ON 6TH STREET. IT WASN'T THE BOOZE SELECTION OR THE CROWD. IT WAS LEROY BOLGER, THE BEST DAMN BARTENDER IN LOS ANGELES.
LEROY HAD WHATEVER YOU NEEDED WHENEVER YOU NEEDED IT. HE KNEW WHEN TO JOIN THE FUN AND WHEN TO WALK AWAY AND LET MEN TALK.
BUT THAT AFTERNOON, SLATER WISHED LEROY WAS ON THE OTHER SIDE OF THE BAR SO HE WOULDN'T HAVE TO LISTEN TO SOMETHING HE DIDN'T WANT TO HEAR.
I'M DONE.
IT DIDN'T MATTER THAT SLATER PROMISED NO MORE BLOOD, OR THAT HE SWORE THINGS WOULD CHANGE.
STICKY HAD MADE HIS CHOICE.
SEE YA, HARVEY.

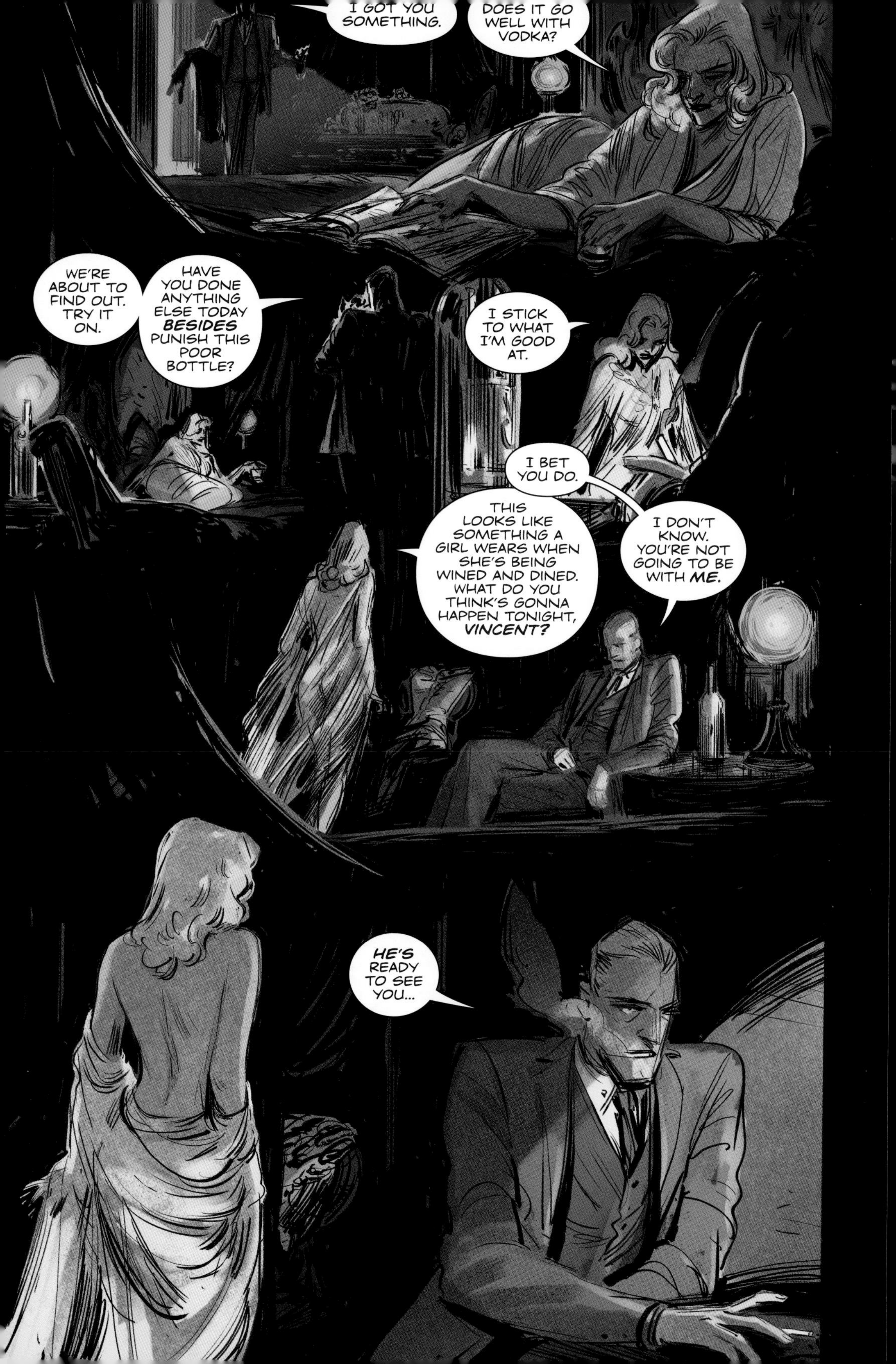

I GOT YOU SOMETHING.
DOES IT GO WELL WITH VODKA?
WE'RE ABOUT TO FIND OUT. TRY IT ON.
HAVE YOU DONE ANYTHING ELSE TODAY BESIDES PUNISH THIS POOR BOTTLE?
I STICK TO WHAT I'M GOOD AT.
I BET YOU DO.
THIS LOOKS LIKE SOMETHING A GIRL WEARS WHEN SHE'S BEING WINED AND DINED. WHAT DO YOU THINK'S GONNA HAPPEN TONIGHT, VINCENT?
I DON'T KNOW. YOU'RE NOT GOING TO BE WITH ME.
HE'S READY TO SEE YOU...

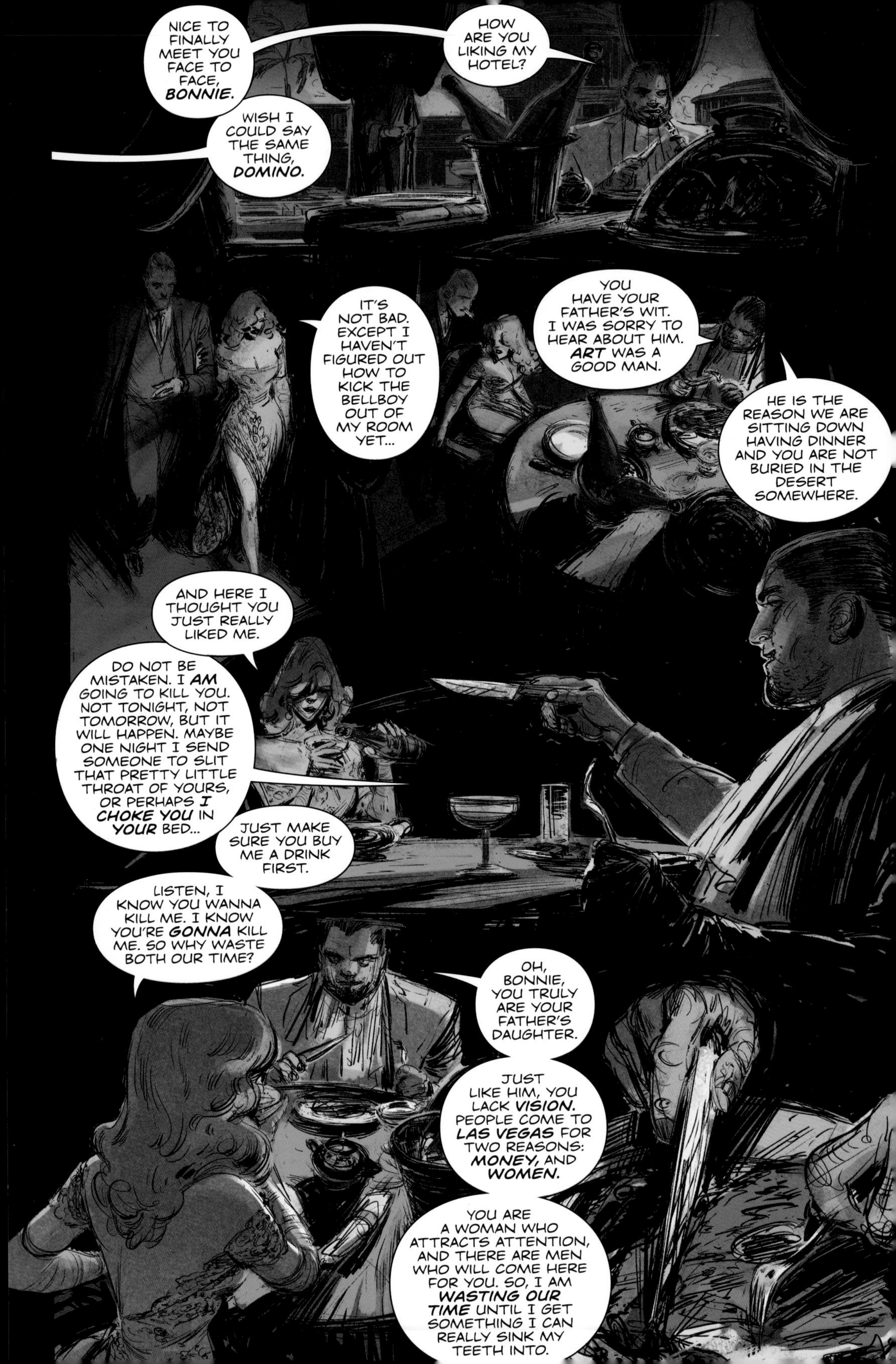
NICE TO FINALLY MEET YOU FACE TO FACE, BONNIE.
HOW ARE YOU LIKING MY HOTEL?
WISH I COULD SAY THE SAME THING, DOMINO.
IT'S NOT BAD. EXCEPT I HAVEN'T FIGURED OUT HOW TO KICK THE BELLBOY OUT OF MY ROOM YET...
YOU HAVE YOUR FATHER'S WIT. I WAS SORRY TO HEAR ABOUT HIM. ART WAS A GOOD MAN.
HE IS THE REASON WE ARE SITTING DOWN HAVING DINNER AND YOU ARE NOT BURIED IN THE DESERT SOMEWHERE.
AND HERE I THOUGHT YOU JUST REALLY LIKED ME.
DO NOT BE MISTAKEN. I AM GOING TO KILL YOU. NOT TONIGHT, NOT TOMORROW, BUT IT WILL HAPPEN. MAYBE ONE NIGHT I SEND SOMEONE TO SLIT THAT PRETTY LITTLE THROAT OF YOURS, OR PERHAPS I CHOKE YOU IN YOUR BED...
JUST MAKE SURE YOU BUY ME A DRINK FIRST.
LISTEN, I KNOW YOU WANNA KILL ME. I KNOW YOU'RE GONNA KILL ME. SO WHY WASTE BOTH OUR TIME?
OH, BONNIE, YOU TRULY ARE YOUR FATHER'S DAUGHTER.
JUST LIKE HIM, YOU LACK VISION. PEOPLE COME TO LAS VEGAS FOR TWO REASONS: MONEY, AND WOMEN.
YOU ARE A WOMAN WHO ATTRACTS ATTENTION, AND THERE ARE MEN WHO WILL COME HERE FOR YOU. SO, I AM WASTING OUR TIME UNTIL I GET SOMETHING I CAN REALLY SINK MY TEETH INTO.

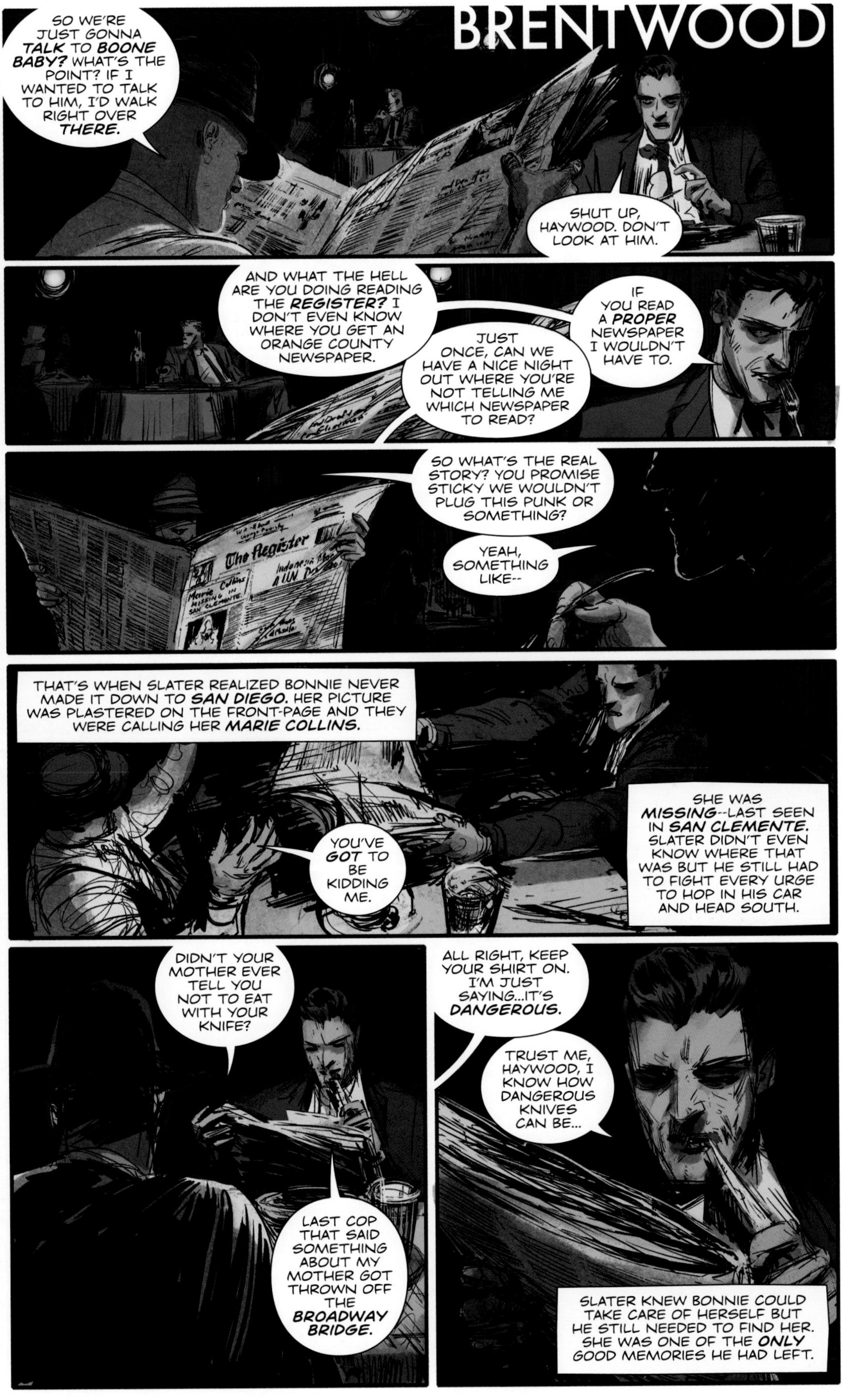
BRENTWOOD
SO WE'RE JUST GONNA TALK TO BOONE BABY? WHAT'S THE POINT? IF I WANTED TO TALK TO HIM, I'D WALK RIGHT OVER THERE.
SHUT UP, HAYWOOD. DON'T LOOK AT HIM.
AND WHAT THE HELL ARE YOU DOING READING THE REGISTER? I DON'T EVEN KNOW WHERE YOU GET AN ORANGE COUNTY NEWSPAPER.
IF YOU READ A PROPER NEWSPAPER I WOULDN'T HAVE TO.
JUST ONCE, CAN WE HAVE A NICE NIGHT OUT WHERE YOU'RE NOT TELLING ME WHICH NEWSPAPER TO READ?
SO WHAT'S THE REAL STORY? YOU PROMISE STICKY WE WOULDN'T PLUG THIS PUNK OR SOMETHING?
YEAH, SOMETHING LIKE--
The Register
THAT'S WHEN SLATER REALIZED BONNIE NEVER MADE IT DOWN TO SAN DIEGO. HER PICTURE WAS PLASTERED ON THE FRONT-PAGE AND THEY WERE CALLING HER MARIE COLLINS.
YOU'VE GOT TO BE KIDDING ME.
SHE WAS MISSING--LAST SEEN IN SAN CLEMENTE. SLATER DIDN'T EVEN KNOW WHERE THAT WAS BUT HE STILL HAD TO FIGHT EVERY URGE TO HOP IN HIS CAR AND HEAD SOUTH.
DIDN'T YOUR MOTHER EVER TELL YOU NOT TO EAT WITH YOUR KNIFE?
LAST COP THAT SAID SOMETHING ABOUT MY MOTHER GOT THROWN OFF THE BROADWAY BRIDGE.
ALL RIGHT, KEEP YOUR SHIRT ON. I'M JUST SAYING...IT'S DANGEROUS.
TRUST ME, HAYWOOD, I KNOW HOW DANGEROUS KNIVES CAN BE...
SLATER KNEW BONNIE COULD TAKE CARE OF HERSELF BUT HE STILL NEEDED TO FIND HER. SHE WAS ONE OF THE ONLY GOOD MEMORIES HE HAD LEFT.

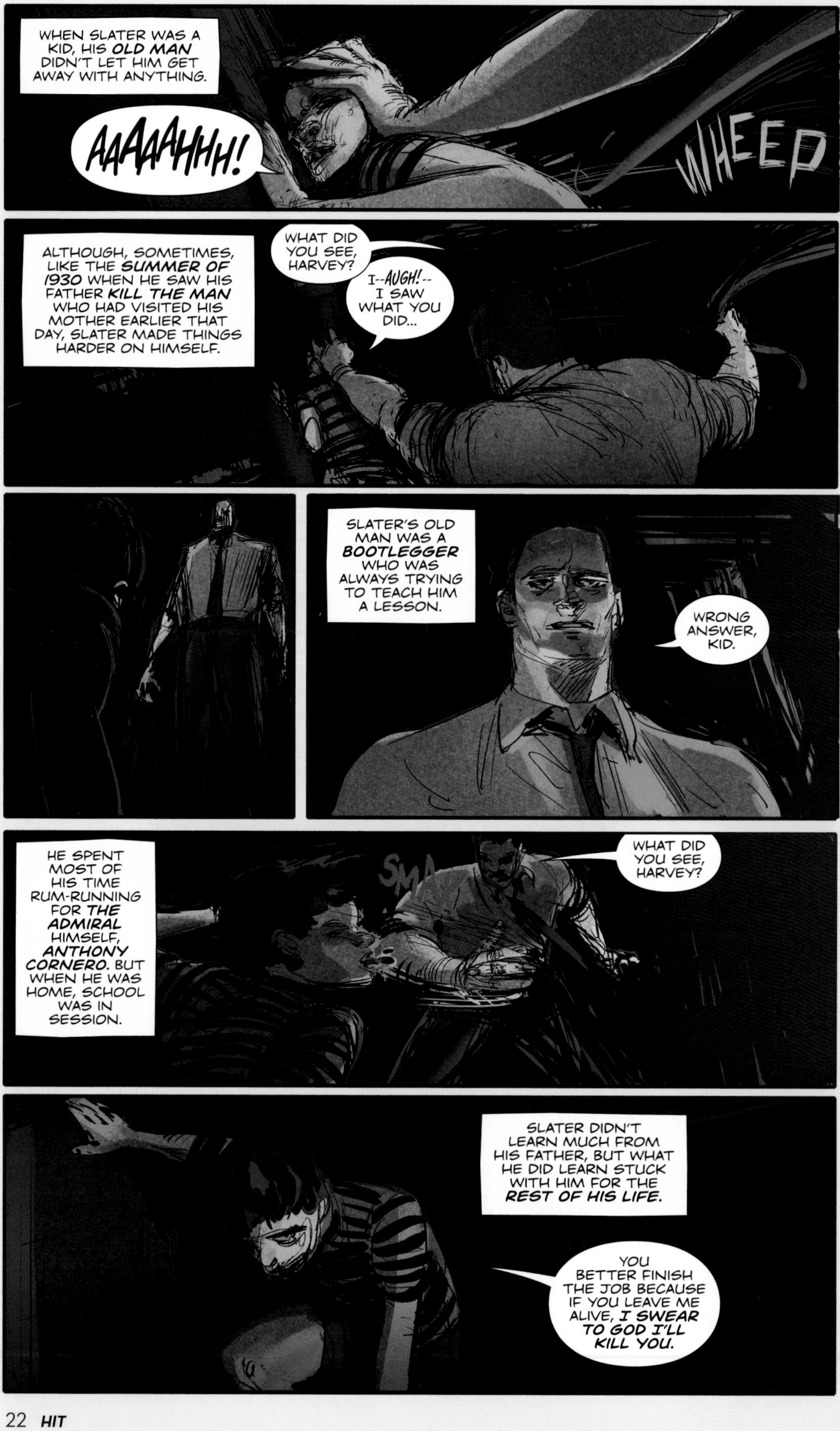
WHEN SLATER WAS A KID, HIS OLD MAN DIDN'T LET HIM GET AWAY WITH ANYTHING.
AAAAAHHH!
WHEEP
ALTHOUGH, SOMETIMES, LIKE THE SUMMER OF 1930 WHEN HE SAW HIS FATHER KILL THE MAN WHO HAD VISITED HIS MOTHER EARLIER THAT DAY, SLATER MADE THINGS HARDER ON HIMSELF.
WHAT DID YOU SEE, HARVEY?
I--AUGH!-- I SAW WHAT YOU DID...
SLATER'S OLD MAN WAS A BOOTLEGGER WHO WAS ALWAYS TRYING TO TEACH HIM A LESSON.
WRONG ANSWER, KID.
HE SPENT MOST OF HIS TIME RUM-RUNNING FOR THE ADMIRAL HIMSELF, ANTHONY CORNERO. BUT WHEN HE WAS HOME, SCHOOL WAS IN SESSION.
WHAT DID YOU SEE, HARVEY?
SLATER DIDN'T LEARN MUCH FROM HIS FATHER, BUT WHAT HE DID LEARN STUCK WITH HIM FOR THE REST OF HIS LIFE.
YOU BETTER FINISH THE JOB BECAUSE IF YOU LEAVE ME ALIVE, I SWEAR TO GOD I'LL KILL YOU.

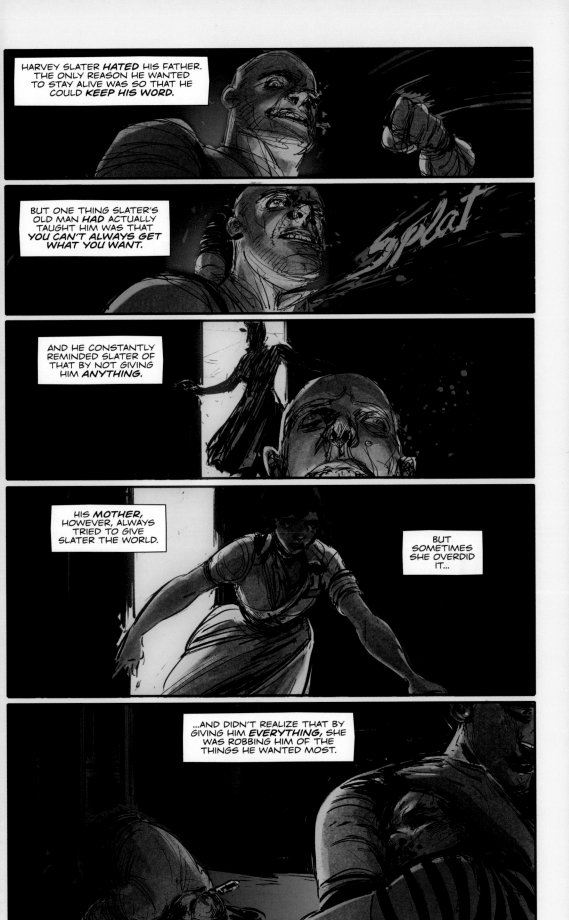

HARVEY SLATER **HATED** HIS FATHER. THE ONLY REASON HE WANTED TO STAY ALIVE WAS SO THAT HE COULD **KEEP HIS WORD.**

BUT ONE THING SLATER'S OLD MAN **HAD** ACTUALLY TAUGHT HIM WAS THAT **YOU CAN'T ALWAYS GET WHAT YOU WANT.**

AND HE CONSTANTLY REMINDED SLATER OF THAT BY NOT GIVING HIM **ANYTHING.**

HIS **MOTHER,** HOWEVER, ALWAYS TRIED TO GIVE SLATER THE WORLD.

BUT SOMETIMES SHE OVERDID IT...

...AND DIDN'T REALIZE THAT BY GIVING HIM **EVERYTHING,** SHE WAS ROBBING HIM OF THE THINGS HE WANTED MOST.

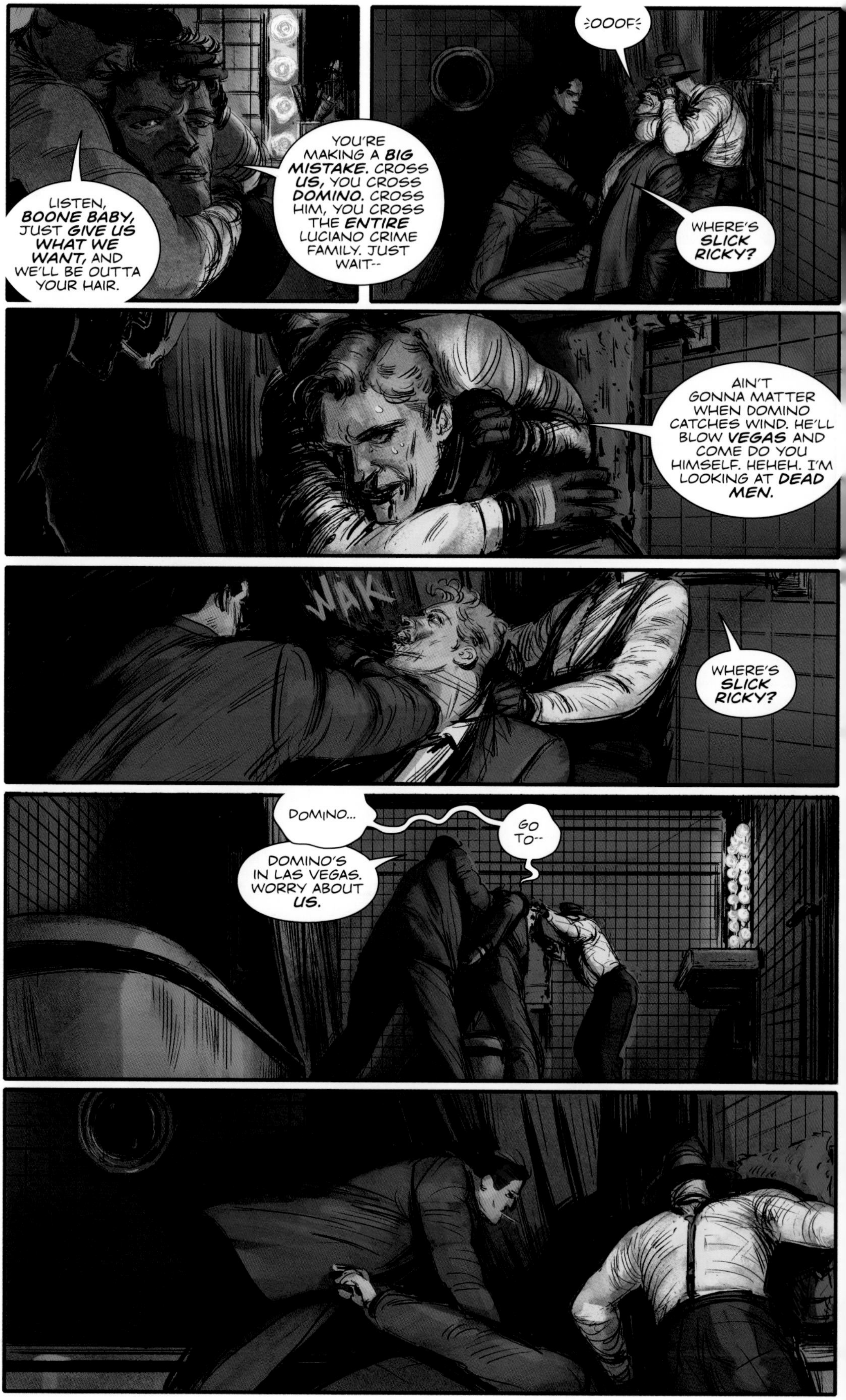
LISTEN, BOONE BABY, JUST GIVE US WHAT WE WANT, AND WE'LL BE OUTTA YOUR HAIR.
YOU'RE MAKING A BIG MISTAKE. CROSS US, YOU CROSS DOMINO. CROSS HIM, YOU CROSS THE ENTIRE LUCIANO CRIME FAMILY. JUST WAIT--
OOOF
WHERE'S SLICK RICKY?
AIN'T GONNA MATTER WHEN DOMINO CATCHES WIND. HE'LL BLOW VEGAS AND COME DO YOU HIMSELF. HEHEH. I'M LOOKING AT DEAD MEN.
WAK
WHERE'S SLICK RICKY?
DOMINO...
GO TO--
DOMINO'S IN LAS VEGAS. WORRY ABOUT US.

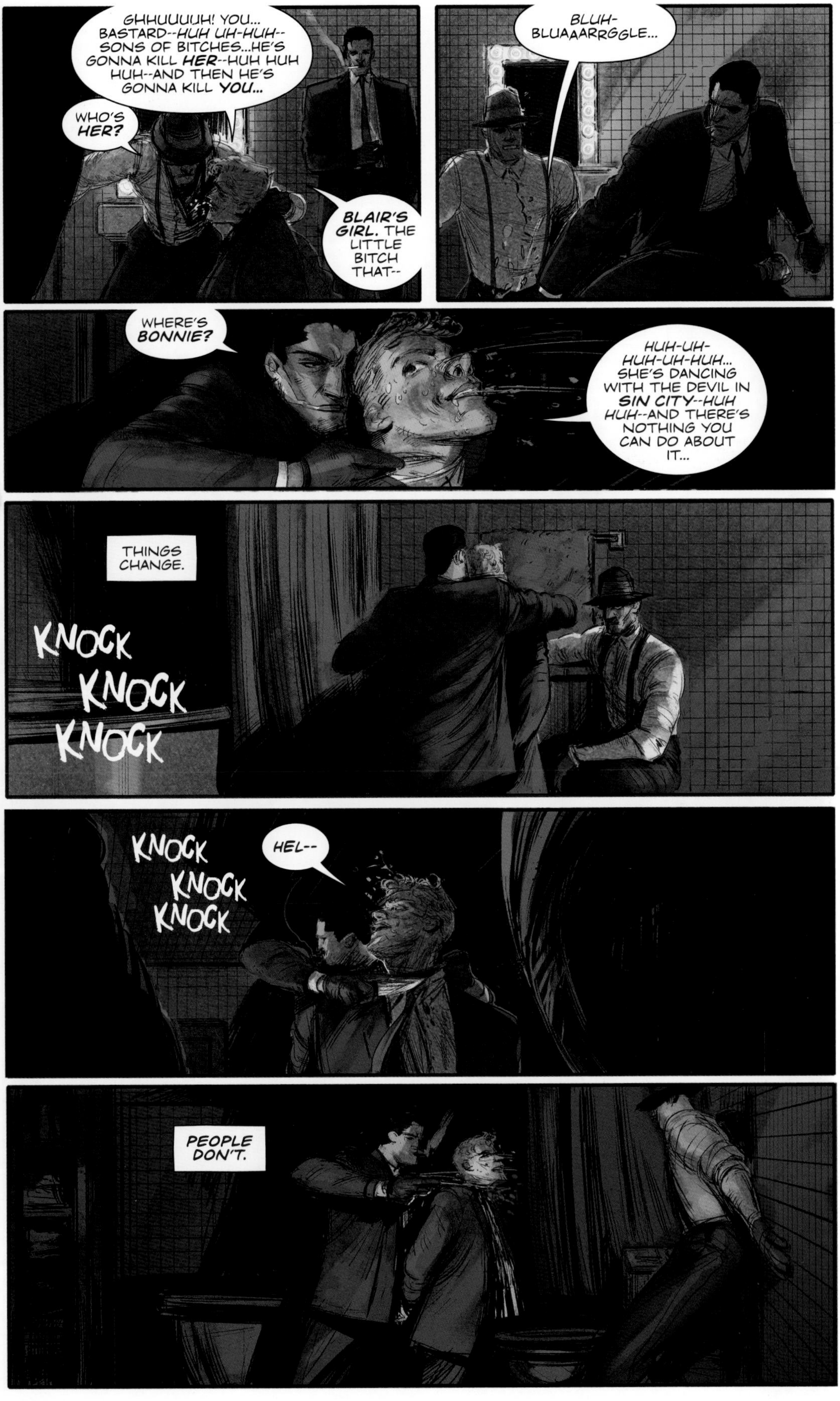
GHHUUUUH! YOU... BASTARD--HUH UH-HUH-- SONS OF BITCHES...HE'S GONNA KILL HER--HUH HUH HUH--AND THEN HE'S GONNA KILL YOU...
WHO'S HER?
BLAIR'S GIRL. THE LITTLE BITCH THAT--
BLUH-BLUAAARRGGLE...
WHERE'S BONNIE?
HUH-UH-HUH-UH-HUH... SHE'S DANCING WITH THE DEVIL IN SIN CITY--HUH HUH--AND THERE'S NOTHING YOU CAN DO ABOUT IT...
THINGS CHANGE.
KNOCK KNOCK KNOCK
KNOCK KNOCK KNOCK
HEL--
PEOPLE DON'T.

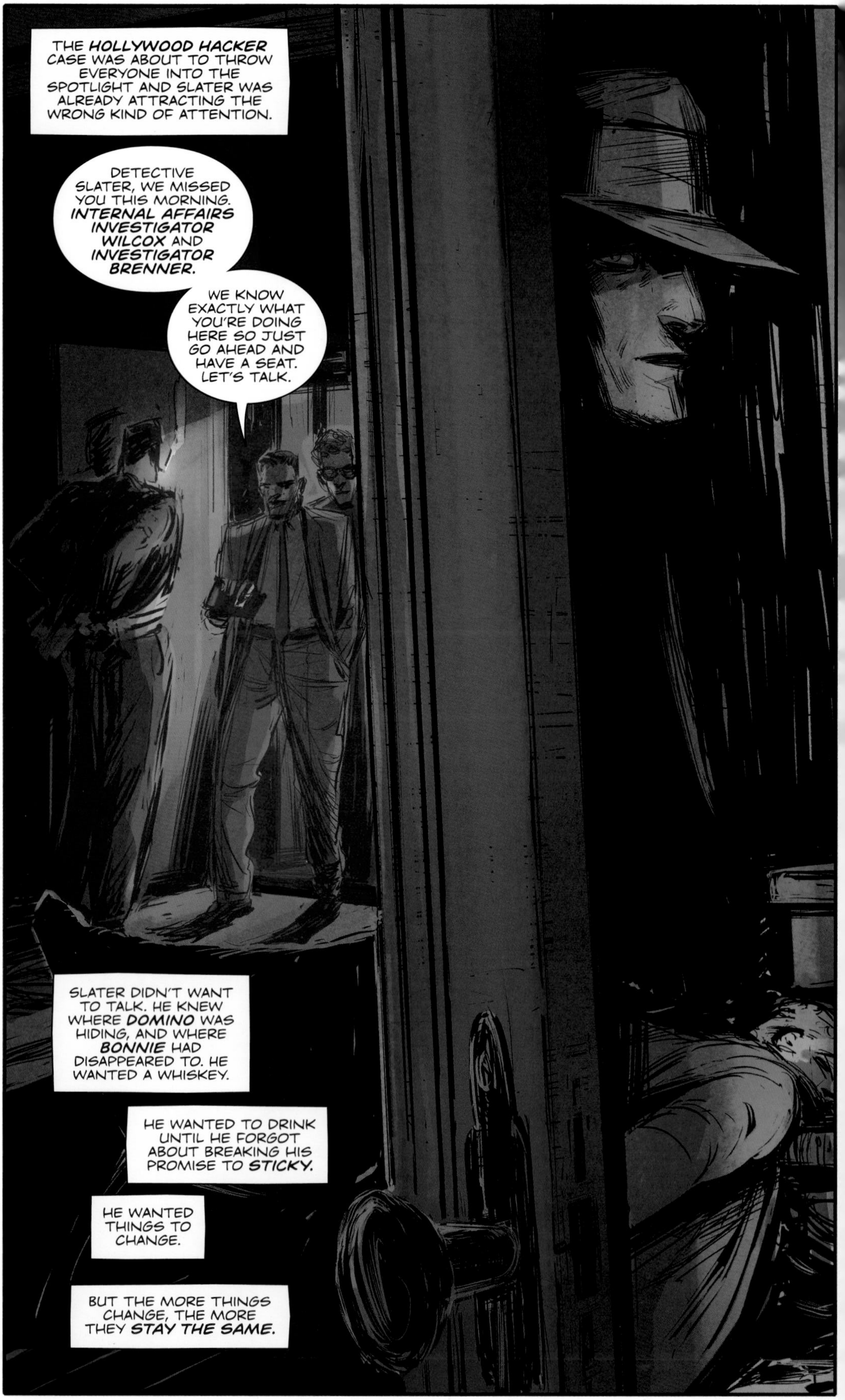
THE **HOLLYWOOD HACKER** CASE WAS ABOUT TO THROW EVERYONE INTO THE SPOTLIGHT AND SLATER WAS ALREADY ATTRACTING THE WRONG KIND OF ATTENTION.
DETECTIVE SLATER, WE MISSED YOU THIS MORNING. **INTERNAL AFFAIRS INVESTIGATOR WILCOX** AND **INVESTIGATOR BRENNER.**
WE KNOW EXACTLY WHAT YOU'RE DOING HERE SO JUST GO AHEAD AND HAVE A SEAT. LET'S TALK.
SLATER DIDN'T WANT TO TALK. HE KNEW WHERE **DOMINO** WAS HIDING, AND WHERE **BONNIE** HAD DISAPPEARED TO. HE WANTED A WHISKEY.
HE WANTED TO DRINK UNTIL HE FORGOT ABOUT BREAKING HIS PROMISE TO **STICKY.**
HE WANTED THINGS TO CHANGE.
BUT THE MORE THINGS CHANGE, THE MORE THEY **STAY THE SAME.**

ISSUE ONE COVER

# VANESA R. DEL REY

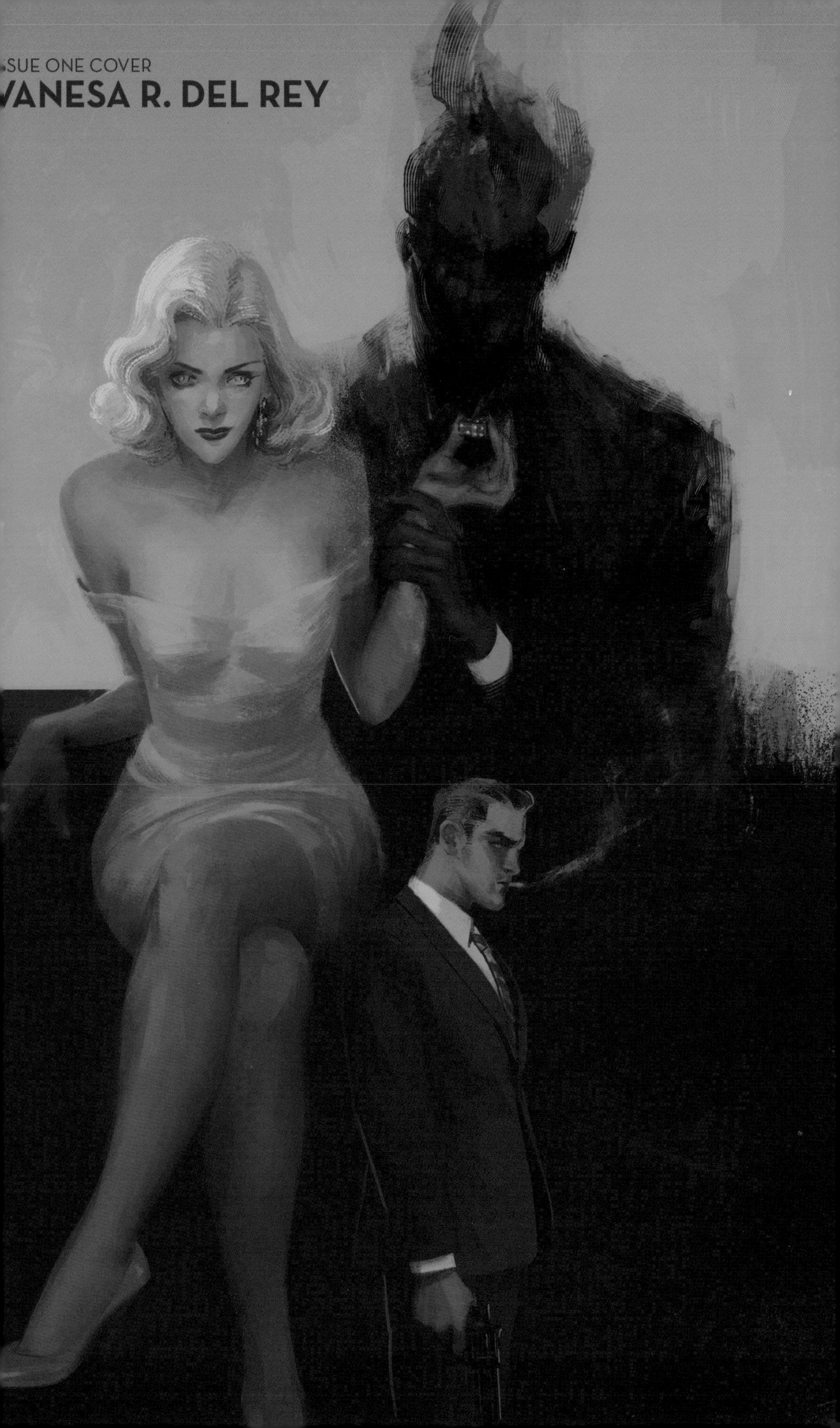

# CHAPTER **TWO**
# INTERNAL AFFAIRS

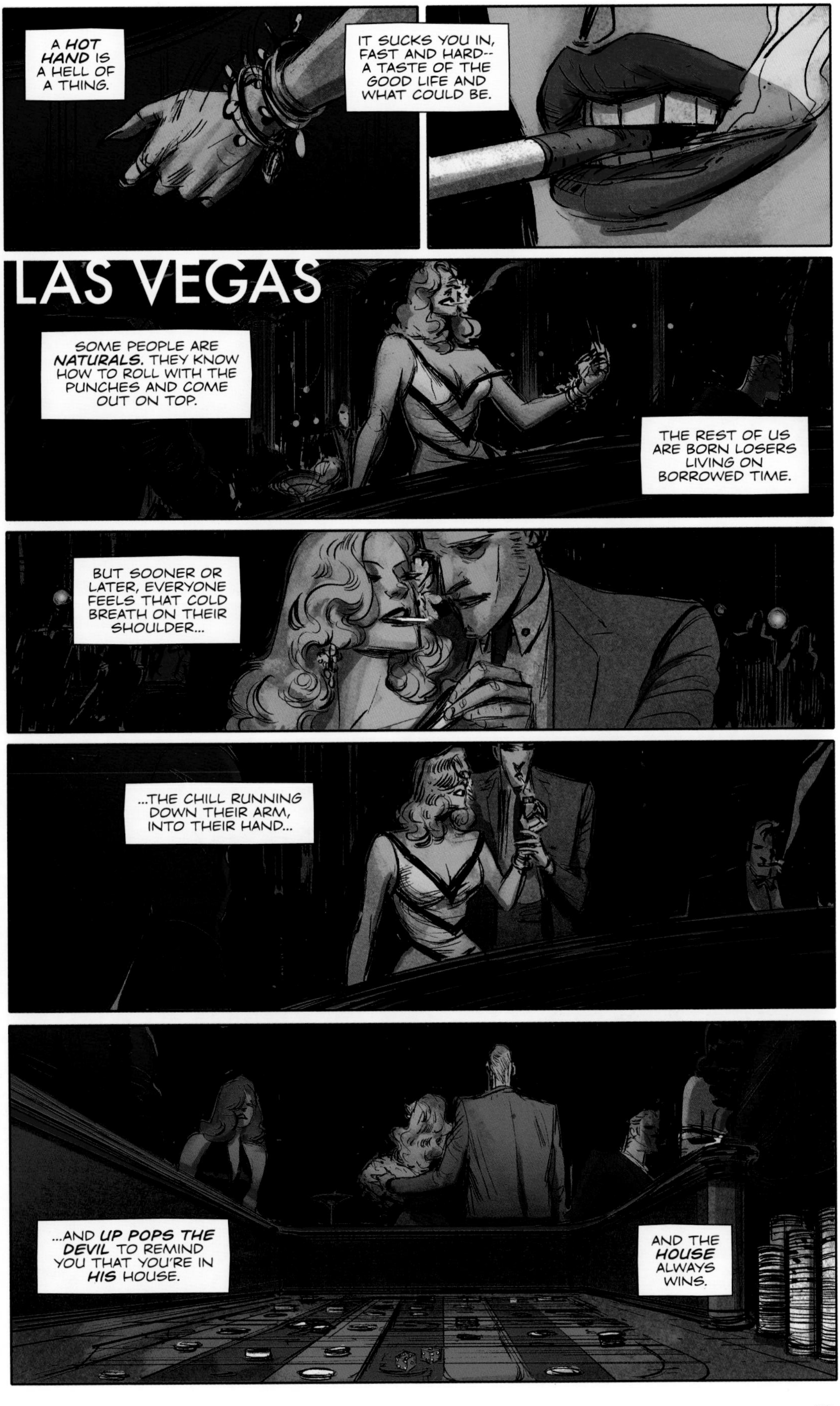
A HOT HAND IS A HELL OF A THING.
IT SUCKS YOU IN, FAST AND HARD-- A TASTE OF THE GOOD LIFE AND WHAT COULD BE.
LAS VEGAS
SOME PEOPLE ARE NATURALS. THEY KNOW HOW TO ROLL WITH THE PUNCHES AND COME OUT ON TOP.
THE REST OF US ARE BORN LOSERS LIVING ON BORROWED TIME.
BUT SOONER OR LATER, EVERYONE FEELS THAT COLD BREATH ON THEIR SHOULDER...
...THE CHILL RUNNING DOWN THEIR ARM, INTO THEIR HAND...
...AND UP POPS THE DEVIL TO REMIND YOU THAT YOU'RE IN HIS HOUSE.
AND THE HOUSE ALWAYS WINS.

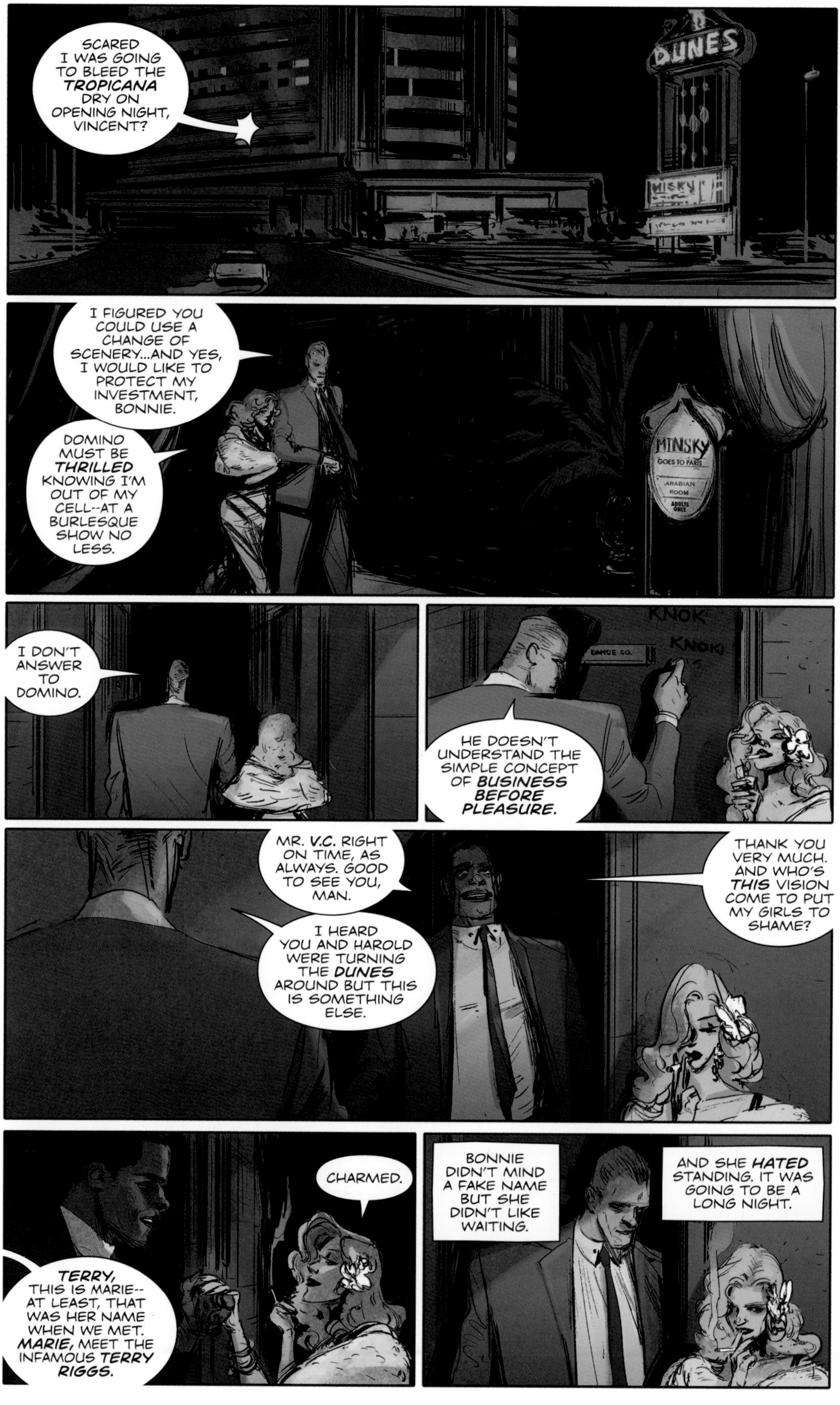
SCARED I WAS GOING TO BLEED THE TROPICANA DRY ON OPENING NIGHT, VINCENT?
DUNES
MINSKY
I FIGURED YOU COULD USE A CHANGE OF SCENERY...AND YES, I WOULD LIKE TO PROTECT MY INVESTMENT, BONNIE.
DOMINO MUST BE THRILLED KNOWING I'M OUT OF MY CELL--AT A BURLESQUE SHOW NO LESS.
MINSKY GOES TO PARIS ARABIAN ROOM ADULTS ONLY
I DON'T ANSWER TO DOMINO.
KNOK
KNOK
DANCE CO.
HE DOESN'T UNDERSTAND THE SIMPLE CONCEPT OF BUSINESS BEFORE PLEASURE.
MR. V.C. RIGHT ON TIME, AS ALWAYS. GOOD TO SEE YOU, MAN.
I HEARD YOU AND HAROLD WERE TURNING THE DUNES AROUND BUT THIS IS SOMETHING ELSE.
THANK YOU VERY MUCH. AND WHO'S THIS VISION COME TO PUT MY GIRLS TO SHAME?
TERRY, THIS IS MARIE--AT LEAST, THAT WAS HER NAME WHEN WE MET. MARIE, MEET THE INFAMOUS TERRY RIGGS.
CHARMED.
BONNIE DIDN'T MIND A FAKE NAME BUT SHE DIDN'T LIKE WAITING.
AND SHE HATED STANDING. IT WAS GOING TO BE A LONG NIGHT.

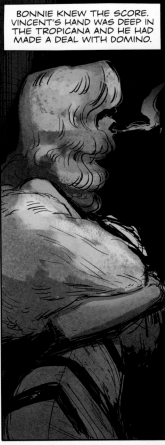

BONNIE KNEW THE SCORE. VINCENT'S HAND WAS DEEP IN THE TROPICANA AND HE HAD MADE A DEAL WITH DOMINO.

BUT HE DIDN'T TRUST HIM. VINCENT KNEW BONNIE WAS SAFER WITH *HIM* THAN ALONE AT THE TROP, BUT HE ALSO KNEW THAT BONNIE COULD TAKE CARE OF HERSELF.

*HOT DAMN,* GIRL--YOU ARE SOMETHING ELSE! YOU IN THE SHOW TONIGHT?

GUESS YOU'LL HAVE TO WAIT AND SEE.

LITTLE BIT OF SASS AND A *WHOLE LOTTA* ASS, I DIG THAT. LET'S TAKE YOU UPSTAIRS, PUT ON A *REAL* SHOW. GOT ENOUGH CASH TO--

THANKS FOR LOOKING AFTER MY GIRL, STRETCH. HAVE A GOOD NIGHT.

≲HURK≳

LET'S GET OUT OF HERE AND TAKE YOU SOMEWHERE NICE.

I'M FOLLOWING *YOU,* HANDSOME.

SOME PEOPLE HAVE A KNACK FOR GETTING *OUT* OF TROUBLE...

# BRENTWOOD

...WHILE OTHERS ALWAYS SEEM TO FIND THEMSELVES RIGHT IN THE THICK OF IT.

WE'VE BEEN WATCHING YOU, *SLATER*.

MOST OF THE DEPARTMENT DOESN'T BELIEVE *HIT SQUADS* EVEN EXIST, BUT WE'VE BEEN LUCKY ENOUGH TO SEE THEM IN ACTION.

YOU AND *KEN COLLINS* KILLED *FIVE* MEN BETWEEN 1948 AND 1950. WHEN IT WAS YOU, *McKNIGHT*, *OVERSTREET*, AND *GOMES*, THAT NUMBER TRIPLED.

BUT LAST NIGHT, THE *MASSACRE* AT SLICK RICKY'S WAREHOUSE WITH *STICKELMAN* AND *HAYWOOD*--YOU OUTDID YOURSELVES AND LEFT NEARLY *TWO DOZEN* DEAD. BRAVO.

SORRY, I DIDN'T HEAR A QUESTION IN THERE.

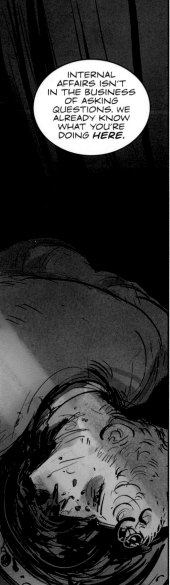

INTERNAL AFFAIRS ISN'T IN THE BUSINESS OF ASKING QUESTIONS. WE ALREADY KNOW WHAT YOU'RE DOING *HERE*.

OKAY, *WILCOX*-- YOU CAUGHT ME.

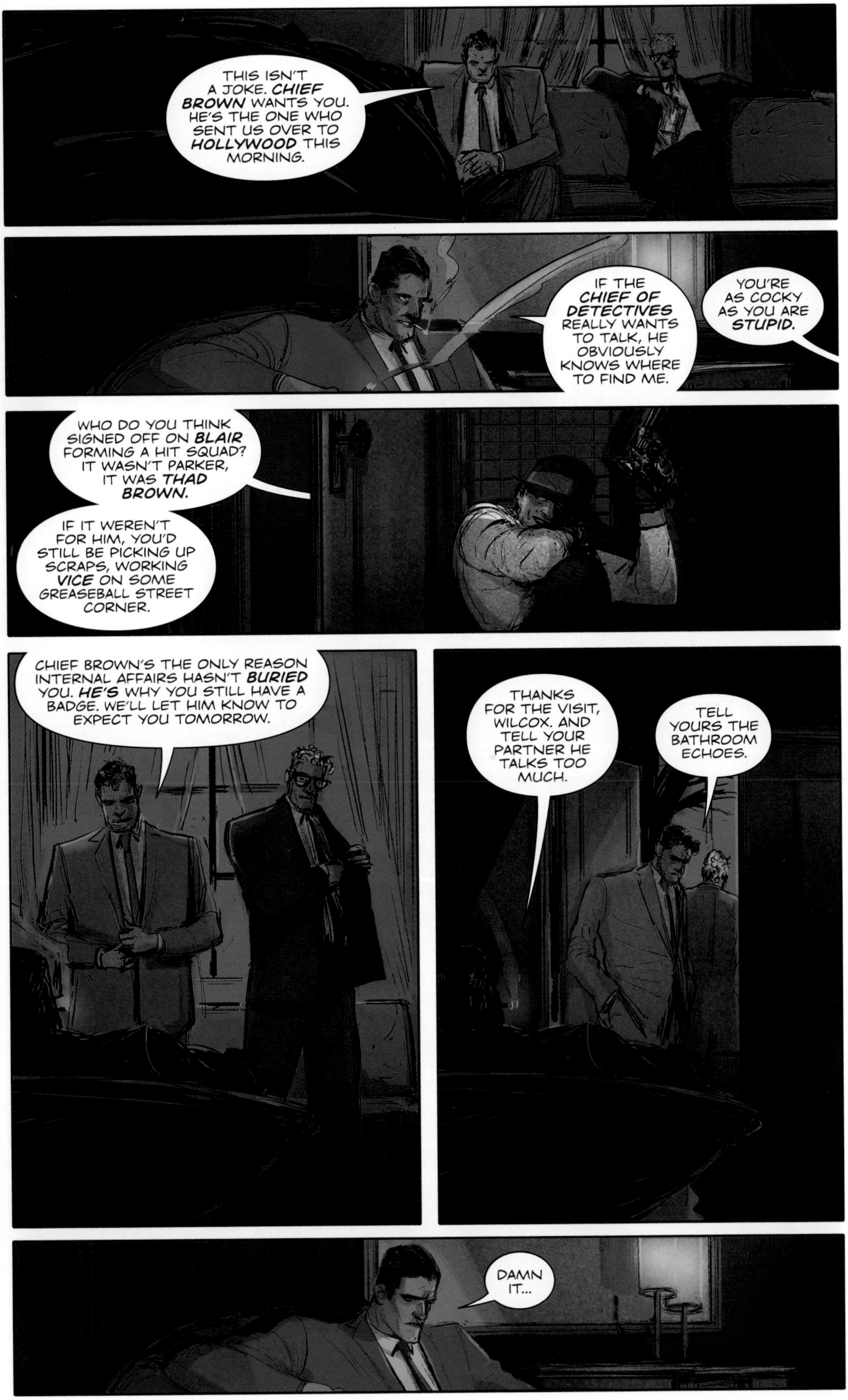
THIS ISN'T A JOKE. CHIEF BROWN WANTS YOU. HE'S THE ONE WHO SENT US OVER TO HOLLYWOOD THIS MORNING.
IF THE CHIEF OF DETECTIVES REALLY WANTS TO TALK, HE OBVIOUSLY KNOWS WHERE TO FIND ME.
YOU'RE AS COCKY AS YOU ARE STUPID.
WHO DO YOU THINK SIGNED OFF ON BLAIR FORMING A HIT SQUAD? IT WASN'T PARKER, IT WAS THAD BROWN.
IF IT WEREN'T FOR HIM, YOU'D STILL BE PICKING UP SCRAPS, WORKING VICE ON SOME GREASEBALL STREET CORNER.
CHIEF BROWN'S THE ONLY REASON INTERNAL AFFAIRS HASN'T BURIED YOU. HE'S WHY YOU STILL HAVE A BADGE. WE'LL LET HIM KNOW TO EXPECT YOU TOMORROW.
THANKS FOR THE VISIT, WILCOX. AND TELL YOUR PARTNER HE TALKS TOO MUCH.
TELL YOURS THE BATHROOM ECHOES.
DAMN IT...

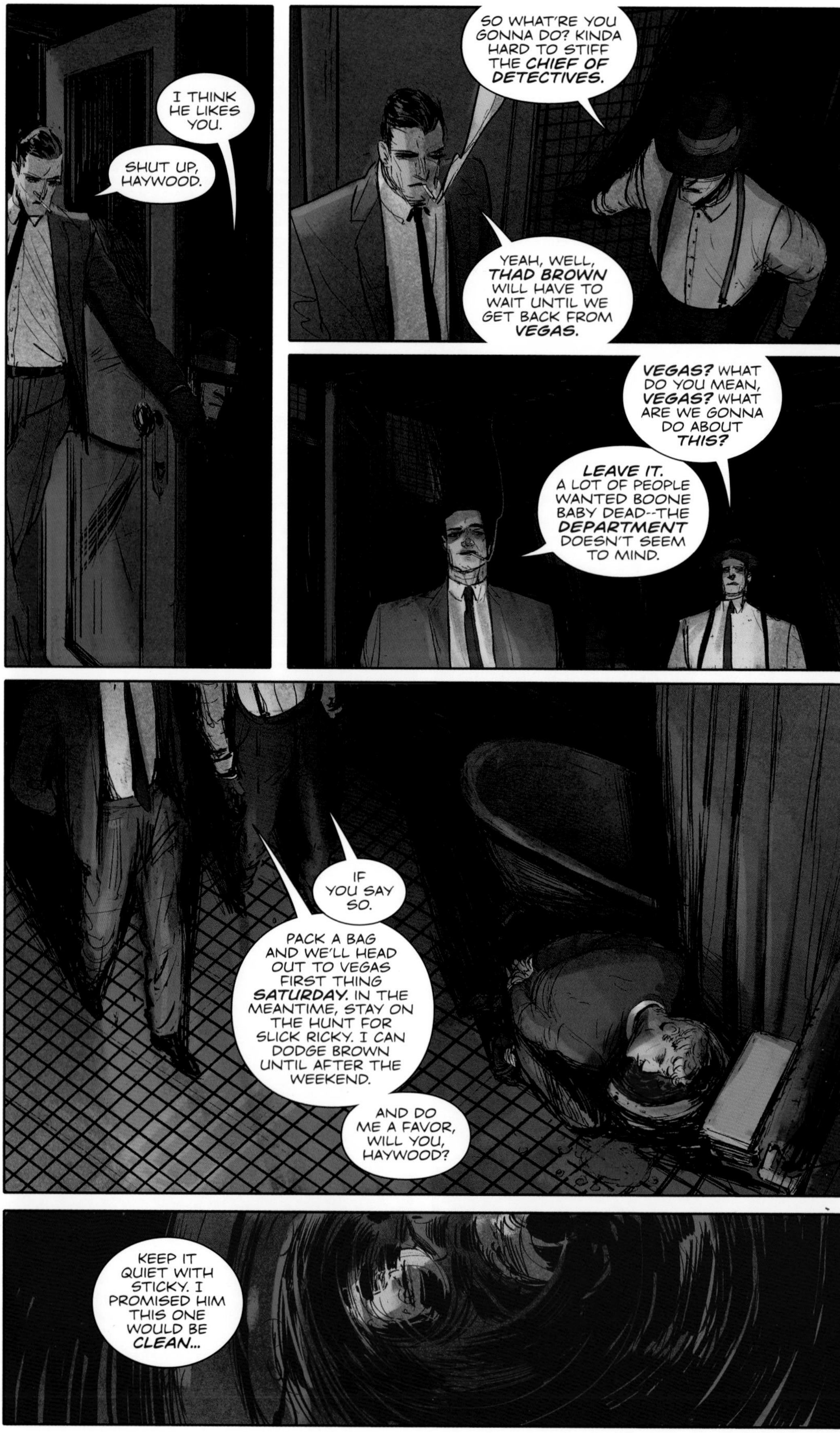
I THINK HE LIKES YOU.
SHUT UP, HAYWOOD.
SO WHAT'RE YOU GONNA DO? KINDA HARD TO STIFF THE **CHIEF OF DETECTIVES.**
YEAH, WELL, **THAD BROWN** WILL HAVE TO WAIT UNTIL WE GET BACK FROM **VEGAS.**
**VEGAS?** WHAT DO YOU MEAN, **VEGAS?** WHAT ARE WE GONNA DO ABOUT **THIS?**
**LEAVE IT.** A LOT OF PEOPLE WANTED BOONE BABY DEAD--THE **DEPARTMENT** DOESN'T SEEM TO MIND.
IF YOU SAY SO.
PACK A BAG AND WE'LL HEAD OUT TO VEGAS FIRST THING **SATURDAY.** IN THE MEANTIME, STAY ON THE HUNT FOR SLICK RICKY. I CAN DODGE BROWN UNTIL AFTER THE WEEKEND.
AND DO ME A FAVOR, WILL YOU, HAYWOOD?
KEEP IT QUIET WITH STICKY. I PROMISED HIM THIS ONE WOULD BE **CLEAN...**

LAS VEGAS

"...AND I DON'T THINK HE CAN HANDLE ANOTHER BROKEN PROMISE RIGHT NOW."

BROKEN PROMISES ARE A HELL OF A THING.

DISHONESTY.

DECEPTION.

BETRAYAL.

A JUDAS KISS.

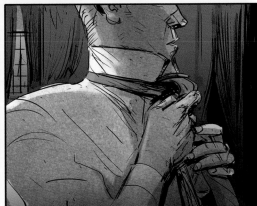

JUST A HANDFUL OF WAYS TO SAY THAT SOMEONE IS *GOING TO DIE.*

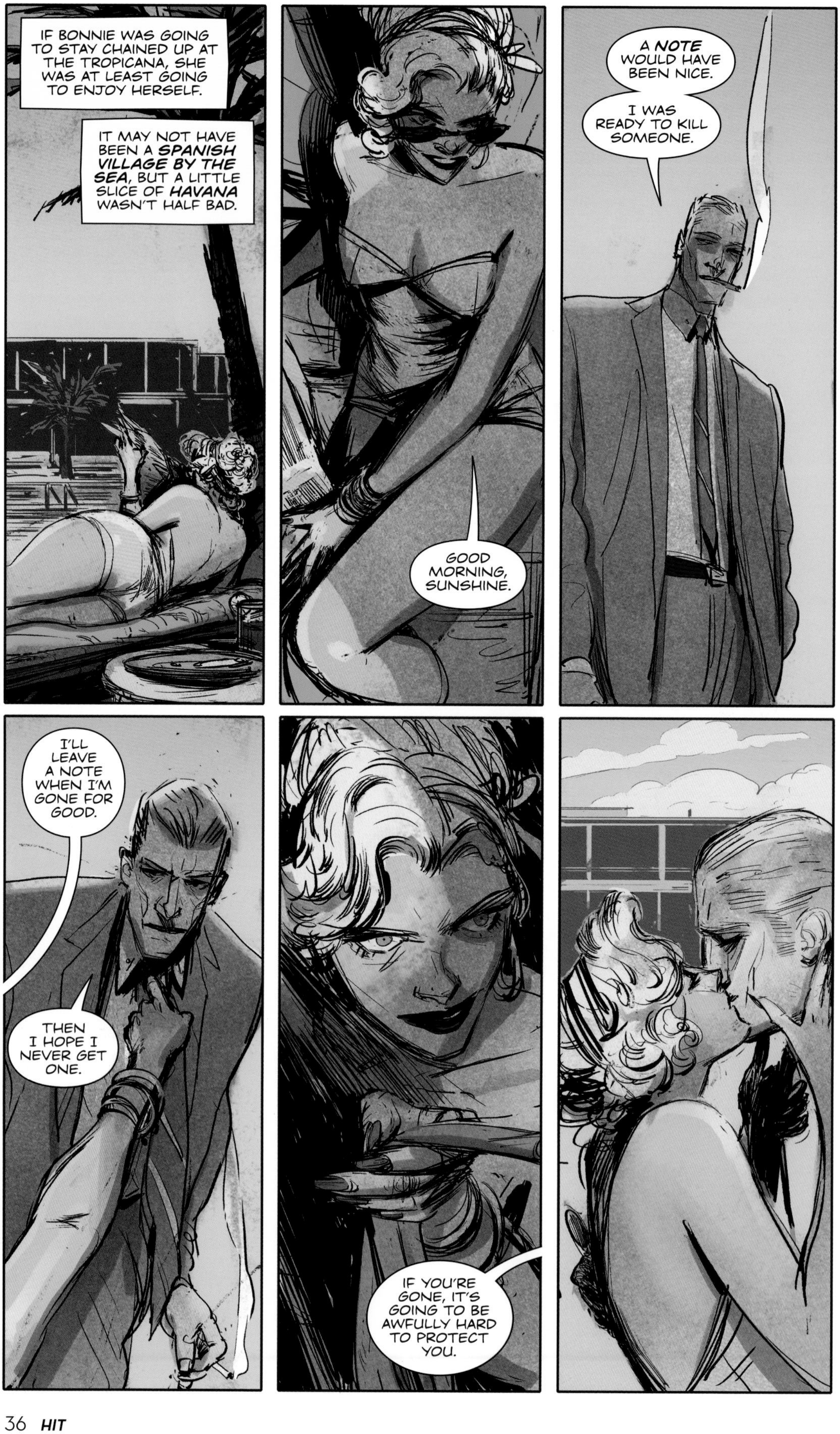

IF BONNIE WAS GOING TO STAY CHAINED UP AT THE TROPICANA, SHE WAS AT LEAST GOING TO ENJOY HERSELF.
IT MAY NOT HAVE BEEN A **SPANISH VILLAGE BY THE SEA**, BUT A LITTLE SLICE OF **HAVANA** WASN'T HALF BAD.
GOOD MORNING, SUNSHINE.
A **NOTE** WOULD HAVE BEEN NICE.
I WAS READY TO KILL SOMEONE.
I'LL LEAVE A NOTE WHEN I'M GONE FOR GOOD.
THEN I HOPE I NEVER GET ONE.
IF YOU'RE GONE, IT'S GOING TO BE AWFULLY HARD TO PROTECT YOU.

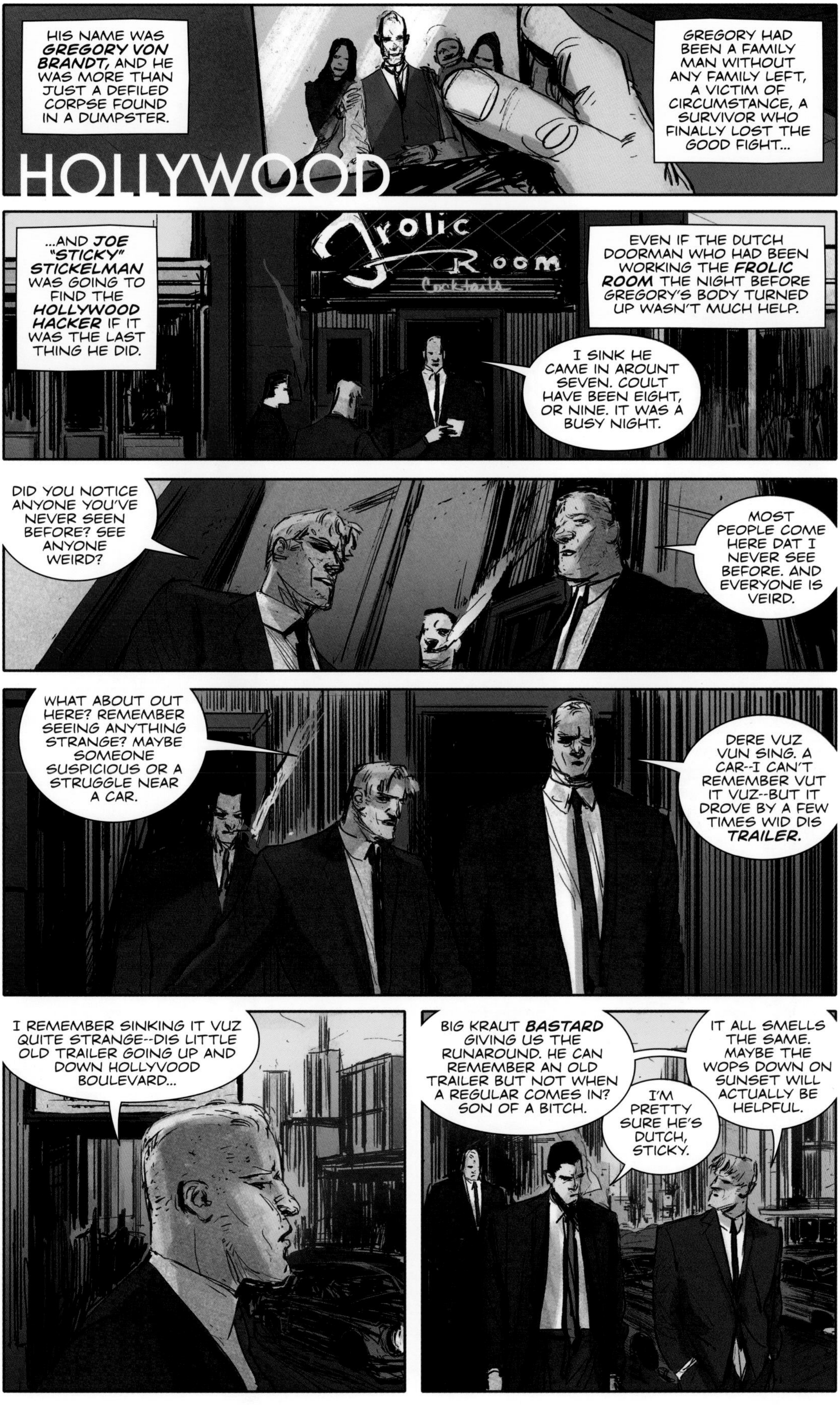
HIS NAME WAS GREGORY VON BRANDT, AND HE WAS MORE THAN JUST A DEFILED CORPSE FOUND IN A DUMPSTER.
GREGORY HAD BEEN A FAMILY MAN WITHOUT ANY FAMILY LEFT, A VICTIM OF CIRCUMSTANCE, A SURVIVOR WHO FINALLY LOST THE GOOD FIGHT...
HOLLYWOOD
...AND JOE "STICKY" STICKELMAN WAS GOING TO FIND THE HOLLYWOOD HACKER IF IT WAS THE LAST THING HE DID.
Frolic Room
Cocktails
EVEN IF THE DUTCH DOORMAN WHO HAD BEEN WORKING THE FROLIC ROOM THE NIGHT BEFORE GREGORY'S BODY TURNED UP WASN'T MUCH HELP.
I SINK HE CAME IN AROUNT SEVEN. COULT HAVE BEEN EIGHT, OR NINE. IT WAS A BUSY NIGHT.
DID YOU NOTICE ANYONE YOU'VE NEVER SEEN BEFORE? SEE ANYONE WEIRD?
MOST PEOPLE COME HERE DAT I NEVER SEE BEFORE. AND EVERYONE IS VEIRD.
WHAT ABOUT OUT HERE? REMEMBER SEEING ANYTHING STRANGE? MAYBE SOMEONE SUSPICIOUS OR A STRUGGLE NEAR A CAR.
DERE VUZ VUN SING. A CAR--I CAN'T REMEMBER VUT IT VUZ--BUT IT DROVE BY A FEW TIMES WID DIS TRAILER.
I REMEMBER SINKING IT VUZ QUITE STRANGE--DIS LITTLE OLD TRAILER GOING UP AND DOWN HOLLYVOOD BOULEVARD...
BIG KRAUT BASTARD GIVING US THE RUNAROUND. HE CAN REMEMBER AN OLD TRAILER BUT NOT WHEN A REGULAR COMES IN? SON OF A BITCH.
I'M PRETTY SURE HE'S DUTCH, STICKY.
IT ALL SMELLS THE SAME. MAYBE THE WOPS DOWN ON SUNSET WILL ACTUALLY BE HELPFUL.

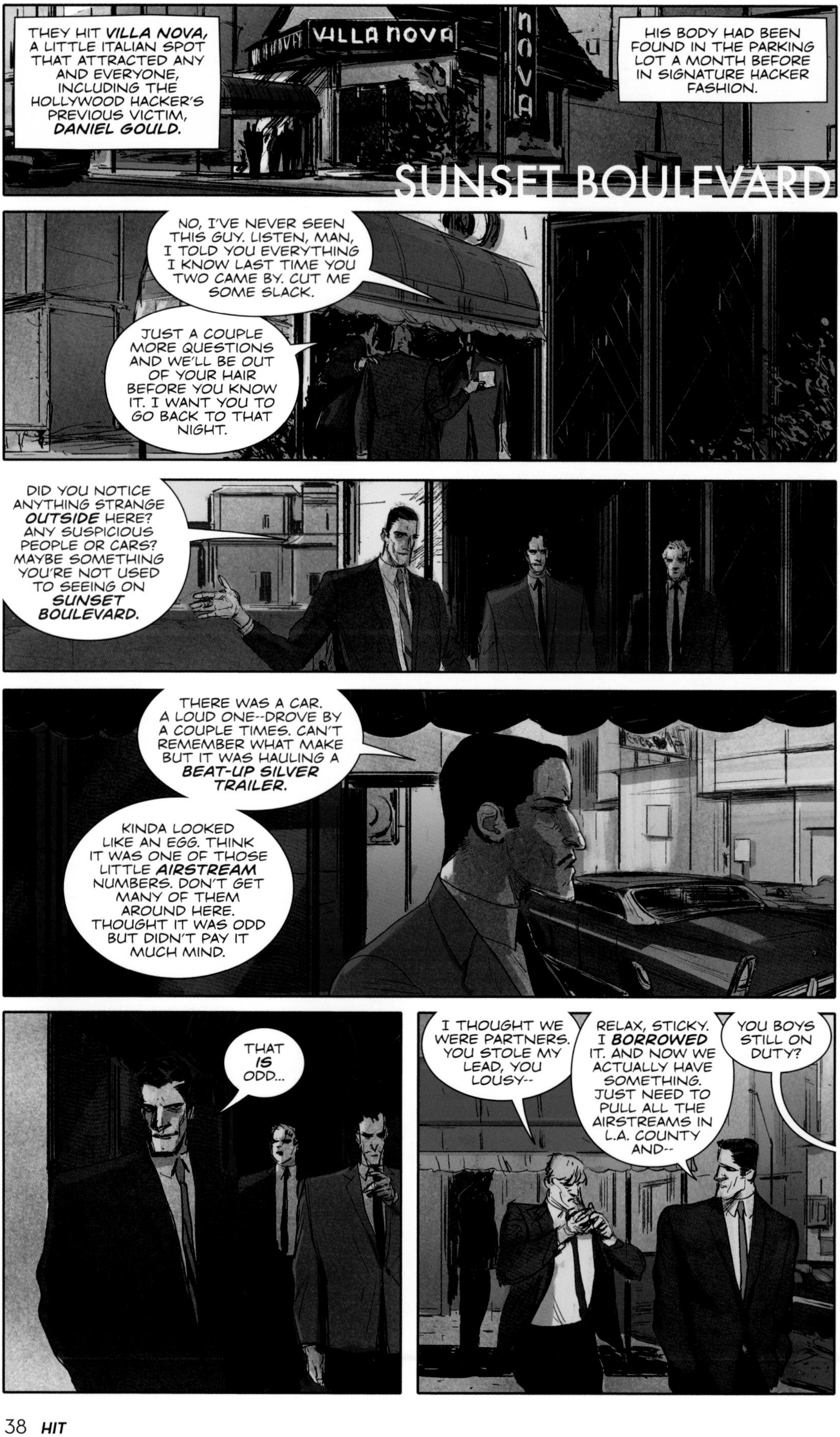
THEY HIT VILLA NOVA, A LITTLE ITALIAN SPOT THAT ATTRACTED ANY AND EVERYONE, INCLUDING THE HOLLYWOOD HACKER'S PREVIOUS VICTIM, DANIEL GOULD.
VILLA NOVA
NOVA
HIS BODY HAD BEEN FOUND IN THE PARKING LOT A MONTH BEFORE IN SIGNATURE HACKER FASHION.
SUNSET BOULEVARD
NO, I'VE NEVER SEEN THIS GUY. LISTEN, MAN, I TOLD YOU EVERYTHING I KNOW LAST TIME YOU TWO CAME BY. CUT ME SOME SLACK.
JUST A COUPLE MORE QUESTIONS AND WE'LL BE OUT OF YOUR HAIR BEFORE YOU KNOW IT. I WANT YOU TO GO BACK TO THAT NIGHT.
DID YOU NOTICE ANYTHING STRANGE OUTSIDE HERE? ANY SUSPICIOUS PEOPLE OR CARS? MAYBE SOMETHING YOU'RE NOT USED TO SEEING ON SUNSET BOULEVARD.
THERE WAS A CAR. A LOUD ONE--DROVE BY A COUPLE TIMES. CAN'T REMEMBER WHAT MAKE BUT IT WAS HAULING A BEAT-UP SILVER TRAILER.
KINDA LOOKED LIKE AN EGG. THINK IT WAS ONE OF THOSE LITTLE AIRSTREAM NUMBERS. DON'T GET MANY OF THEM AROUND HERE. THOUGHT IT WAS ODD BUT DIDN'T PAY IT MUCH MIND.
THAT IS ODD...
I THOUGHT WE WERE PARTNERS. YOU STOLE MY LEAD, YOU LOUSY--
RELAX, STICKY. I BORROWED IT. AND NOW WE ACTUALLY HAVE SOMETHING. JUST NEED TO PULL ALL THE AIRSTREAMS IN L.A. COUNTY AND--
YOU BOYS STILL ON DUTY?

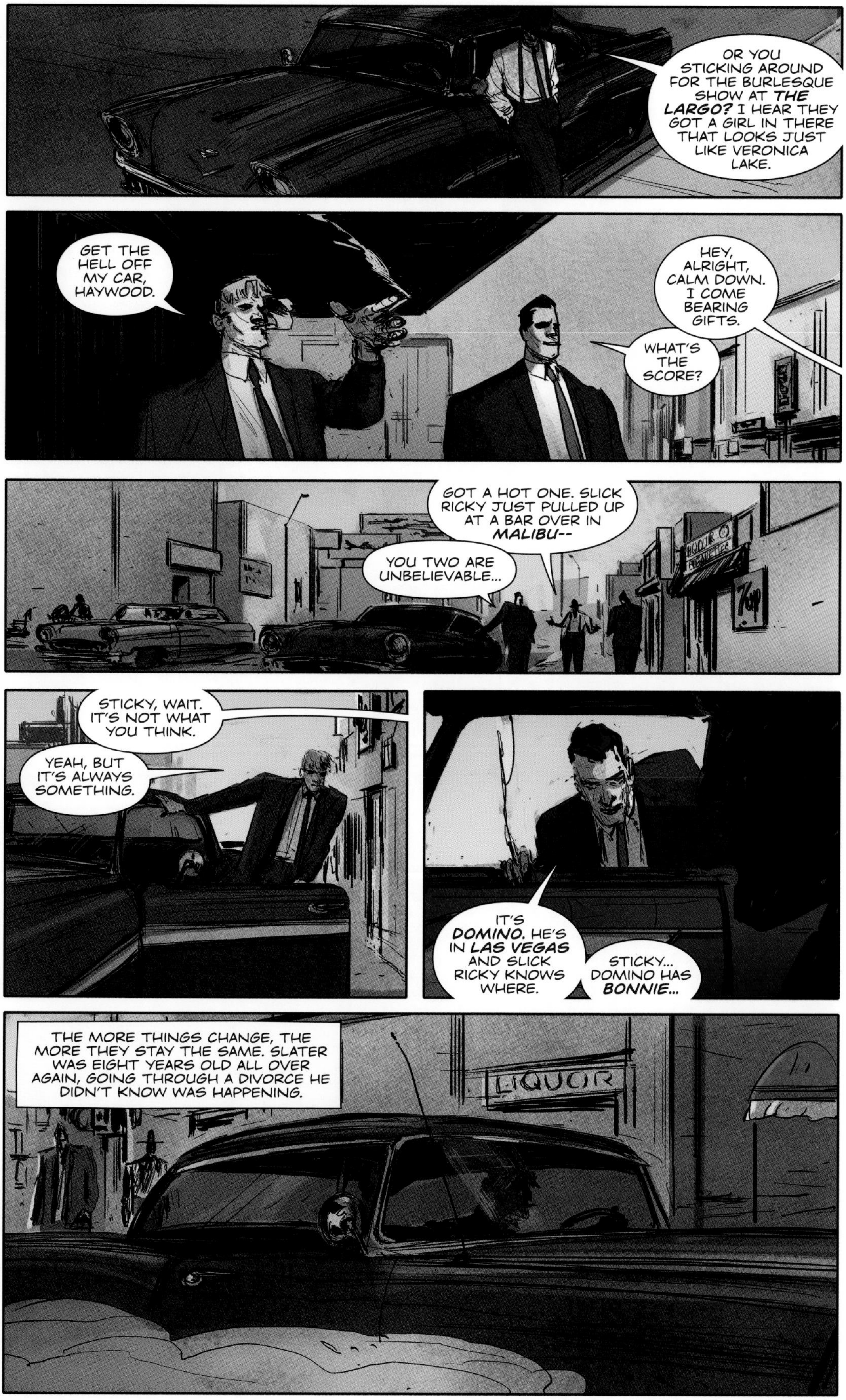
OR YOU STICKING AROUND FOR THE BURLESQUE SHOW AT **THE LARGO?** I HEAR THEY GOT A GIRL IN THERE THAT LOOKS JUST LIKE VERONICA LAKE.
GET THE HELL OFF MY CAR, HAYWOOD.
HEY, ALRIGHT, CALM DOWN. I COME BEARING GIFTS.
WHAT'S THE SCORE?
GOT A HOT ONE. SLICK RICKY JUST PULLED UP AT A BAR OVER IN **MALIBU--**
YOU TWO ARE UNBELIEVABLE...
LIQUOR CIGARETTES
STICKY, WAIT. IT'S NOT WHAT YOU THINK.
YEAH, BUT IT'S ALWAYS SOMETHING.
IT'S **DOMINO.** HE'S IN **LAS VEGAS** AND SLICK RICKY KNOWS WHERE.
STICKY... DOMINO HAS **BONNIE...**
THE MORE THINGS CHANGE, THE MORE THEY STAY THE SAME. SLATER WAS EIGHT YEARS OLD ALL OVER AGAIN, GOING THROUGH A DIVORCE HE DIDN'T KNOW WAS HAPPENING.
LIQUOR

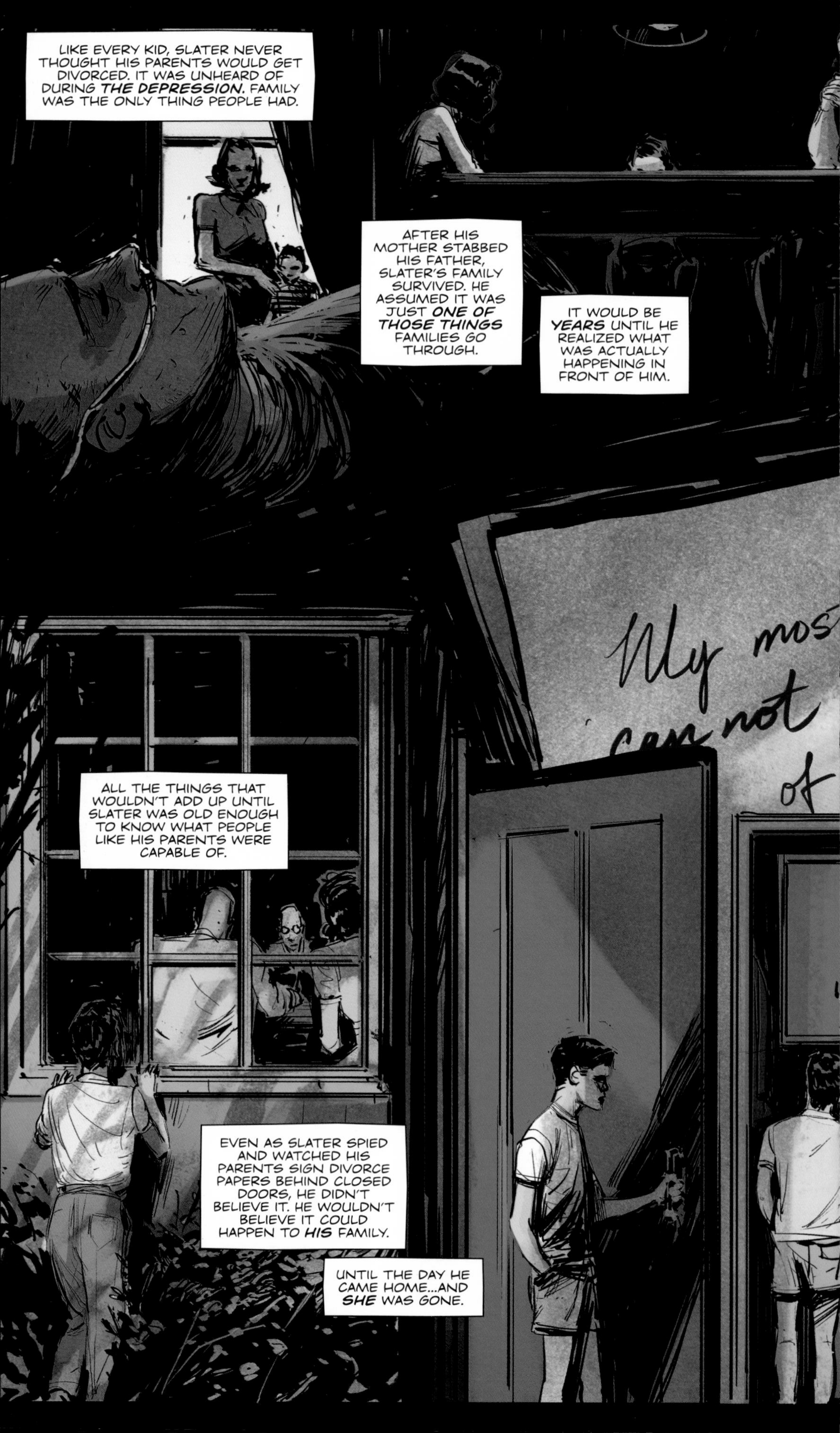
LIKE EVERY KID, SLATER NEVER THOUGHT HIS PARENTS WOULD GET DIVORCED. IT WAS UNHEARD OF DURING THE DEPRESSION. FAMILY WAS THE ONLY THING PEOPLE HAD.
AFTER HIS MOTHER STABBED HIS FATHER, SLATER'S FAMILY SURVIVED. HE ASSUMED IT WAS JUST ONE OF THOSE THINGS FAMILIES GO THROUGH.
IT WOULD BE YEARS UNTIL HE REALIZED WHAT WAS ACTUALLY HAPPENING IN FRONT OF HIM.
My mos
can not
of
ALL THE THINGS THAT WOULDN'T ADD UP UNTIL SLATER WAS OLD ENOUGH TO KNOW WHAT PEOPLE LIKE HIS PARENTS WERE CAPABLE OF.
EVEN AS SLATER SPIED AND WATCHED HIS PARENTS SIGN DIVORCE PAPERS BEHIND CLOSED DOORS, HE DIDN'T BELIEVE IT. HE WOULDN'T BELIEVE IT COULD HAPPEN TO HIS FAMILY.
UNTIL THE DAY HE CAME HOME...AND SHE WAS GONE.

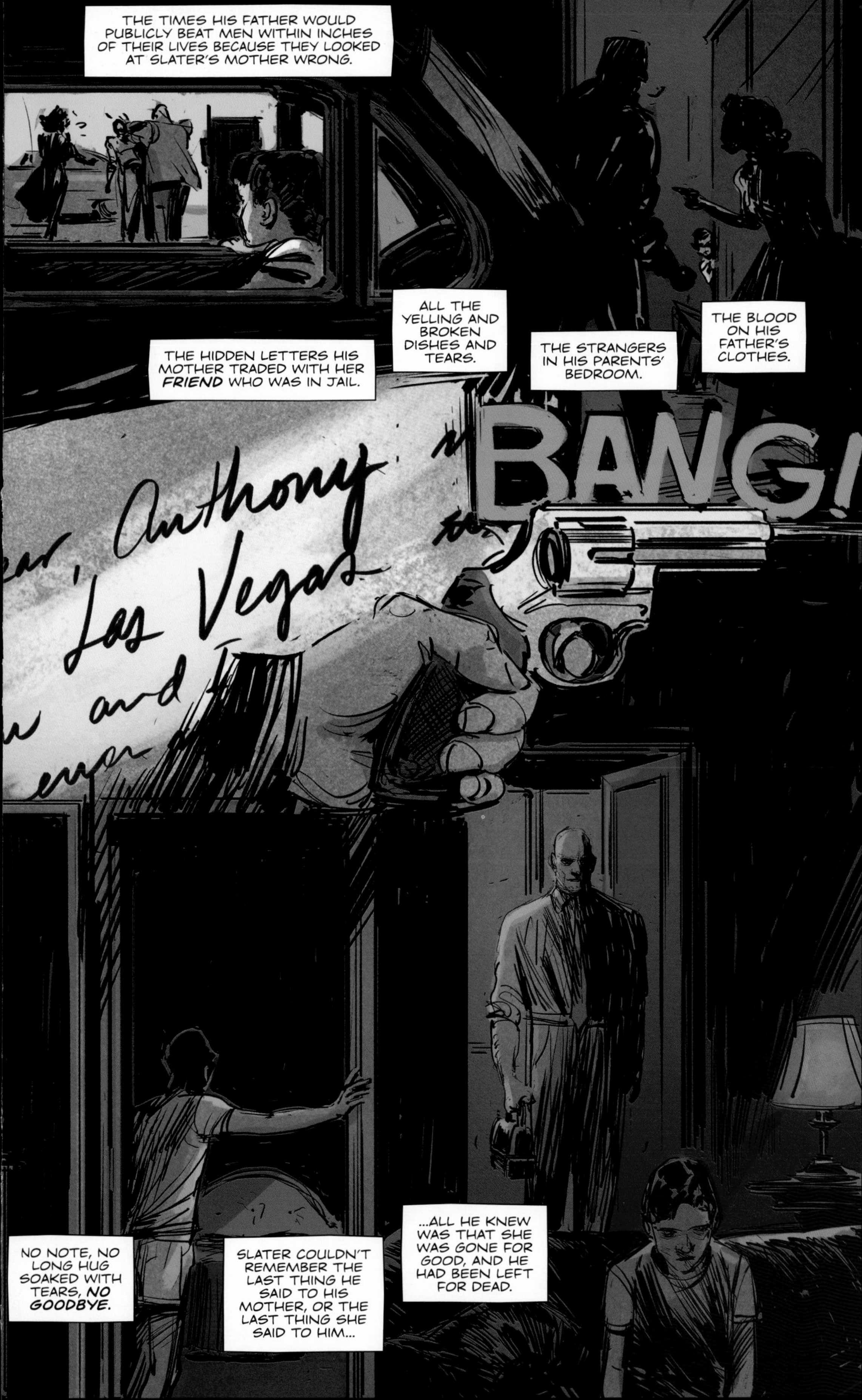
THE TIMES HIS FATHER WOULD PUBLICLY BEAT MEN WITHIN INCHES OF THEIR LIVES BECAUSE THEY LOOKED AT SLATER'S MOTHER WRONG.
THE HIDDEN LETTERS HIS MOTHER TRADED WITH HER *FRIEND* WHO WAS IN JAIL.
ALL THE YELLING AND BROKEN DISHES AND TEARS.
THE STRANGERS IN HIS PARENTS' BEDROOM.
THE BLOOD ON HIS FATHER'S CLOTHES.
Anthony
Las Vegas
and
BANG!
NO NOTE, NO LONG HUG SOAKED WITH TEARS, ***NO GOODBYE***.
SLATER COULDN'T REMEMBER THE LAST THING HE SAID TO HIS MOTHER, OR THE LAST THING SHE SAID TO HIM...
...ALL HE KNEW WAS THAT SHE WAS GONE FOR GOOD, AND HE HAD BEEN LEFT FOR DEAD.

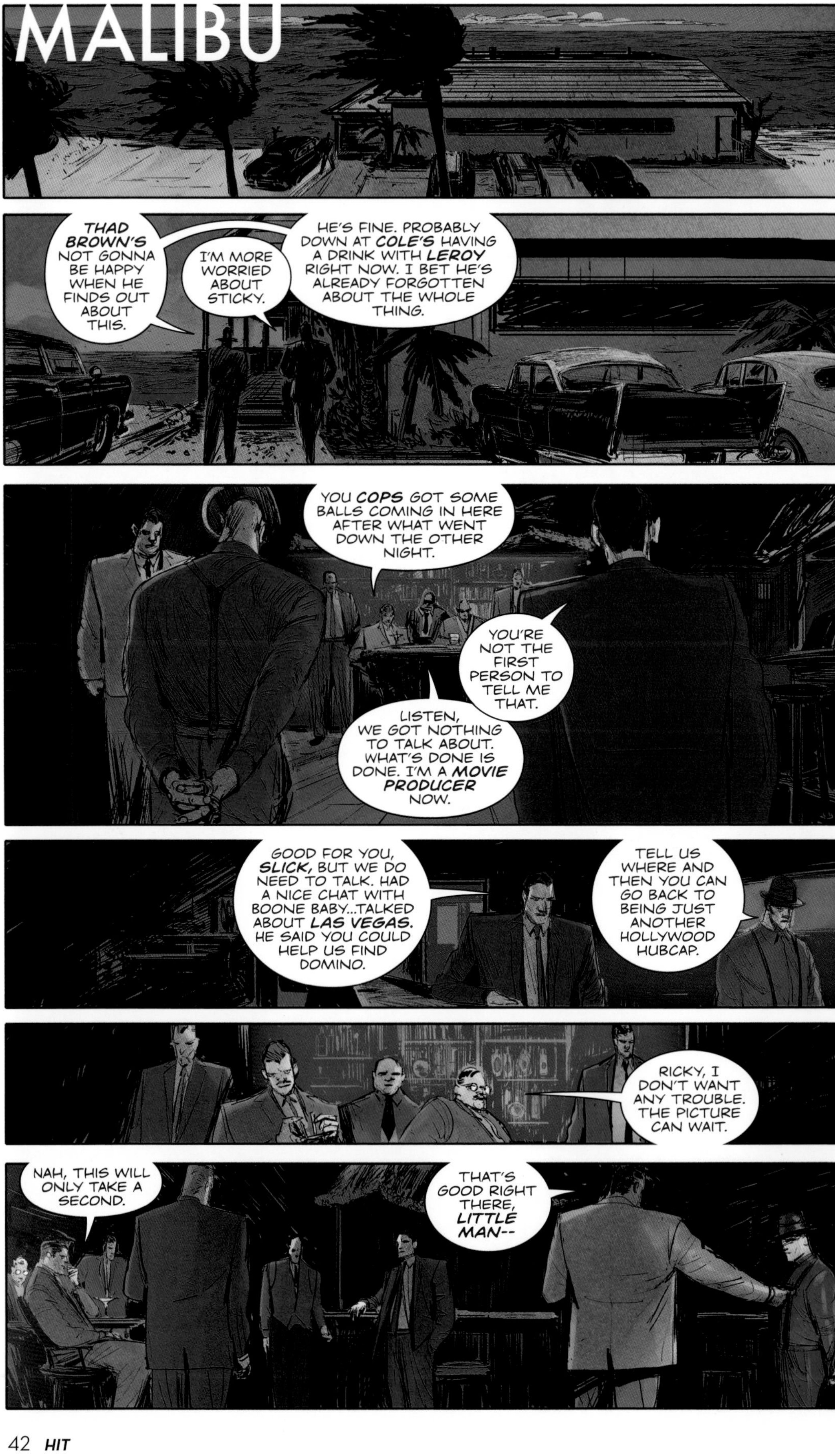
MALIBU
THAD BROWN'S NOT GONNA BE HAPPY WHEN HE FINDS OUT ABOUT THIS.
I'M MORE WORRIED ABOUT STICKY.
HE'S FINE. PROBABLY DOWN AT COLE'S HAVING A DRINK WITH LEROY RIGHT NOW. I BET HE'S ALREADY FORGOTTEN ABOUT THE WHOLE THING.
YOU COPS GOT SOME BALLS COMING IN HERE AFTER WHAT WENT DOWN THE OTHER NIGHT.
YOU'RE NOT THE FIRST PERSON TO TELL ME THAT.
LISTEN, WE GOT NOTHING TO TALK ABOUT. WHAT'S DONE IS DONE. I'M A MOVIE PRODUCER NOW.
GOOD FOR YOU, SLICK, BUT WE DO NEED TO TALK. HAD A NICE CHAT WITH BOONE BABY...TALKED ABOUT LAS VEGAS. HE SAID YOU COULD HELP US FIND DOMINO.
TELL US WHERE AND THEN YOU CAN GO BACK TO BEING JUST ANOTHER HOLLYWOOD HUBCAP.
RICKY, I DON'T WANT ANY TROUBLE. THE PICTURE CAN WAIT.
NAH, THIS WILL ONLY TAKE A SECOND.
THAT'S GOOD RIGHT THERE, LITTLE MAN--

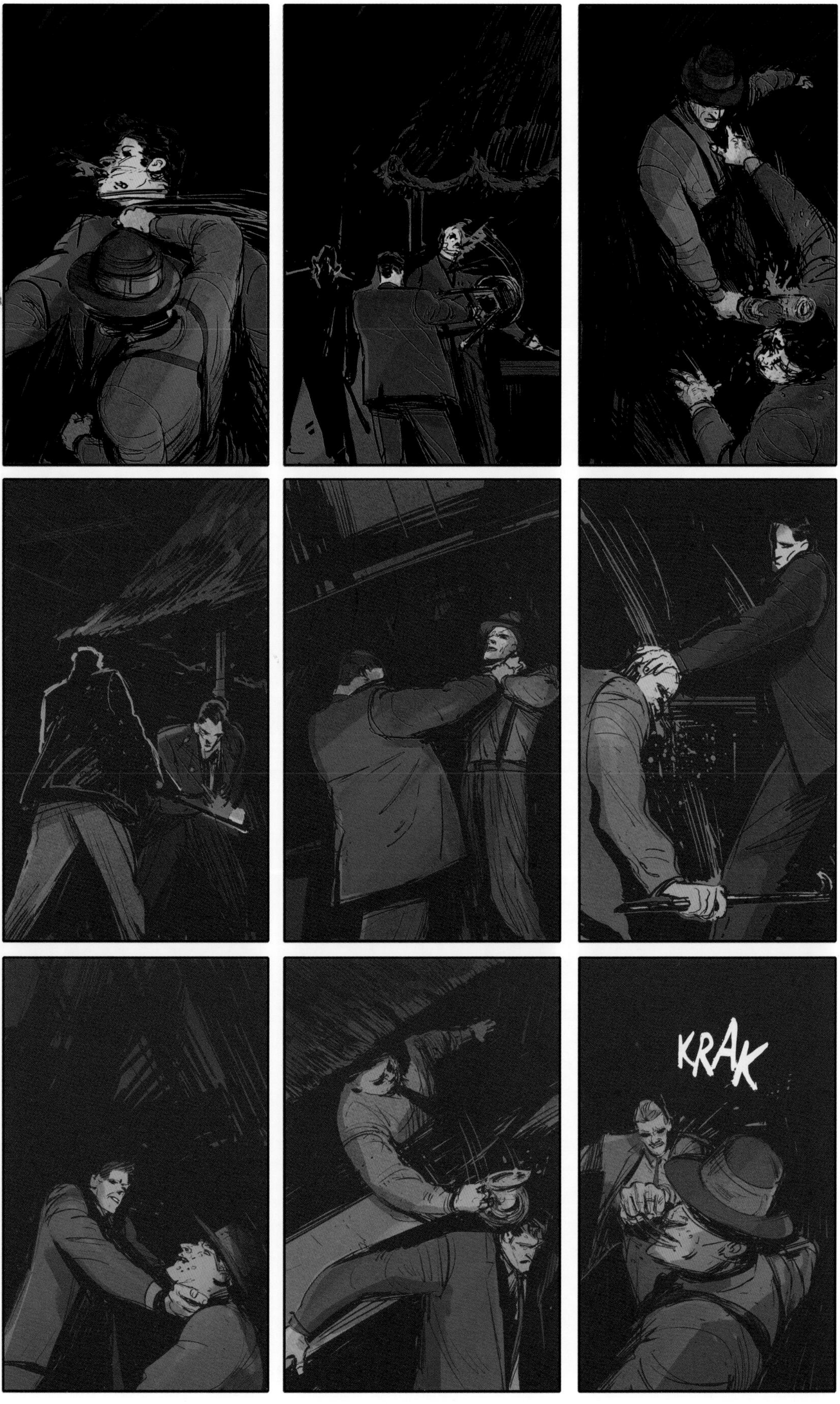
KRAK

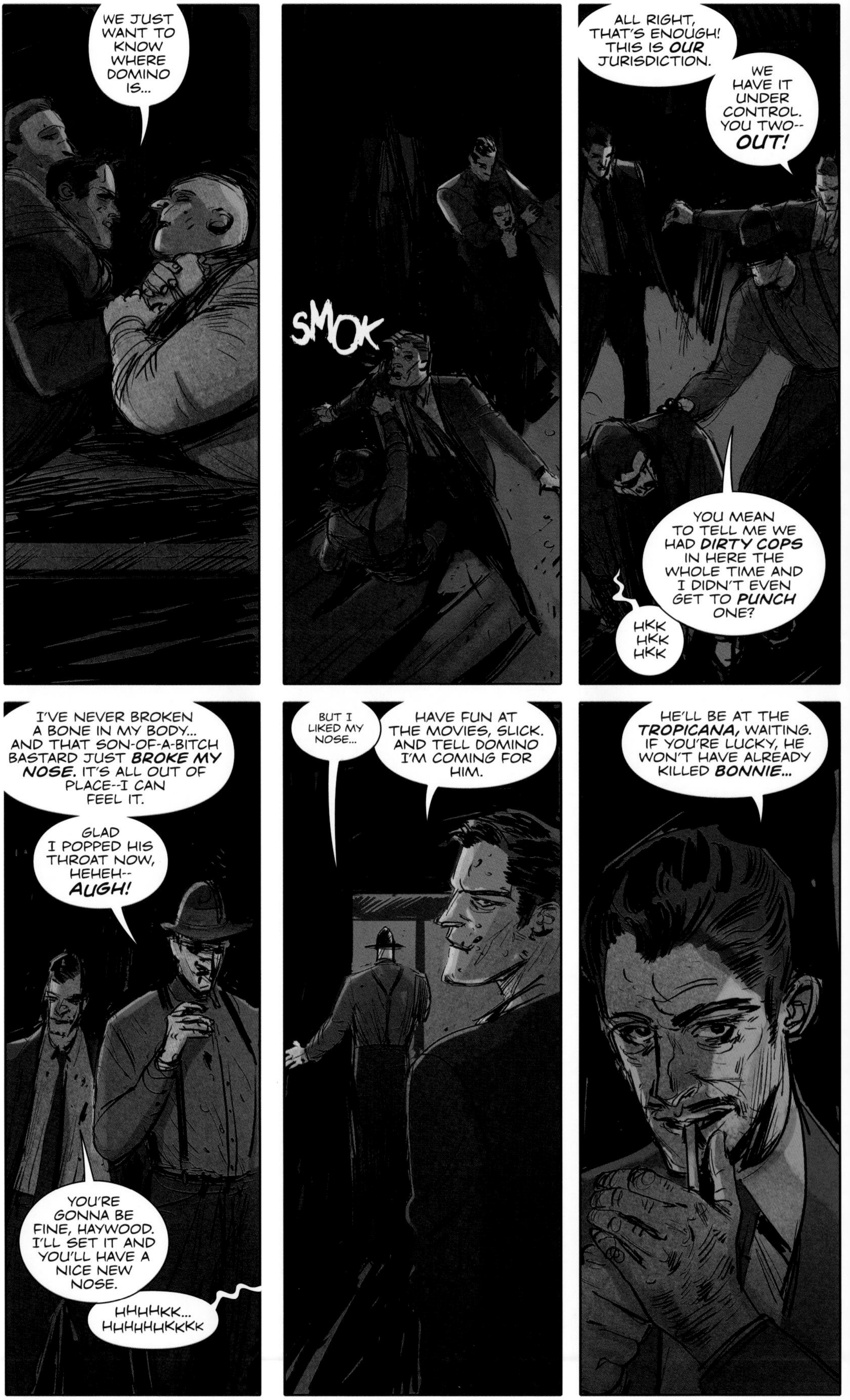

WE JUST WANT TO KNOW WHERE DOMINO IS...
SMOK
ALL RIGHT, THAT'S ENOUGH! THIS IS **OUR** JURISDICTION.
WE HAVE IT UNDER CONTROL. YOU TWO-- **OUT!**
YOU MEAN TO TELL ME WE HAD **DIRTY COPS** IN HERE THE WHOLE TIME AND I DIDN'T EVEN GET TO **PUNCH** ONE?
HKK HKK HKK
I'VE NEVER BROKEN A BONE IN MY BODY... AND THAT SON-OF-A-BITCH BASTARD JUST **BROKE MY NOSE.** IT'S ALL OUT OF PLACE--I CAN FEEL IT.
GLAD I POPPED HIS THROAT NOW, HEHEH-- **AUGH!**
YOU'RE GONNA BE FINE, HAYWOOD. I'LL SET IT AND YOU'LL HAVE A NICE NEW NOSE.
HHHHKK... HHHHHHKKKK
BUT I LIKED MY NOSE...
HAVE FUN AT THE MOVIES, SLICK. AND TELL DOMINO I'M COMING FOR HIM.
HE'LL BE AT THE **TROPICANA,** WAITING. IF YOU'RE LUCKY, HE WON'T HAVE ALREADY KILLED **BONNIE...**

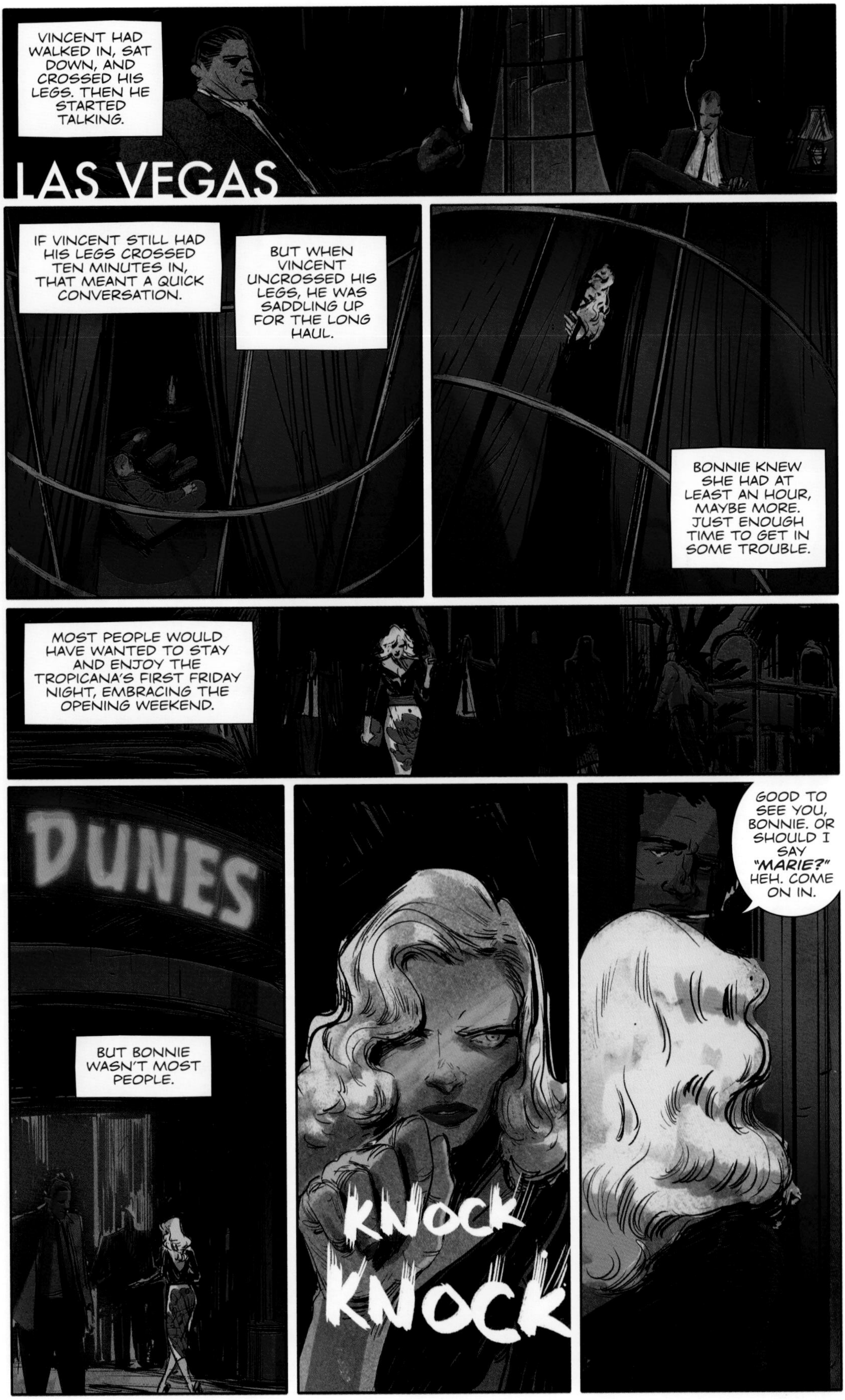
VINCENT HAD WALKED IN, SAT DOWN, AND CROSSED HIS LEGS. THEN HE STARTED TALKING.
LAS VEGAS
IF VINCENT STILL HAD HIS LEGS CROSSED TEN MINUTES IN, THAT MEANT A QUICK CONVERSATION.
BUT WHEN VINCENT UNCROSSED HIS LEGS, HE WAS SADDLING UP FOR THE LONG HAUL.
BONNIE KNEW SHE HAD AT LEAST AN HOUR, MAYBE MORE. JUST ENOUGH TIME TO GET IN SOME TROUBLE.
MOST PEOPLE WOULD HAVE WANTED TO STAY AND ENJOY THE TROPICANA'S FIRST FRIDAY NIGHT, EMBRACING THE OPENING WEEKEND.
DUNES
BUT BONNIE WASN'T MOST PEOPLE.
KNOCK KNOCK
GOOD TO SEE YOU, BONNIE. OR SHOULD I SAY *"MARIE?"* HEH. COME ON IN.

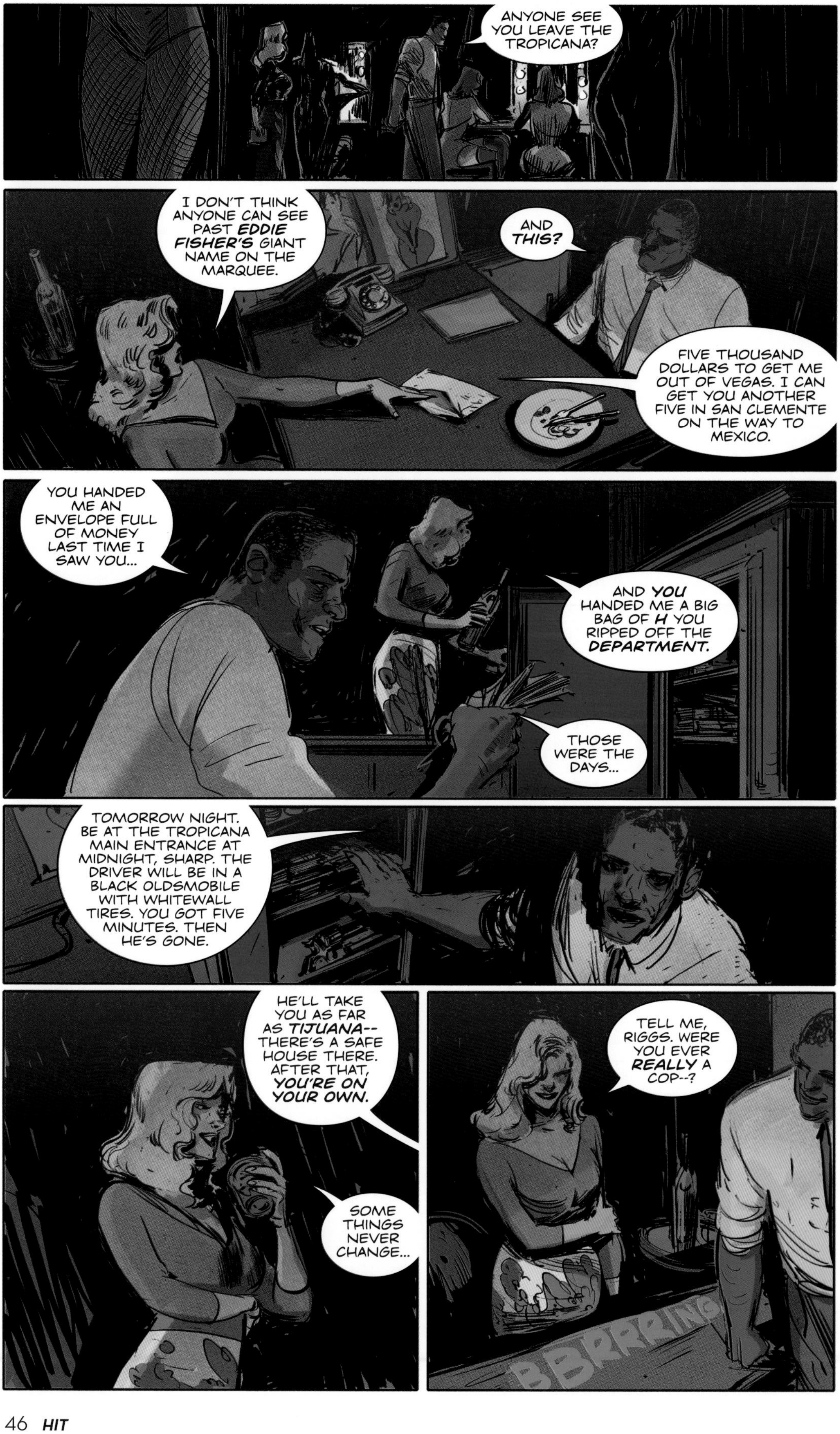
ANYONE SEE YOU LEAVE THE TROPICANA?
I DON'T THINK ANYONE CAN SEE PAST EDDIE FISHER'S GIANT NAME ON THE MARQUEE.
AND THIS?
FIVE THOUSAND DOLLARS TO GET ME OUT OF VEGAS. I CAN GET YOU ANOTHER FIVE IN SAN CLEMENTE ON THE WAY TO MEXICO.
YOU HANDED ME AN ENVELOPE FULL OF MONEY LAST TIME I SAW YOU...
AND YOU HANDED ME A BIG BAG OF H YOU RIPPED OFF THE DEPARTMENT.
THOSE WERE THE DAYS...
TOMORROW NIGHT. BE AT THE TROPICANA MAIN ENTRANCE AT MIDNIGHT, SHARP. THE DRIVER WILL BE IN A BLACK OLDSMOBILE WITH WHITEWALL TIRES. YOU GOT FIVE MINUTES. THEN HE'S GONE.
HE'LL TAKE YOU AS FAR AS TIJUANA-- THERE'S A SAFE HOUSE THERE. AFTER THAT, YOU'RE ON YOUR OWN.
SOME THINGS NEVER CHANGE...
TELL ME, RIGGS. WERE YOU EVER REALLY A COP--?
BBRRRING

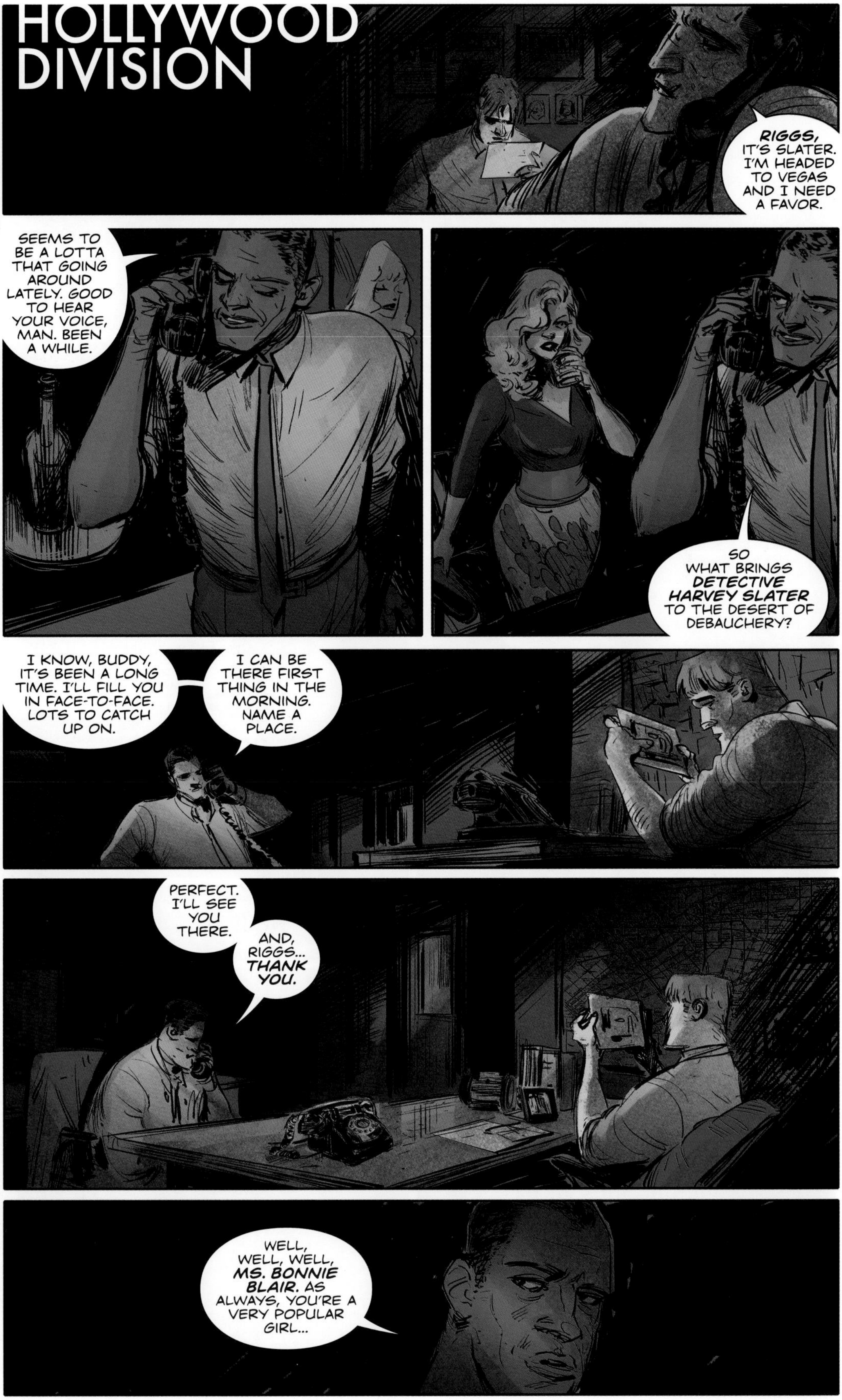
HOLLYWOOD DIVISION
RIGGS, IT'S SLATER. I'M HEADED TO VEGAS AND I NEED A FAVOR.
SEEMS TO BE A LOTTA THAT GOING AROUND LATELY. GOOD TO HEAR YOUR VOICE, MAN. BEEN A WHILE.
SO WHAT BRINGS DETECTIVE HARVEY SLATER TO THE DESERT OF DEBAUCHERY?
I KNOW, BUDDY, IT'S BEEN A LONG TIME. I'LL FILL YOU IN FACE-TO-FACE. LOTS TO CATCH UP ON.
I CAN BE THERE FIRST THING IN THE MORNING. NAME A PLACE.
PERFECT. I'LL SEE YOU THERE.
AND, RIGGS... THANK YOU.
WELL, WELL, WELL, MS. BONNIE BLAIR. AS ALWAYS, YOU'RE A VERY POPULAR GIRL...

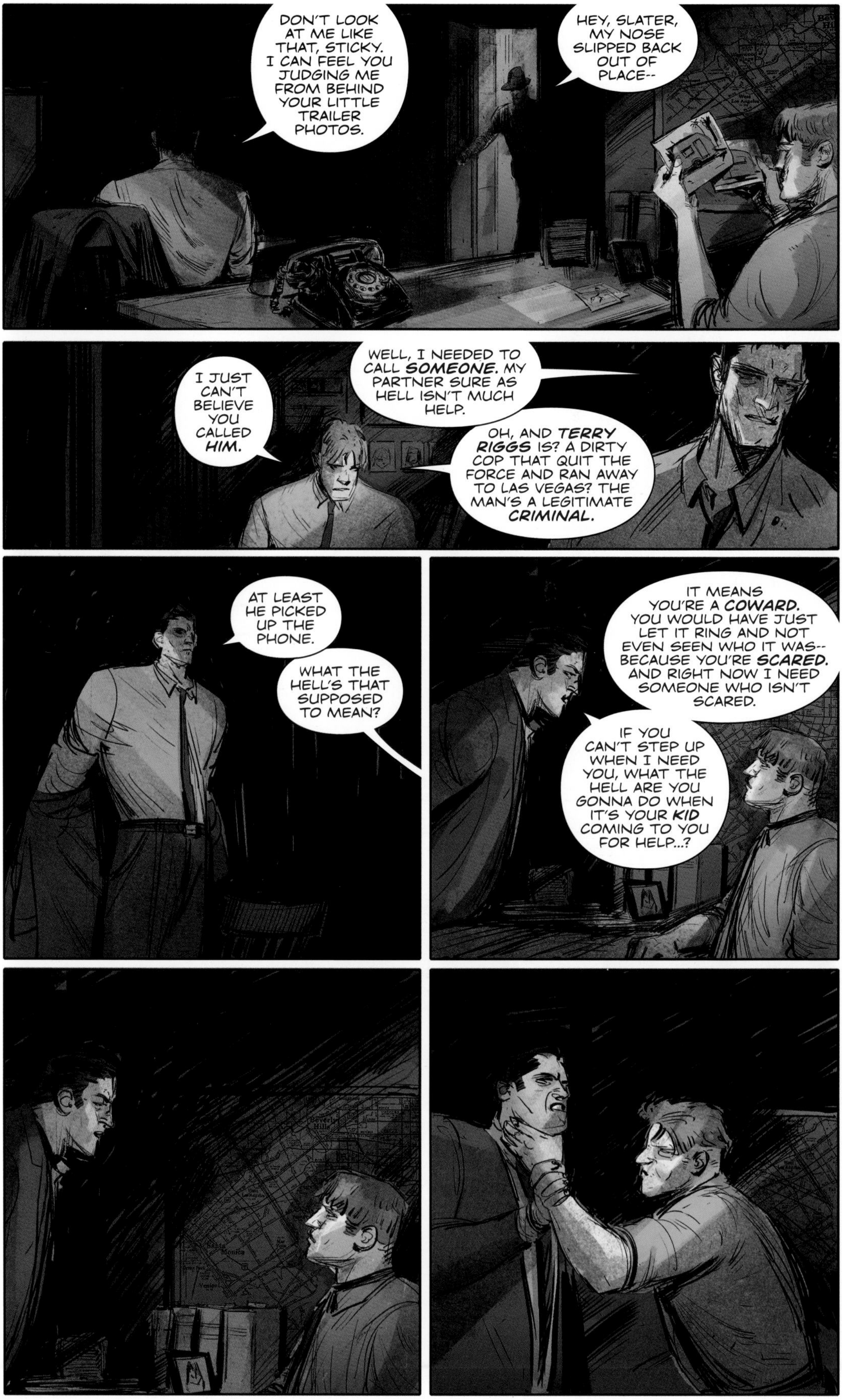
DON'T LOOK AT ME LIKE THAT, STICKY. I CAN FEEL YOU JUDGING ME FROM BEHIND YOUR LITTLE TRAILER PHOTOS.
HEY, SLATER, MY NOSE SLIPPED BACK OUT OF PLACE--
I JUST CAN'T BELIEVE YOU CALLED ***HIM.***
WELL, I NEEDED TO CALL ***SOMEONE.*** MY PARTNER SURE AS HELL ISN'T MUCH HELP.
OH, AND ***TERRY RIGGS*** IS? A DIRTY COP THAT QUIT THE FORCE AND RAN AWAY TO LAS VEGAS? THE MAN'S A LEGITIMATE ***CRIMINAL.***
AT LEAST HE PICKED UP THE PHONE.
WHAT THE HELL'S THAT SUPPOSED TO MEAN?
IT MEANS YOU'RE A ***COWARD.*** YOU WOULD HAVE JUST LET IT RING AND NOT EVEN SEEN WHO IT WAS-- BECAUSE YOU'RE ***SCARED.*** AND RIGHT NOW I NEED SOMEONE WHO ISN'T SCARED.
IF YOU CAN'T STEP UP WHEN I NEED YOU, WHAT THE HELL ARE YOU GONNA DO WHEN IT'S YOUR ***KID*** COMING TO YOU FOR HELP...?

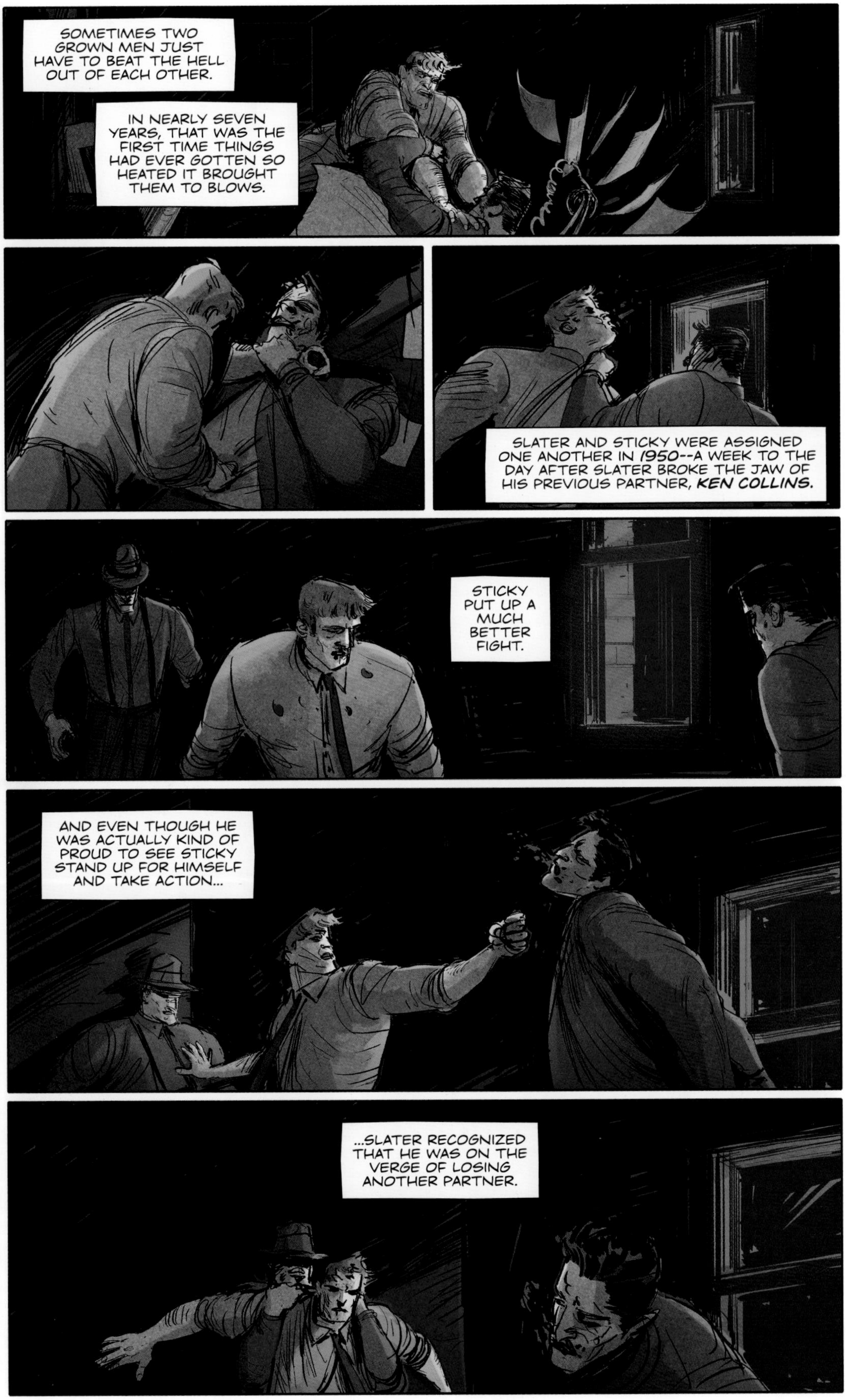
SOMETIMES TWO GROWN MEN JUST HAVE TO BEAT THE HELL OUT OF EACH OTHER.
IN NEARLY SEVEN YEARS, THAT WAS THE FIRST TIME THINGS HAD EVER GOTTEN SO HEATED IT BROUGHT THEM TO BLOWS.
SLATER AND STICKY WERE ASSIGNED ONE ANOTHER IN *1950*--A WEEK TO THE DAY AFTER SLATER BROKE THE JAW OF HIS PREVIOUS PARTNER, ***KEN COLLINS.***
STICKY PUT UP A MUCH BETTER FIGHT.
AND EVEN THOUGH HE WAS ACTUALLY KIND OF PROUD TO SEE STICKY STAND UP FOR HIMSELF AND TAKE ACTION...
...SLATER RECOGNIZED THAT HE WAS ON THE VERGE OF LOSING ANOTHER PARTNER.

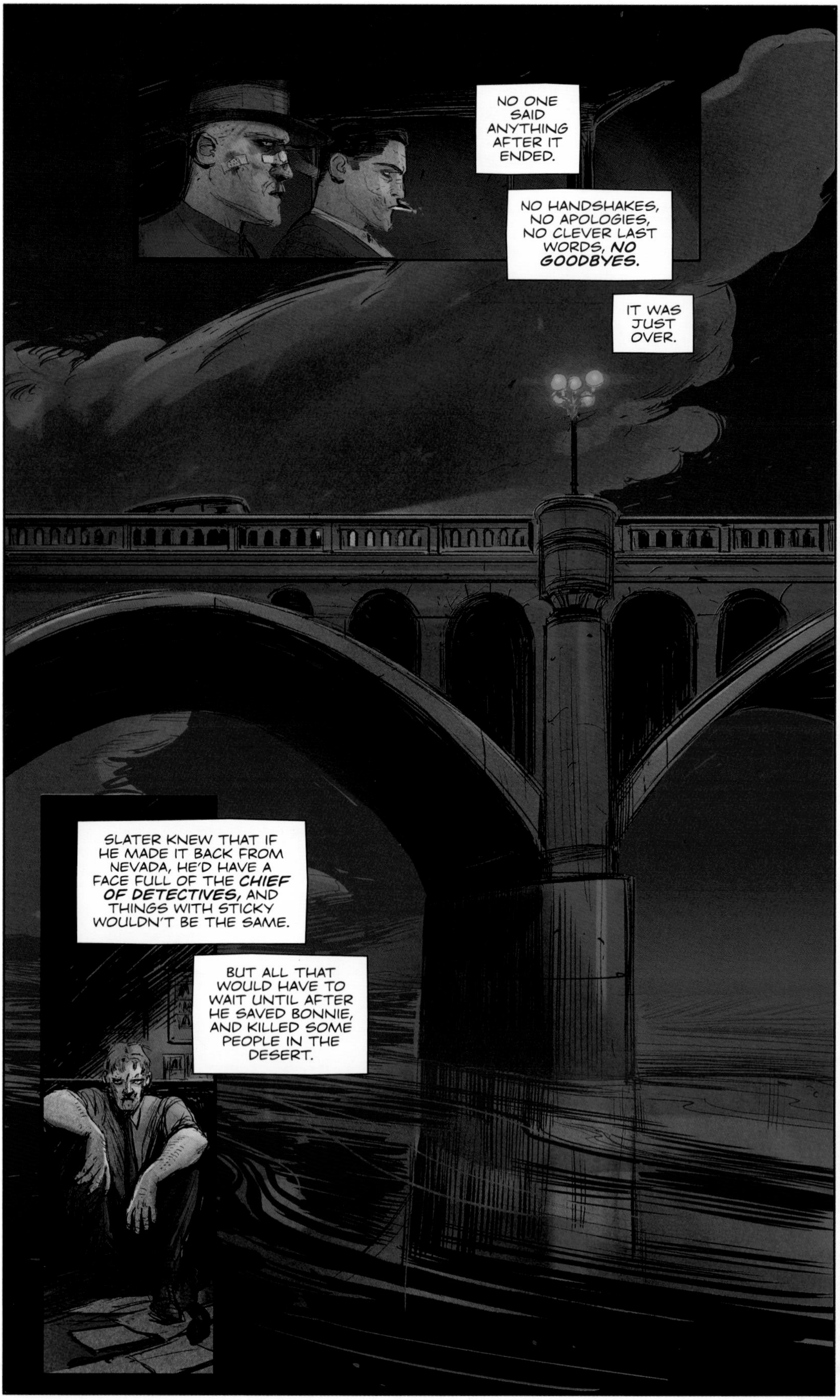
NO ONE SAID ANYTHING AFTER IT ENDED.
NO HANDSHAKES, NO APOLOGIES, NO CLEVER LAST WORDS, NO GOODBYES.
IT WAS JUST OVER.
SLATER KNEW THAT IF HE MADE IT BACK FROM NEVADA, HE'D HAVE A FACE FULL OF THE CHIEF OF DETECTIVES, AND THINGS WITH STICKY WOULDN'T BE THE SAME.
BUT ALL THAT WOULD HAVE TO WAIT UNTIL AFTER HE SAVED BONNIE, AND KILLED SOME PEOPLE IN THE DESERT.

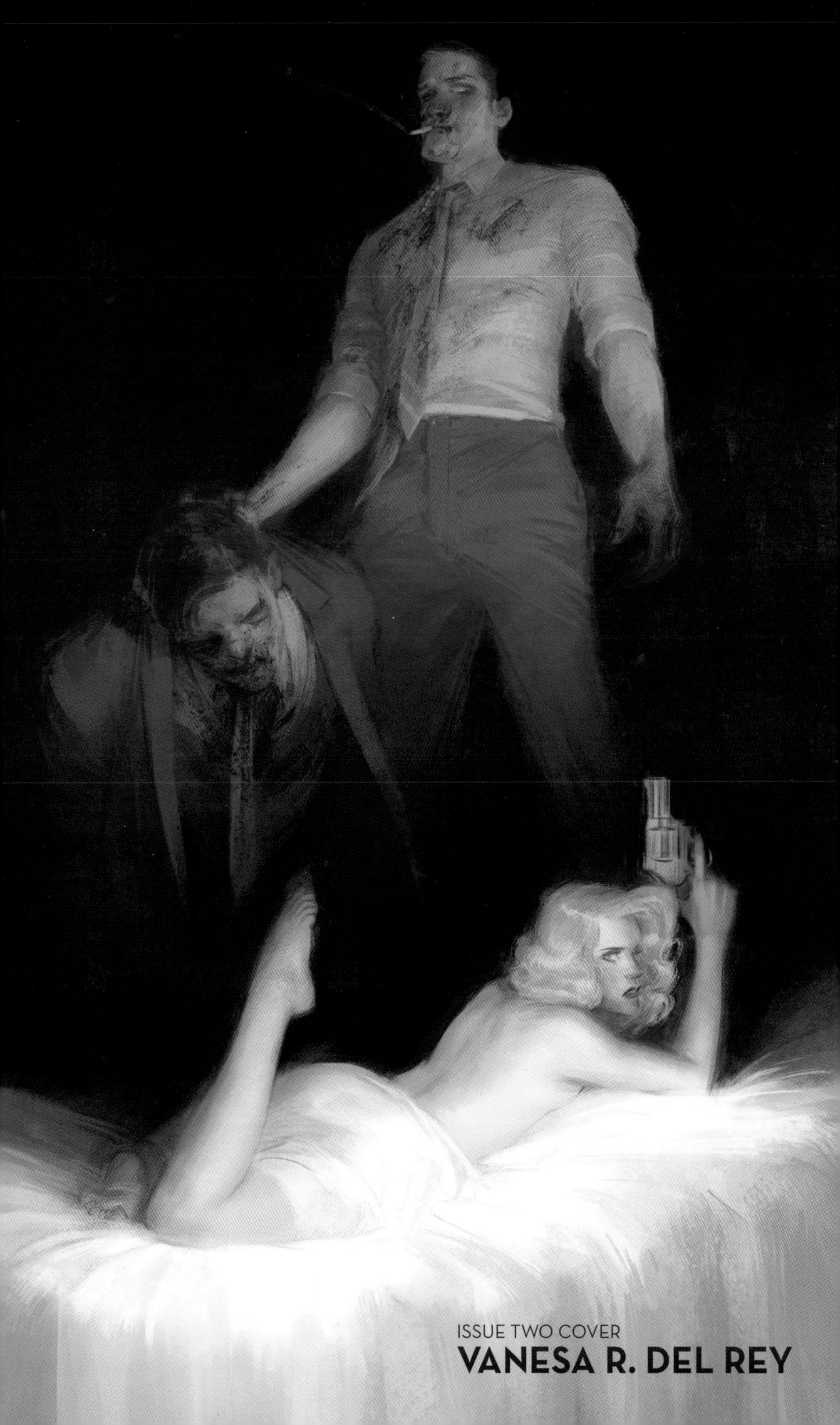

ISSUE TWO COVER
**VANESA R. DEL REY**

CHAPTER **THREE**
# **MUERE** LAS VEGAS

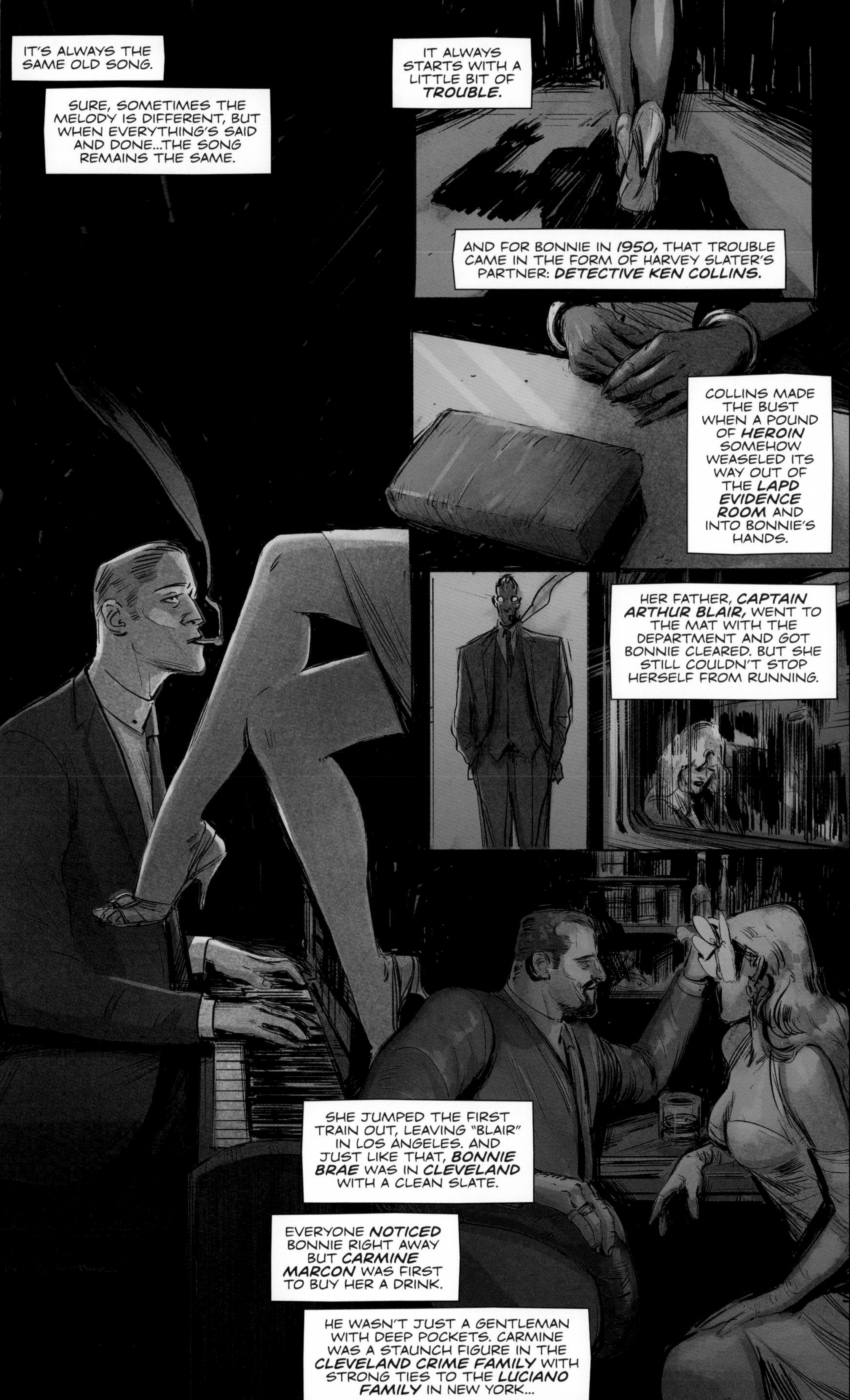

IT'S ALWAYS THE SAME OLD SONG.
SURE, SOMETIMES THE MELODY IS DIFFERENT, BUT WHEN EVERYTHING'S SAID AND DONE...THE SONG REMAINS THE SAME.
IT ALWAYS STARTS WITH A LITTLE BIT OF TROUBLE.
AND FOR BONNIE IN 1950, THAT TROUBLE CAME IN THE FORM OF HARVEY SLATER'S PARTNER: DETECTIVE KEN COLLINS.
COLLINS MADE THE BUST WHEN A POUND OF HEROIN SOMEHOW WEASELED ITS WAY OUT OF THE LAPD EVIDENCE ROOM AND INTO BONNIE'S HANDS.
HER FATHER, CAPTAIN ARTHUR BLAIR, WENT TO THE MAT WITH THE DEPARTMENT AND GOT BONNIE CLEARED. BUT SHE STILL COULDN'T STOP HERSELF FROM RUNNING.
SHE JUMPED THE FIRST TRAIN OUT, LEAVING "BLAIR" IN LOS ANGELES. AND JUST LIKE THAT, BONNIE BRAE WAS IN CLEVELAND WITH A CLEAN SLATE.
EVERYONE NOTICED BONNIE RIGHT AWAY BUT CARMINE MARCON WAS FIRST TO BUY HER A DRINK.
HE WASN'T JUST A GENTLEMAN WITH DEEP POCKETS. CARMINE WAS A STAUNCH FIGURE IN THE CLEVELAND CRIME FAMILY WITH STRONG TIES TO THE LUCIANO FAMILY IN NEW YORK...

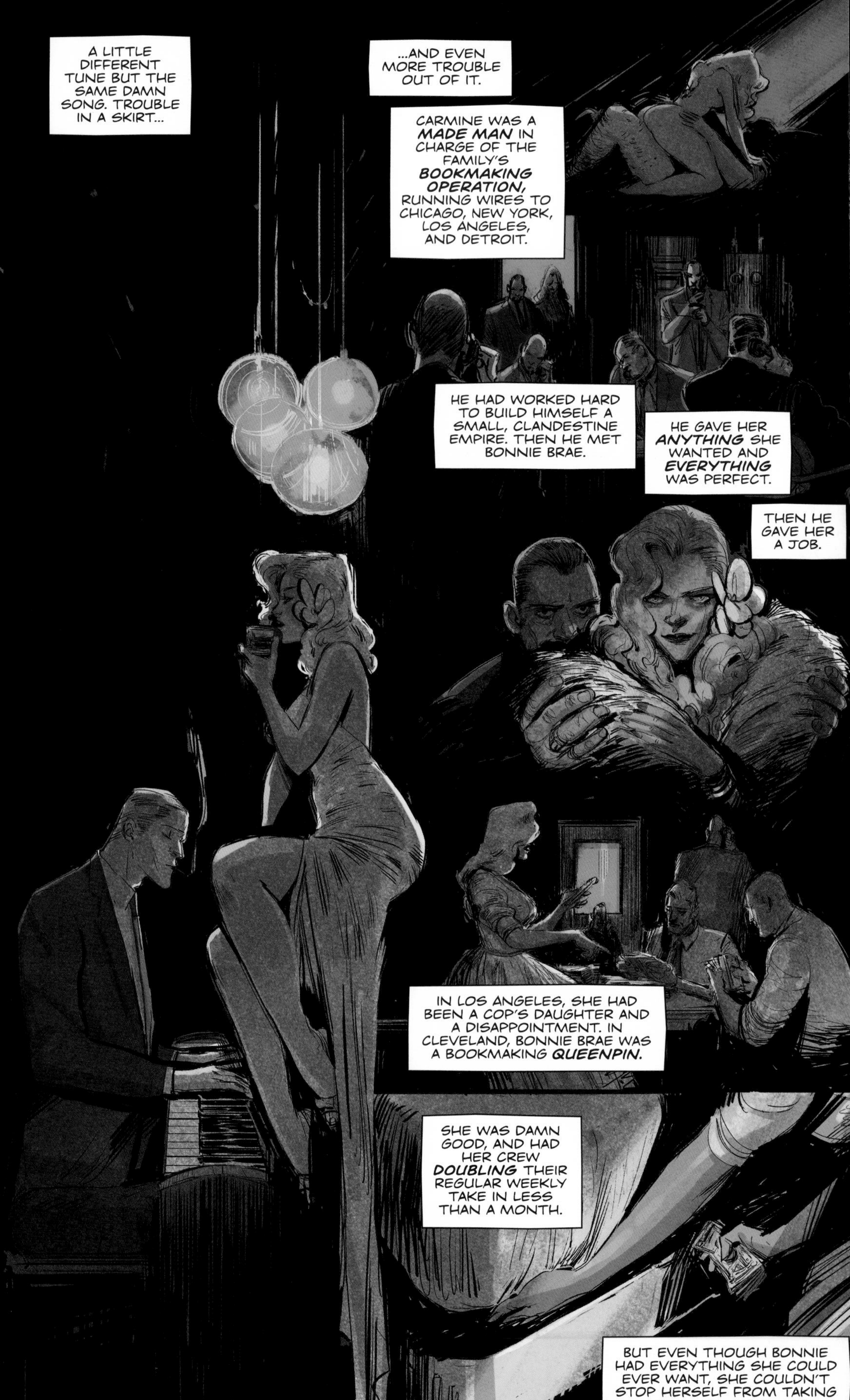
A LITTLE DIFFERENT TUNE BUT THE SAME DAMN SONG. TROUBLE IN A SKIRT...
...AND EVEN MORE TROUBLE OUT OF IT.
CARMINE WAS A MADE MAN IN CHARGE OF THE FAMILY'S BOOKMAKING OPERATION, RUNNING WIRES TO CHICAGO, NEW YORK, LOS ANGELES, AND DETROIT.
HE HAD WORKED HARD TO BUILD HIMSELF A SMALL, CLANDESTINE EMPIRE. THEN HE MET BONNIE BRAE.
HE GAVE HER ANYTHING SHE WANTED AND EVERYTHING WAS PERFECT.
THEN HE GAVE HER A JOB.
IN LOS ANGELES, SHE HAD BEEN A COP'S DAUGHTER AND A DISAPPOINTMENT. IN CLEVELAND, BONNIE BRAE WAS A BOOKMAKING QUEENPIN.
SHE WAS DAMN GOOD, AND HAD HER CREW DOUBLING THEIR REGULAR WEEKLY TAKE IN LESS THAN A MONTH.
BUT EVEN THOUGH BONNIE HAD EVERYTHING SHE COULD EVER WANT, SHE COULDN'T STOP HERSELF FROM TAKING

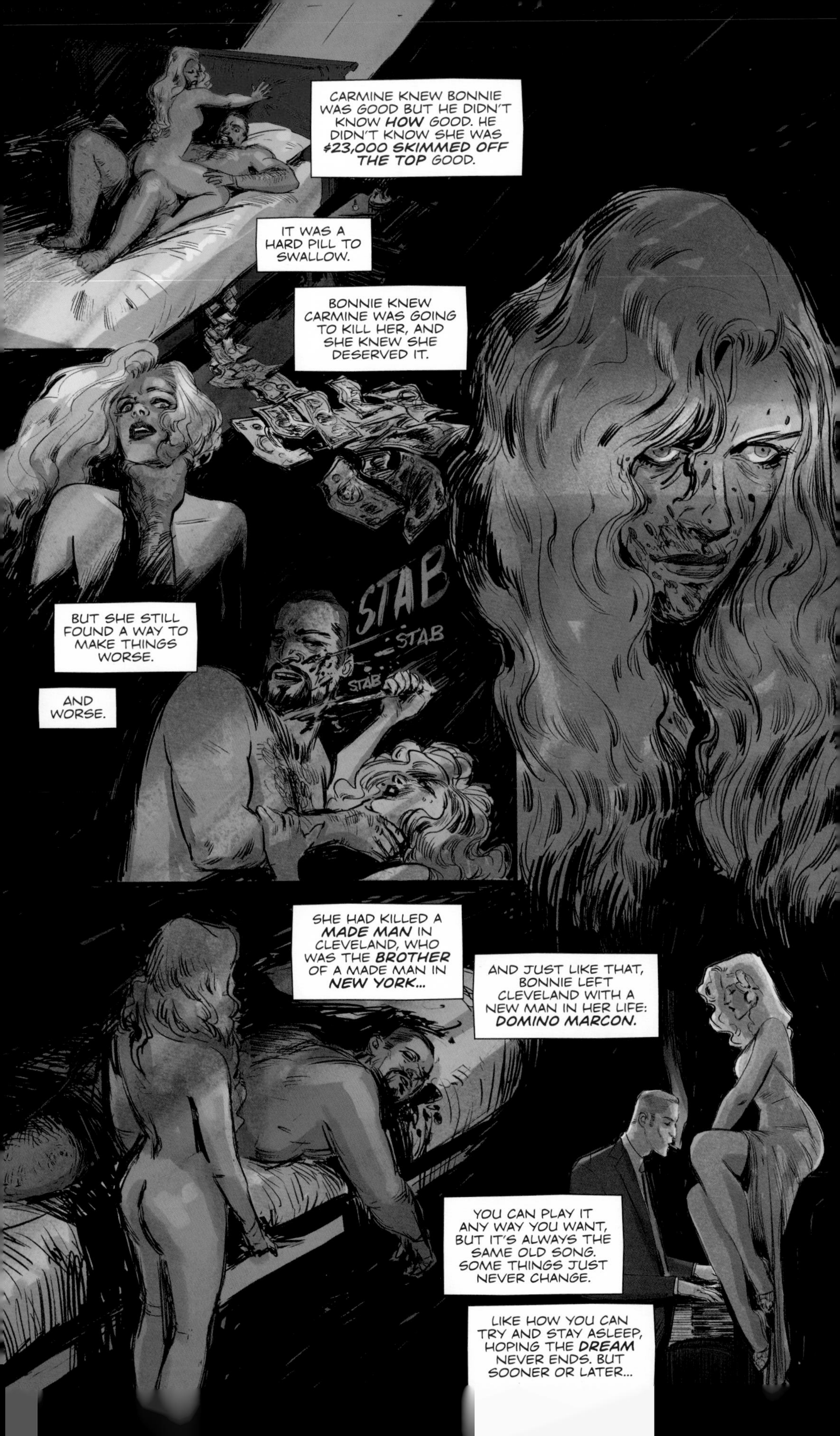
CARMINE KNEW BONNIE WAS GOOD BUT HE DIDN'T KNOW **HOW** GOOD. HE DIDN'T KNOW SHE WAS **$23,000 SKIMMED OFF THE TOP** GOOD.
IT WAS A HARD PILL TO SWALLOW.
BONNIE KNEW CARMINE WAS GOING TO KILL HER, AND SHE KNEW SHE DESERVED IT.
BUT SHE STILL FOUND A WAY TO MAKE THINGS WORSE.
AND WORSE.
STAB
STAB
STAB
SHE HAD KILLED A **MADE MAN** IN CLEVELAND, WHO WAS THE **BROTHER** OF A MADE MAN IN **NEW YORK...**
AND JUST LIKE THAT, BONNIE LEFT CLEVELAND WITH A NEW MAN IN HER LIFE: **DOMINO MARCON.**
YOU CAN PLAY IT ANY WAY YOU WANT, BUT IT'S ALWAYS THE SAME OLD SONG. SOME THINGS JUST NEVER CHANGE.
LIKE HOW YOU CAN TRY AND STAY ASLEEP, HOPING THE **DREAM** NEVER ENDS. BUT SOONER OR LATER...

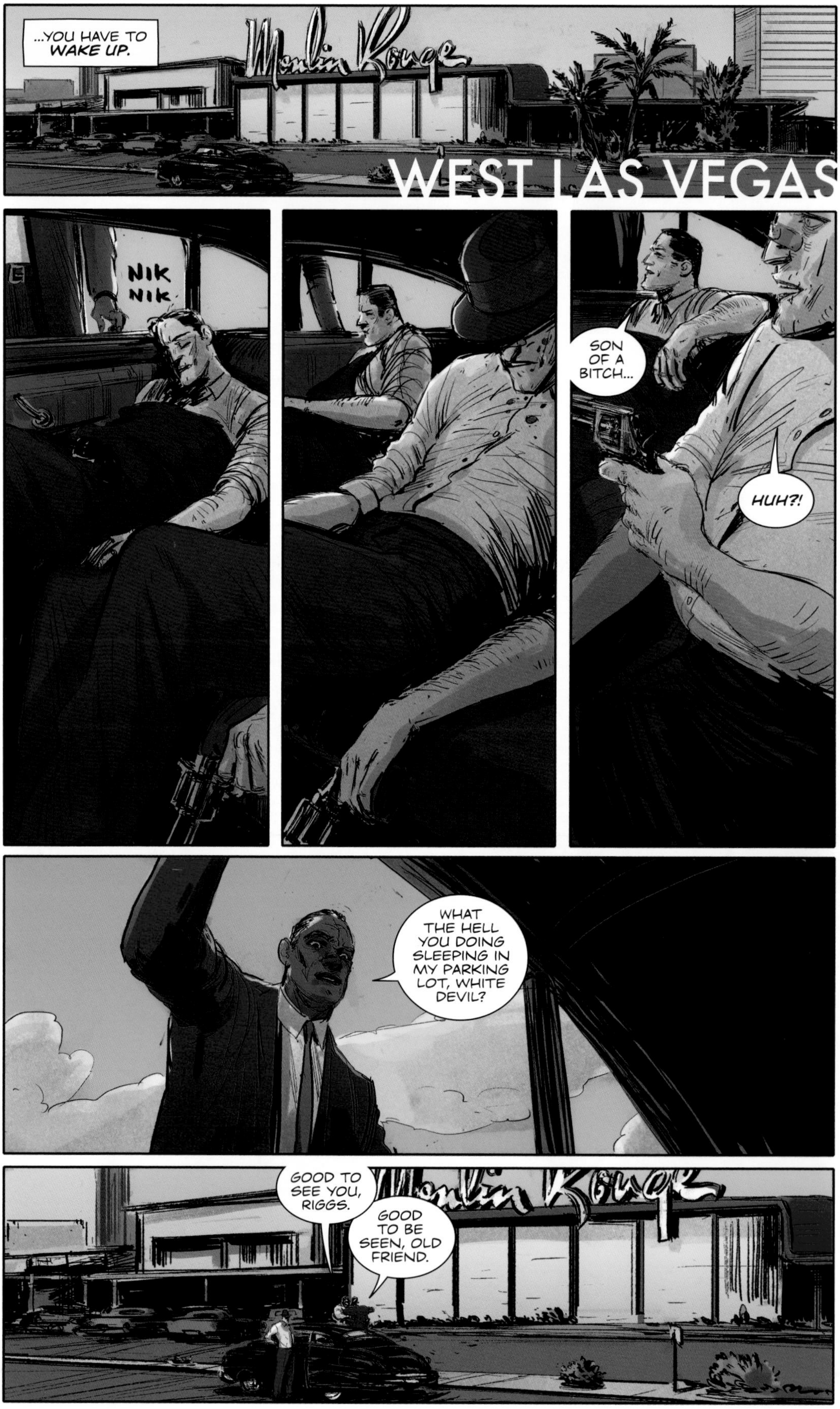
...YOU HAVE TO WAKE UP.
Moulin Rouge
WEST LAS VEGAS
NIK NIK
SON OF A BITCH...
HUH?!
WHAT THE HELL YOU DOING SLEEPING IN MY PARKING LOT, WHITE DEVIL?
Moulin Rouge
GOOD TO SEE YOU, RIGGS.
GOOD TO BE SEEN, OLD FRIEND.

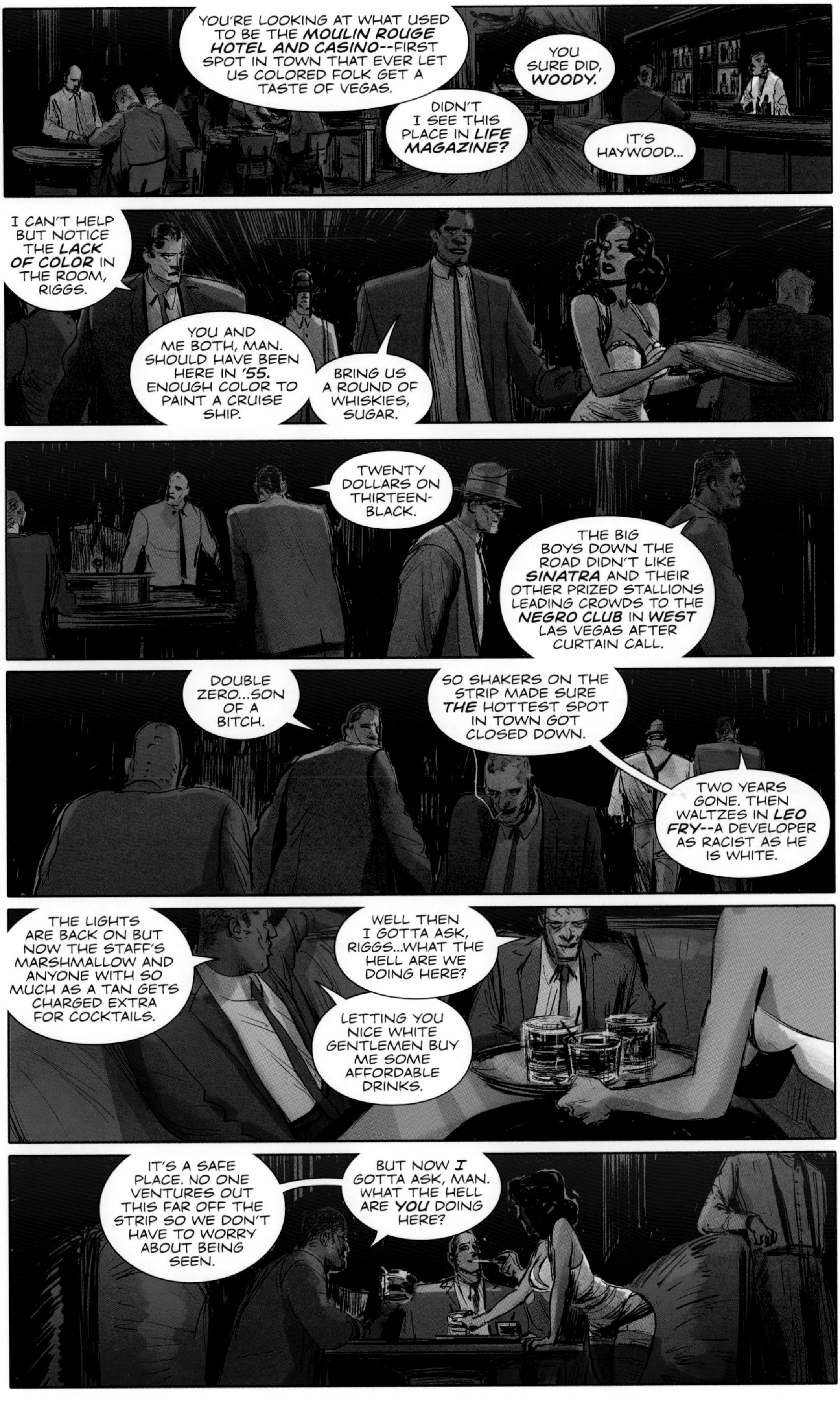

YOU'RE LOOKING AT WHAT USED TO BE THE MOULIN ROUGE HOTEL AND CASINO--FIRST SPOT IN TOWN THAT EVER LET US COLORED FOLK GET A TASTE OF VEGAS.
DIDN'T I SEE THIS PLACE IN LIFE MAGAZINE?
YOU SURE DID, WOODY.
IT'S HAYWOOD...
I CAN'T HELP BUT NOTICE THE LACK OF COLOR IN THE ROOM, RIGGS.
YOU AND ME BOTH, MAN. SHOULD HAVE BEEN HERE IN '55. ENOUGH COLOR TO PAINT A CRUISE SHIP.
BRING US A ROUND OF WHISKIES, SUGAR.
TWENTY DOLLARS ON THIRTEEN-BLACK.
THE BIG BOYS DOWN THE ROAD DIDN'T LIKE SINATRA AND THEIR OTHER PRIZED STALLIONS LEADING CROWDS TO THE NEGRO CLUB IN WEST LAS VEGAS AFTER CURTAIN CALL.
DOUBLE ZERO...SON OF A BITCH.
SO SHAKERS ON THE STRIP MADE SURE THE HOTTEST SPOT IN TOWN GOT CLOSED DOWN.
TWO YEARS GONE. THEN WALTZES IN LEO FRY--A DEVELOPER AS RACIST AS HE IS WHITE.
THE LIGHTS ARE BACK ON BUT NOW THE STAFF'S MARSHMALLOW AND ANYONE WITH SO MUCH AS A TAN GETS CHARGED EXTRA FOR COCKTAILS.
WELL THEN I GOTTA ASK, RIGGS...WHAT THE HELL ARE WE DOING HERE?
LETTING YOU NICE WHITE GENTLEMEN BUY ME SOME AFFORDABLE DRINKS.
IT'S A SAFE PLACE. NO ONE VENTURES OUT THIS FAR OFF THE STRIP SO WE DON'T HAVE TO WORRY ABOUT BEING SEEN.
BUT NOW I GOTTA ASK, MAN. WHAT THE HELL ARE YOU DOING HERE?

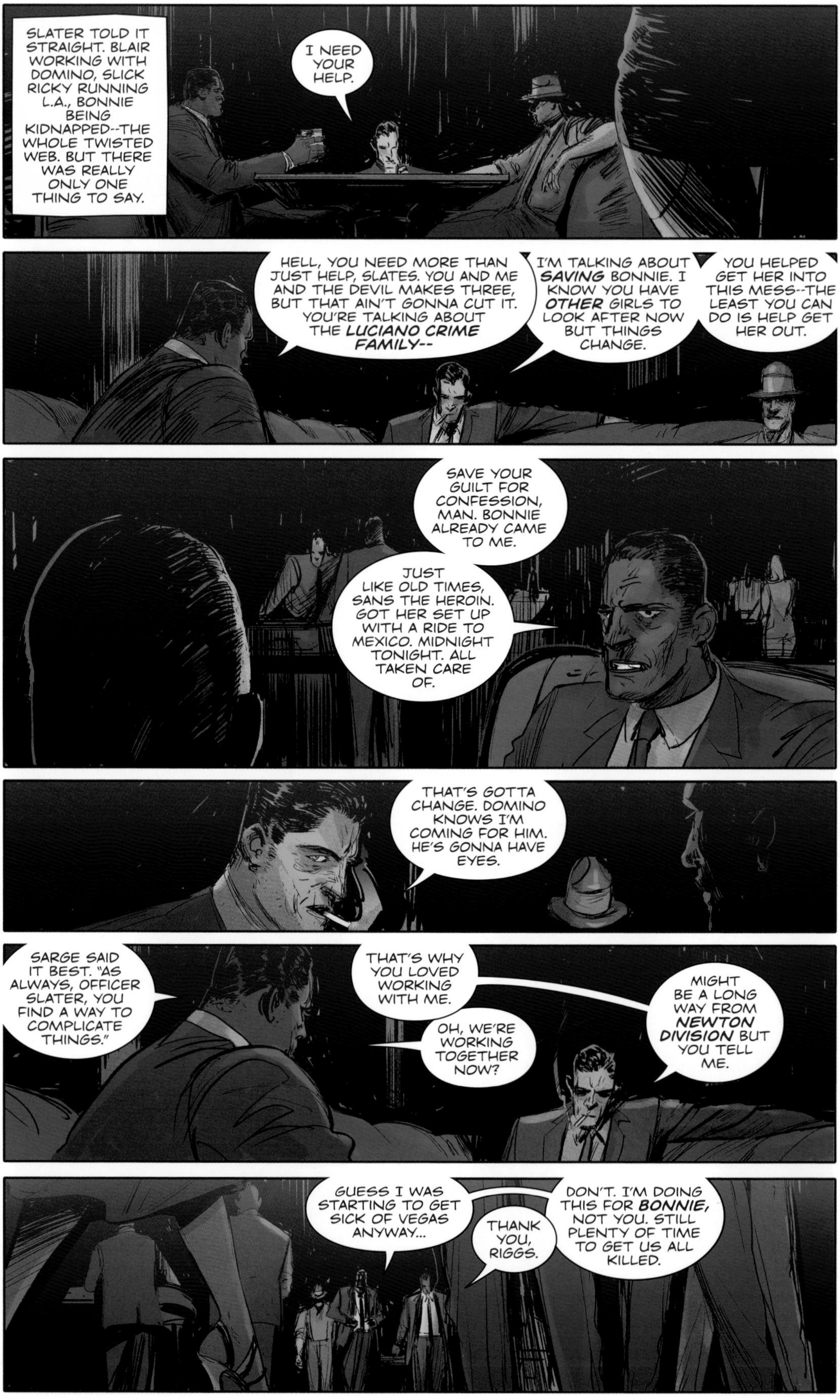
SLATER TOLD IT STRAIGHT. BLAIR WORKING WITH DOMINO, SLICK RICKY RUNNING L.A., BONNIE BEING KIDNAPPED--THE WHOLE TWISTED WEB. BUT THERE WAS REALLY ONLY ONE THING TO SAY.
I NEED YOUR HELP.
HELL, YOU NEED MORE THAN JUST HELP, SLATES. YOU AND ME AND THE DEVIL MAKES THREE, BUT THAT AIN'T GONNA CUT IT. YOU'RE TALKING ABOUT THE **LUCIANO CRIME FAMILY**--
I'M TALKING ABOUT **SAVING** BONNIE. I KNOW YOU HAVE **OTHER** GIRLS TO LOOK AFTER NOW BUT THINGS CHANGE.
YOU HELPED GET HER INTO THIS MESS--THE LEAST YOU CAN DO IS HELP GET HER OUT.
SAVE YOUR GUILT FOR CONFESSION, MAN. BONNIE ALREADY CAME TO ME.
JUST LIKE OLD TIMES, SANS THE HEROIN. GOT HER SET UP WITH A RIDE TO MEXICO. MIDNIGHT TONIGHT. ALL TAKEN CARE OF.
THAT'S GOTTA CHANGE. DOMINO KNOWS I'M COMING FOR HIM. HE'S GONNA HAVE EYES.
SARGE SAID IT BEST. "AS ALWAYS, OFFICER SLATER, YOU FIND A WAY TO COMPLICATE THINGS."
THAT'S WHY YOU LOVED WORKING WITH ME.
OH, WE'RE WORKING TOGETHER NOW?
MIGHT BE A LONG WAY FROM **NEWTON DIVISION** BUT YOU TELL ME.
GUESS I WAS STARTING TO GET SICK OF VEGAS ANYWAY...
THANK YOU, RIGGS.
DON'T. I'M DOING THIS FOR **BONNIE,** NOT YOU. STILL PLENTY OF TIME TO GET US ALL KILLED.

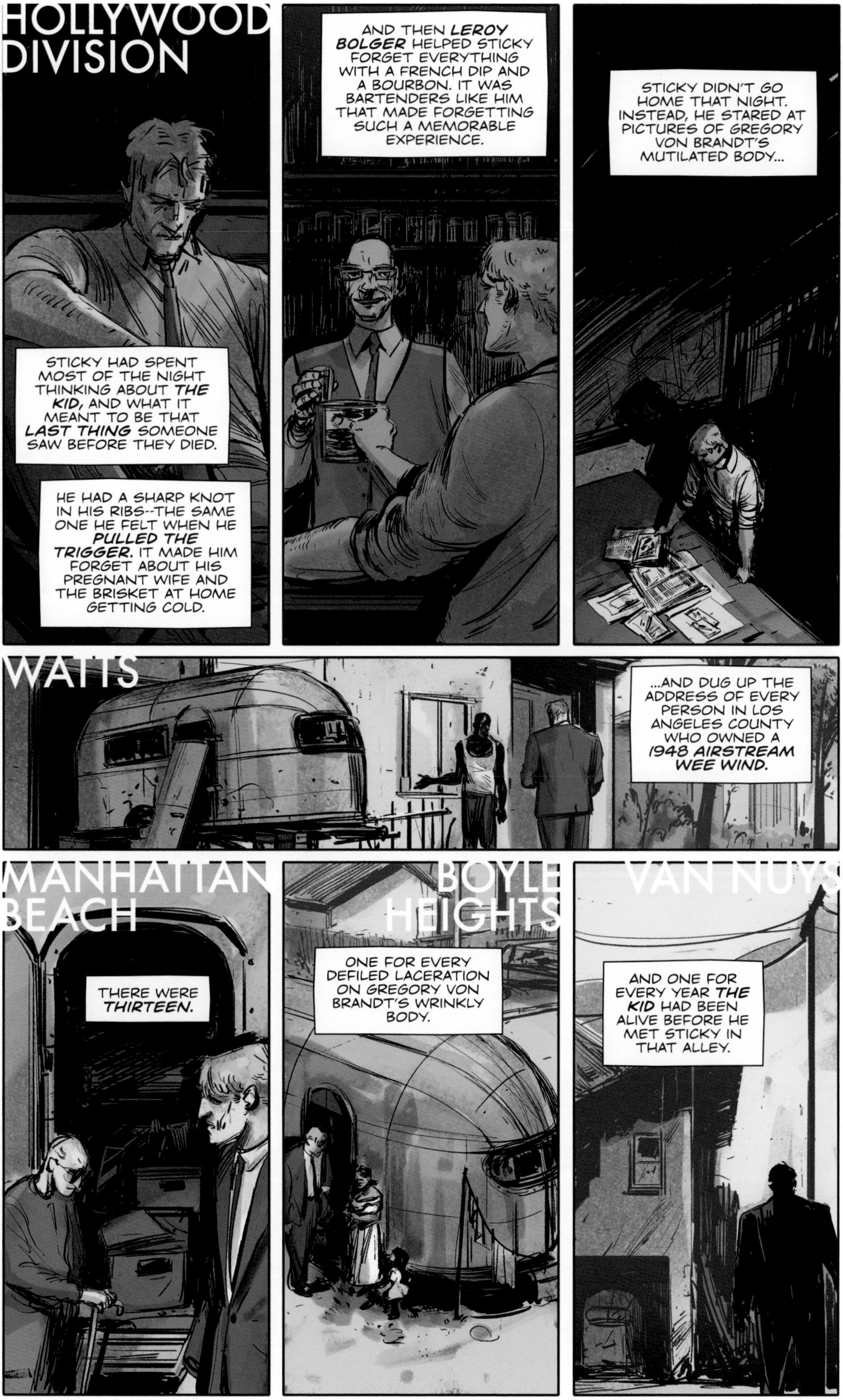
HOLLYWOOD DIVISION
STICKY HAD SPENT MOST OF THE NIGHT THINKING ABOUT THE KID, AND WHAT IT MEANT TO BE THAT LAST THING SOMEONE SAW BEFORE THEY DIED.
HE HAD A SHARP KNOT IN HIS RIBS--THE SAME ONE HE FELT WHEN HE PULLED THE TRIGGER. IT MADE HIM FORGET ABOUT HIS PREGNANT WIFE AND THE BRISKET AT HOME GETTING COLD.
AND THEN LEROY BOLGER HELPED STICKY FORGET EVERYTHING WITH A FRENCH DIP AND A BOURBON. IT WAS BARTENDERS LIKE HIM THAT MADE FORGETTING SUCH A MEMORABLE EXPERIENCE.
STICKY DIDN'T GO HOME THAT NIGHT. INSTEAD, HE STARED AT PICTURES OF GREGORY VON BRANDT'S MUTILATED BODY...
WATTS
...AND DUG UP THE ADDRESS OF EVERY PERSON IN LOS ANGELES COUNTY WHO OWNED A 1948 AIRSTREAM WEE WIND.
MANHATTAN BEACH
THERE WERE THIRTEEN.
BOYLE HEIGHTS
ONE FOR EVERY DEFILED LACERATION ON GREGORY VON BRANDT'S WRINKLY BODY.
VAN NUYS
AND ONE FOR EVERY YEAR THE KID HAD BEEN ALIVE BEFORE HE MET STICKY IN THAT ALLEY.

# DOWNTOWN

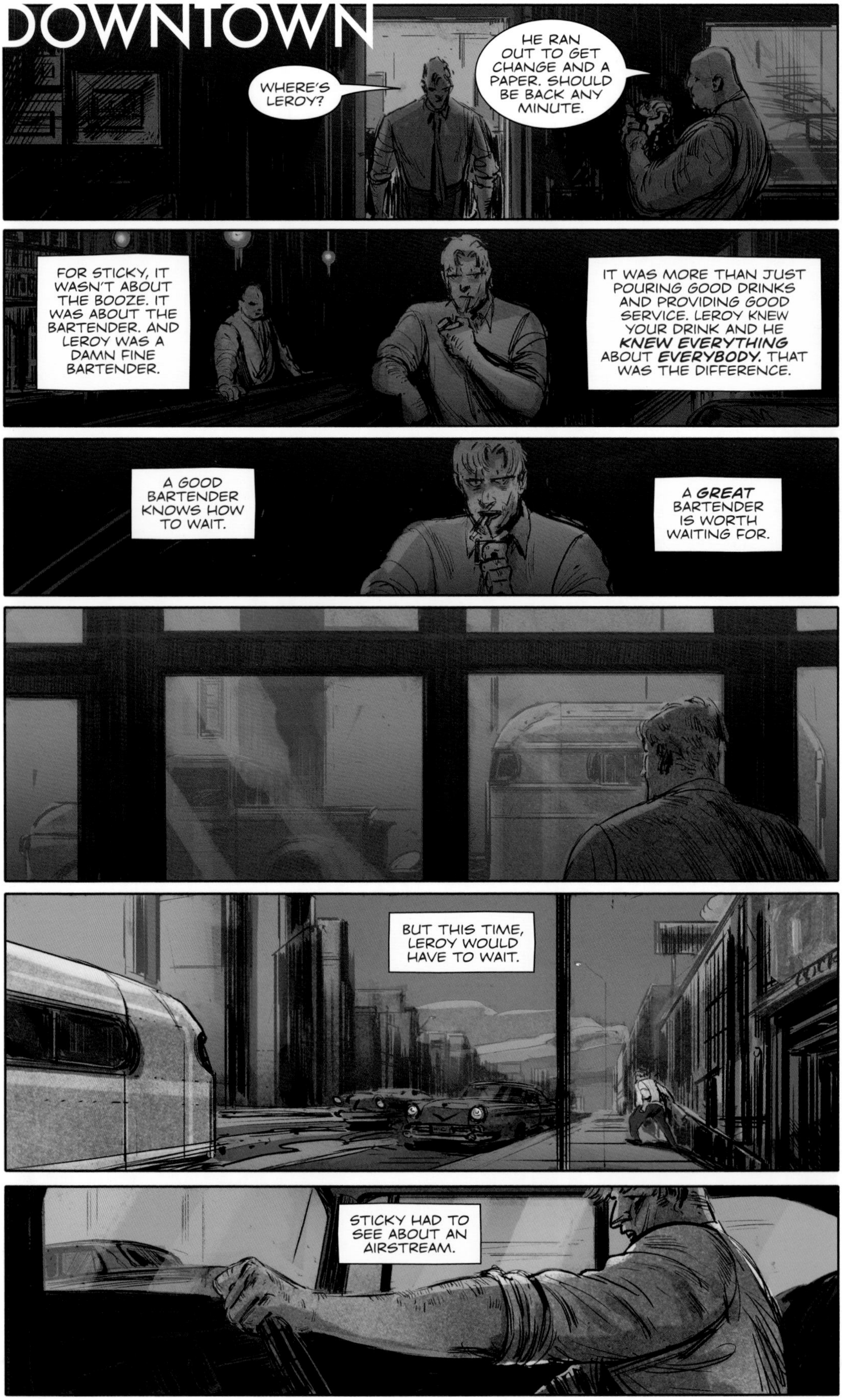
WHERE'S LEROY?
HE RAN OUT TO GET CHANGE AND A PAPER. SHOULD BE BACK ANY MINUTE.
FOR STICKY, IT WASN'T ABOUT THE BOOZE. IT WAS ABOUT THE BARTENDER. AND LEROY WAS A DAMN FINE BARTENDER.
IT WAS MORE THAN JUST POURING GOOD DRINKS AND PROVIDING GOOD SERVICE. LEROY KNEW YOUR DRINK AND HE ***KNEW EVERYTHING*** ABOUT ***EVERYBODY.*** THAT WAS THE DIFFERENCE.
A GOOD BARTENDER KNOWS HOW TO WAIT.
A ***GREAT*** BARTENDER IS WORTH WAITING FOR.
BUT THIS TIME, LEROY WOULD HAVE TO WAIT.
STICKY HAD TO SEE ABOUT AN AIRSTREAM.

I OWE YOU ONE, *FLETCH.* DROP BY THE DUNES ANYTIME YOU'RE LOOKING TO FALL IN LOVE.

I'M ALWAYS LOOKING TO FALL IN LOVE.

BUT JUST KEEP ME OUT OF WHATEVER IT IS YOU'RE ABOUT TO DO AND WE'LL CALL IT EVEN.

NOTHING IN VEGAS WAS EVER EVEN. THE ODDS WERE STACKED AND THERE WAS ALWAYS AN ANGLE.

RIGGS KNEW BONNIE WAS SHARING A SUITE UPSTAIRS WITH VINCENT. ONCE VINCENT WENT TO HIS NIGHTLY SIT-DOWN WITH DOMINO, "*ROOM SERVICE*" WOULD SMUGGLE BONNIE OUT.

THEN THEY'D HOLE UP IN THE SUITE AND STAKEOUT DOMINO UNTIL THEY HAD A CLEAR SHOT. AS ALWAYS, THE DEVIL WAS IN THE DETAILS.

LOSE THE HAT, WOODY. DRESS CODE.

C'MON, REALLY?

YOU HEARD HIM.

ALRIGHT, GET IT ALL OUT. HERE'S YOUR CHANCE. CUE BALL, CHROME DOME, PEANUT HEAD, C'MON. I DON'T WANNA HEAR ABOUT IT LATER WHEN--

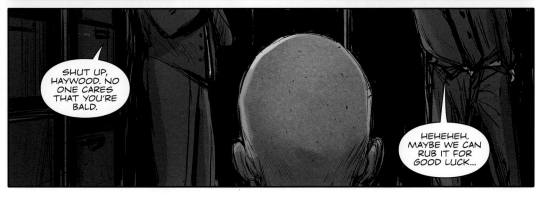

SHUT UP, HAYWOOD. NO ONE CARES THAT YOU'RE BALD.

HEHEHEH. MAYBE WE CAN RUB IT FOR GOOD LUCK...

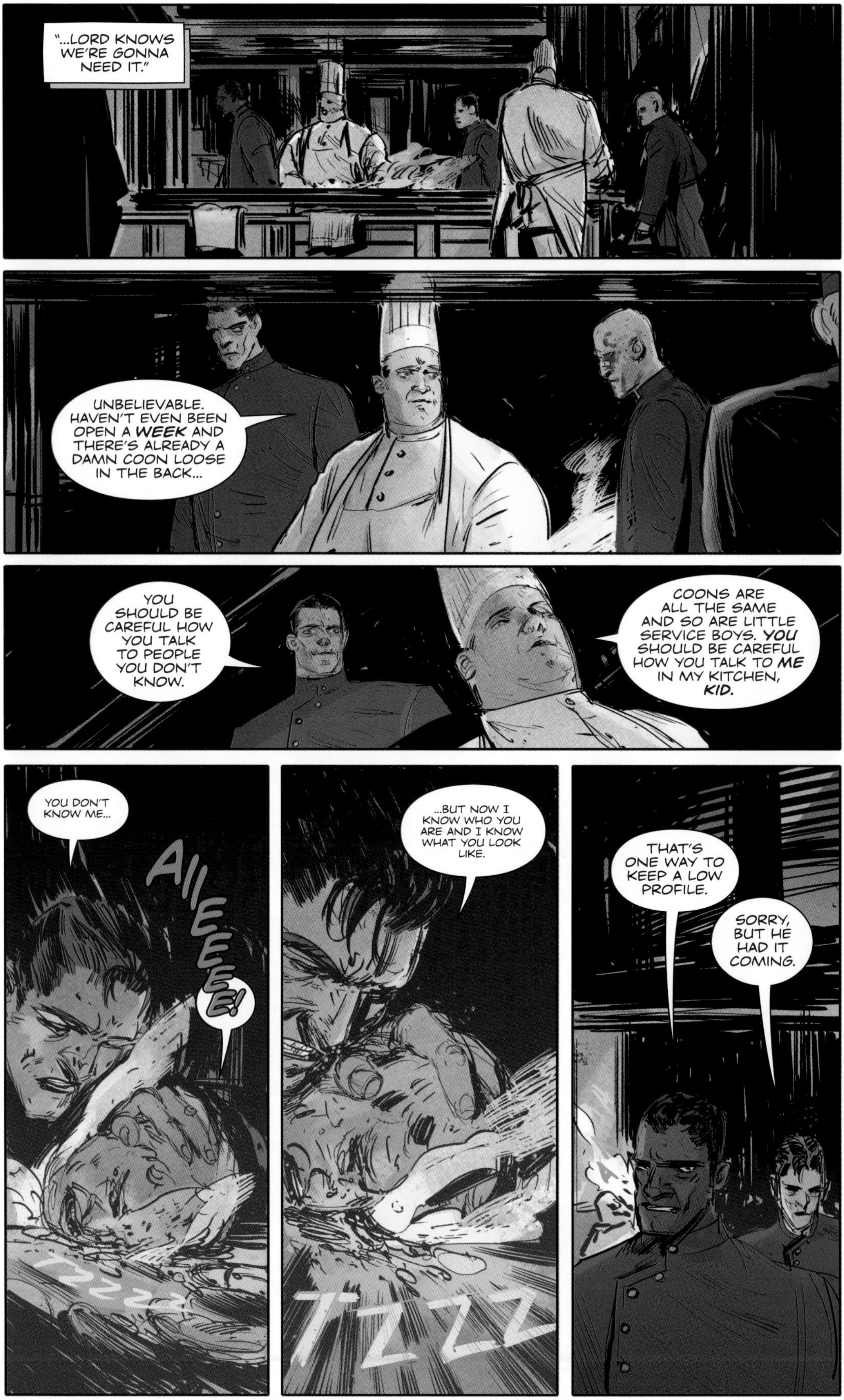

"...LORD KNOWS WE'RE GONNA NEED IT."
UNBELIEVABLE. HAVEN'T EVEN BEEN OPEN A WEEK AND THERE'S ALREADY A DAMN COON LOOSE IN THE BACK...
YOU SHOULD BE CAREFUL HOW YOU TALK TO PEOPLE YOU DON'T KNOW.
COONS ARE ALL THE SAME AND SO ARE LITTLE SERVICE BOYS. YOU SHOULD BE CAREFUL HOW YOU TALK TO ME IN MY KITCHEN, KID.
YOU DON'T KNOW ME...
AIIEEEEE!
TZZZZ
...BUT NOW I KNOW WHO YOU ARE AND I KNOW WHAT YOU LOOK LIKE.
TZZZ
THAT'S ONE WAY TO KEEP A LOW PROFILE.
SORRY, BUT HE HAD IT COMING.

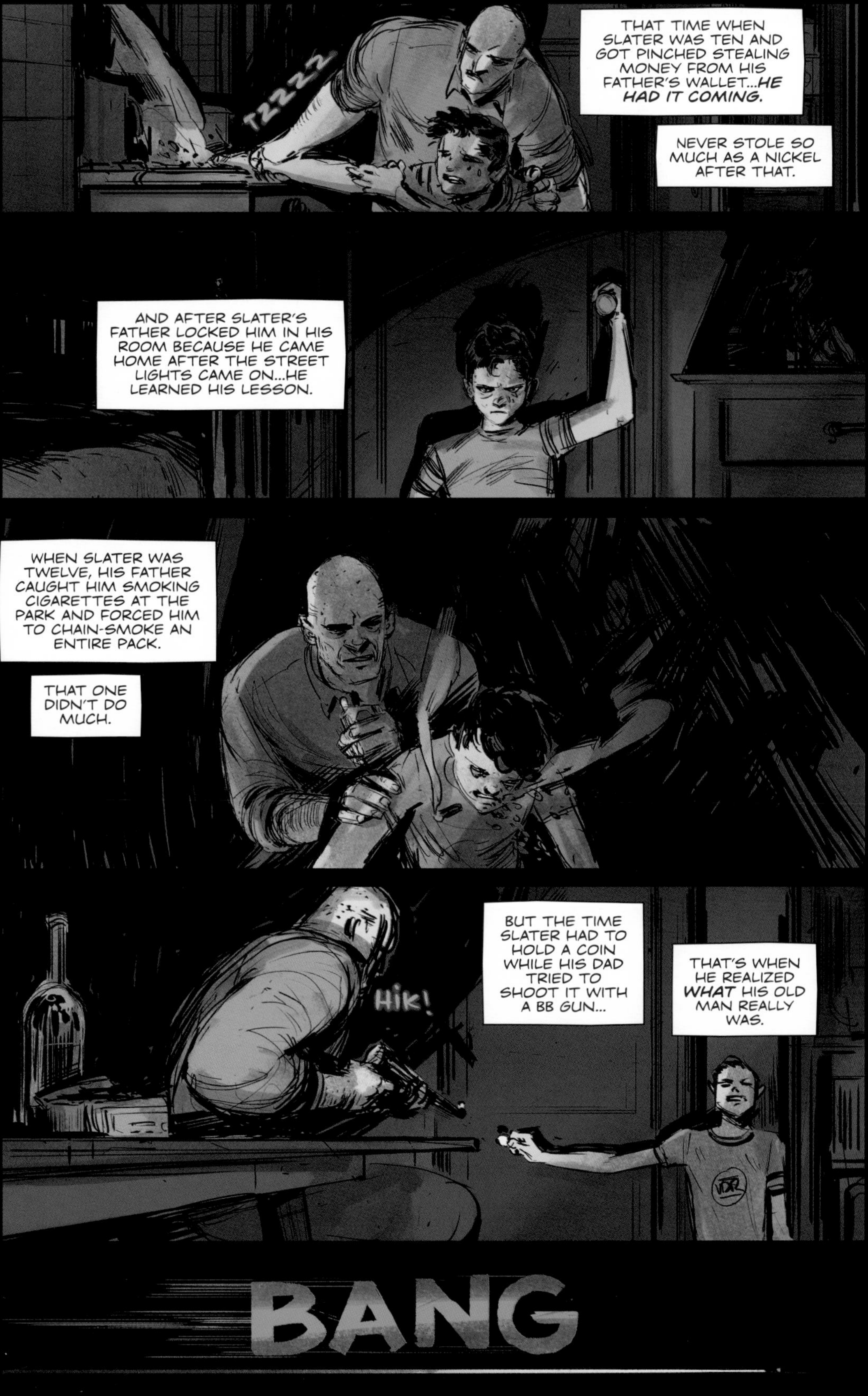
THAT TIME WHEN SLATER WAS TEN AND GOT PINCHED STEALING MONEY FROM HIS FATHER'S WALLET...*HE HAD IT COMING.*
TZZZZ
NEVER STOLE SO MUCH AS A NICKEL AFTER THAT.
AND AFTER SLATER'S FATHER LOCKED HIM IN HIS ROOM BECAUSE HE CAME HOME AFTER THE STREET LIGHTS CAME ON...HE LEARNED HIS LESSON.
WHEN SLATER WAS TWELVE, HIS FATHER CAUGHT HIM SMOKING CIGARETTES AT THE PARK AND FORCED HIM TO CHAIN-SMOKE AN ENTIRE PACK.
THAT ONE DIDN'T DO MUCH.
HIK!
BUT THE TIME SLATER HAD TO HOLD A COIN WHILE HIS DAD TRIED TO SHOOT IT WITH A BB GUN...
THAT'S WHEN HE REALIZED *WHAT* HIS OLD MAN REALLY WAS.
BANG

A BITTER OLD MAN WITH A LIFETIME OF SCARS IN HIS WAKE, AND NOTHING TO SHOW FOR IT.

HARVEY SLATER HATED HIS FATHER. THE DRINKING, THE VIOLENCE, THE TOXICITY.

HE COULD FORGIVE HIS FATHER FOR BEING ANGRY, BUT HE COULD NEVER FORGIVE HIM FOR DRIVING HIS MOTHER AWAY.

THE SAME WAY SLATER COULD NEVER FORGIVE HIS **MOTHER** FOR ABANDONING HIM.

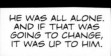

HE WAS ALL ALONE. AND IF THAT WAS GOING TO CHANGE, IT WAS UP TO HIM.

SLATER FINALLY REALIZED THAT IF YOU WANT TO GET RID OF THE **DARKNESS...**

...YOU HAVE TO FIND A WAY TO SHUT IT OUT *YOURSELF*.
LOOKS LIKE SOMEBODY COULD USE A PICK-ME-UP.
THIS SHOULD DO THE TRICK.
THANKS.
YOU'RE TOO PRETTY TO BE DRINKING ALONE.
I'M NOT ALONE ANYMORE.
THERE'S NO RING ON THAT FINGER. YOU GOT A MAN?
IT'S COMPLICATED.

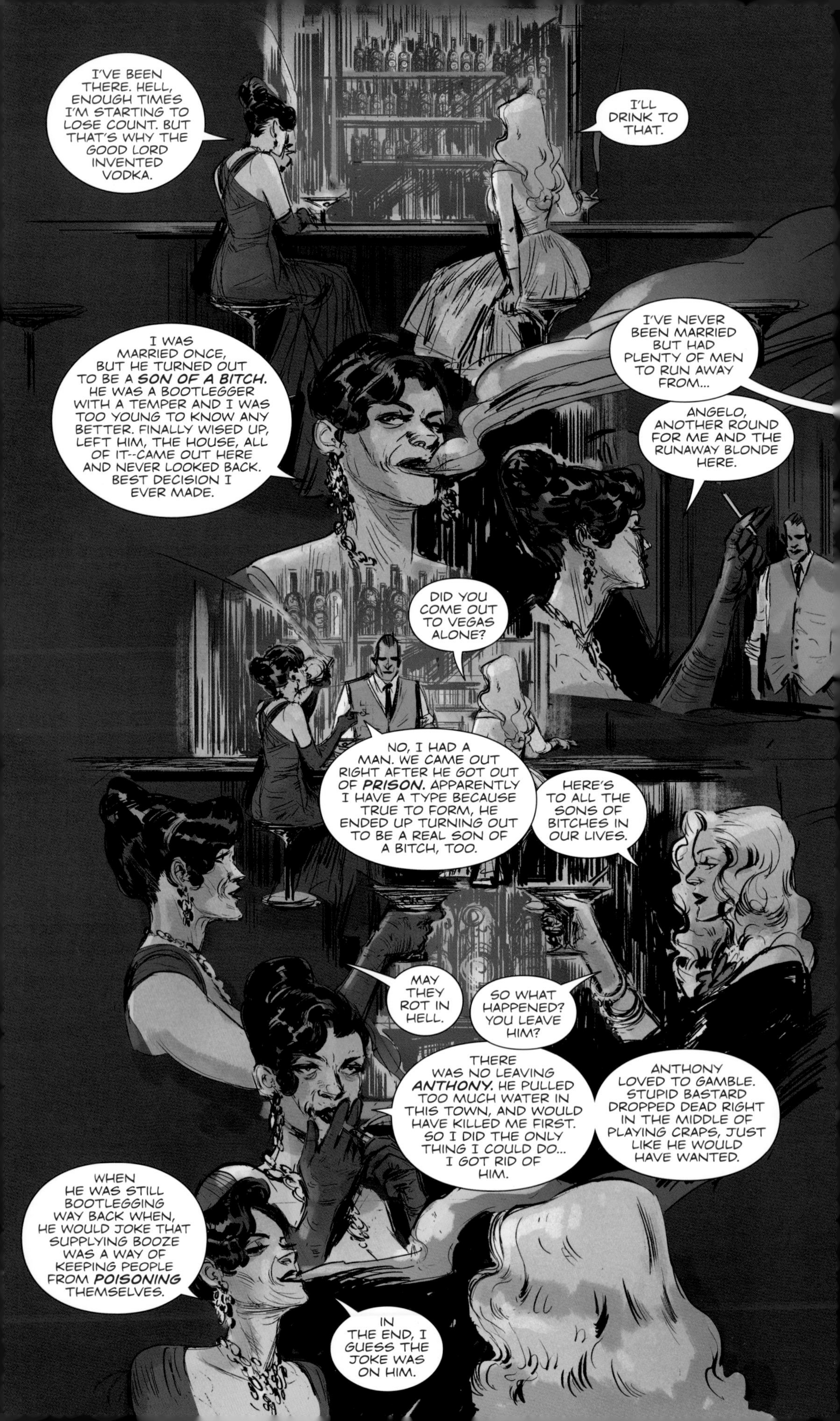
I'VE BEEN THERE. HELL, ENOUGH TIMES I'M STARTING TO LOSE COUNT. BUT THAT'S WHY THE GOOD LORD INVENTED VODKA.
I'LL DRINK TO THAT.
I WAS MARRIED ONCE, BUT HE TURNED OUT TO BE A ***SON OF A BITCH.*** HE WAS A BOOTLEGGER WITH A TEMPER AND I WAS TOO YOUNG TO KNOW ANY BETTER. FINALLY WISED UP, LEFT HIM, THE HOUSE, ALL OF IT--CAME OUT HERE AND NEVER LOOKED BACK. BEST DECISION I EVER MADE.
I'VE NEVER BEEN MARRIED BUT HAD PLENTY OF MEN TO RUN AWAY FROM...
ANGELO, ANOTHER ROUND FOR ME AND THE RUNAWAY BLONDE HERE.
DID YOU COME OUT TO VEGAS ALONE?
NO, I HAD A MAN. WE CAME OUT RIGHT AFTER HE GOT OUT OF ***PRISON.*** APPARENTLY I HAVE A TYPE BECAUSE TRUE TO FORM, HE ENDED UP TURNING OUT TO BE A REAL SON OF A BITCH, TOO.
HERE'S TO ALL THE SONS OF BITCHES IN OUR LIVES.
MAY THEY ROT IN HELL.
SO WHAT HAPPENED? YOU LEAVE HIM?
THERE WAS NO LEAVING ***ANTHONY.*** HE PULLED TOO MUCH WATER IN THIS TOWN, AND WOULD HAVE KILLED ME FIRST. SO I DID THE ONLY THING I COULD DO... I GOT RID OF HIM.
ANTHONY LOVED TO GAMBLE. STUPID BASTARD DROPPED DEAD RIGHT IN THE MIDDLE OF PLAYING CRAPS, JUST LIKE HE WOULD HAVE WANTED.
WHEN HE WAS STILL BOOTLEGGING WAY BACK WHEN, HE WOULD JOKE THAT SUPPLYING BOOZE WAS A WAY OF KEEPING PEOPLE FROM ***POISONING*** THEMSELVES.
IN THE END, I GUESS THE JOKE WAS ON HIM.

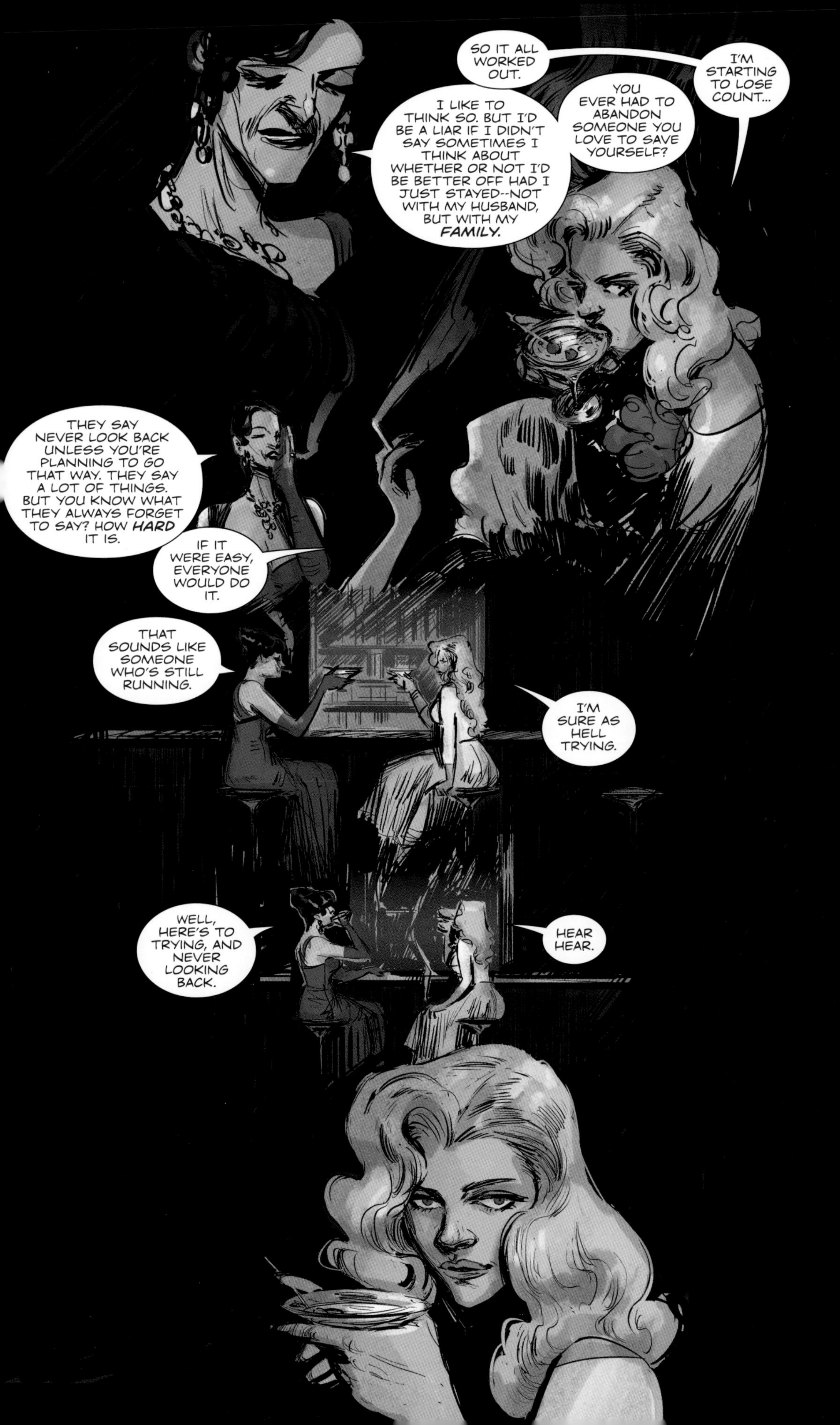
SO IT ALL WORKED OUT.
I'M STARTING TO LOSE COUNT...
I LIKE TO THINK SO. BUT I'D BE A LIAR IF I DIDN'T SAY SOMETIMES I THINK ABOUT WHETHER OR NOT I'D BE BETTER OFF HAD I JUST STAYED--NOT WITH MY HUSBAND, BUT WITH MY *FAMILY.*
YOU EVER HAD TO ABANDON SOMEONE YOU LOVE TO SAVE YOURSELF?
THEY SAY NEVER LOOK BACK UNLESS YOU'RE PLANNING TO GO THAT WAY. THEY SAY A LOT OF THINGS. BUT YOU KNOW WHAT THEY ALWAYS FORGET TO SAY? HOW *HARD* IT IS.
IF IT WERE EASY, EVERYONE WOULD DO IT.
THAT SOUNDS LIKE SOMEONE WHO'S STILL RUNNING.
I'M SURE AS HELL TRYING.
WELL, HERE'S TO TRYING, AND NEVER LOOKING BACK.
HEAR HEAR.

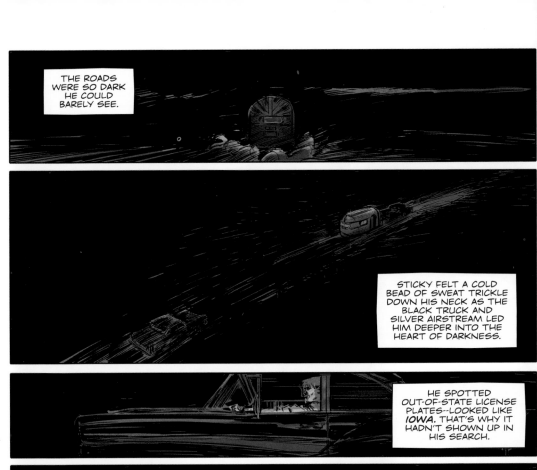

THE ROADS WERE SO DARK HE COULD BARELY SEE.

STICKY FELT A COLD BEAD OF SWEAT TRICKLE DOWN HIS NECK AS THE BLACK TRUCK AND SILVER AIRSTREAM LED HIM DEEPER INTO THE HEART OF DARKNESS.

HE SPOTTED OUT-OF-STATE LICENSE PLATES--LOOKED LIKE *IOWA*. THAT'S WHY IT HADN'T SHOWN UP IN HIS SEARCH.

EVERYTHING WAS DEADLY STILL, A POOL OF BLACK SILENTLY SWALLOWING EVERYTHING IN SIGHT...

# HIGHLAND PARK

...LEADING STICKY INTO THE MOUTH OF SOMETHING HE COULDN'T BEGIN TO UNDERSTAND.

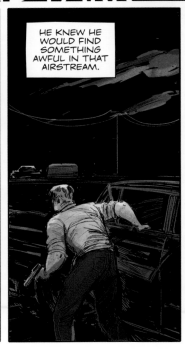

HE KNEW HE WOULD FIND SOMETHING AWFUL IN THAT AIRSTREAM.

BUT REALLY, HE HAD NO IDEA...

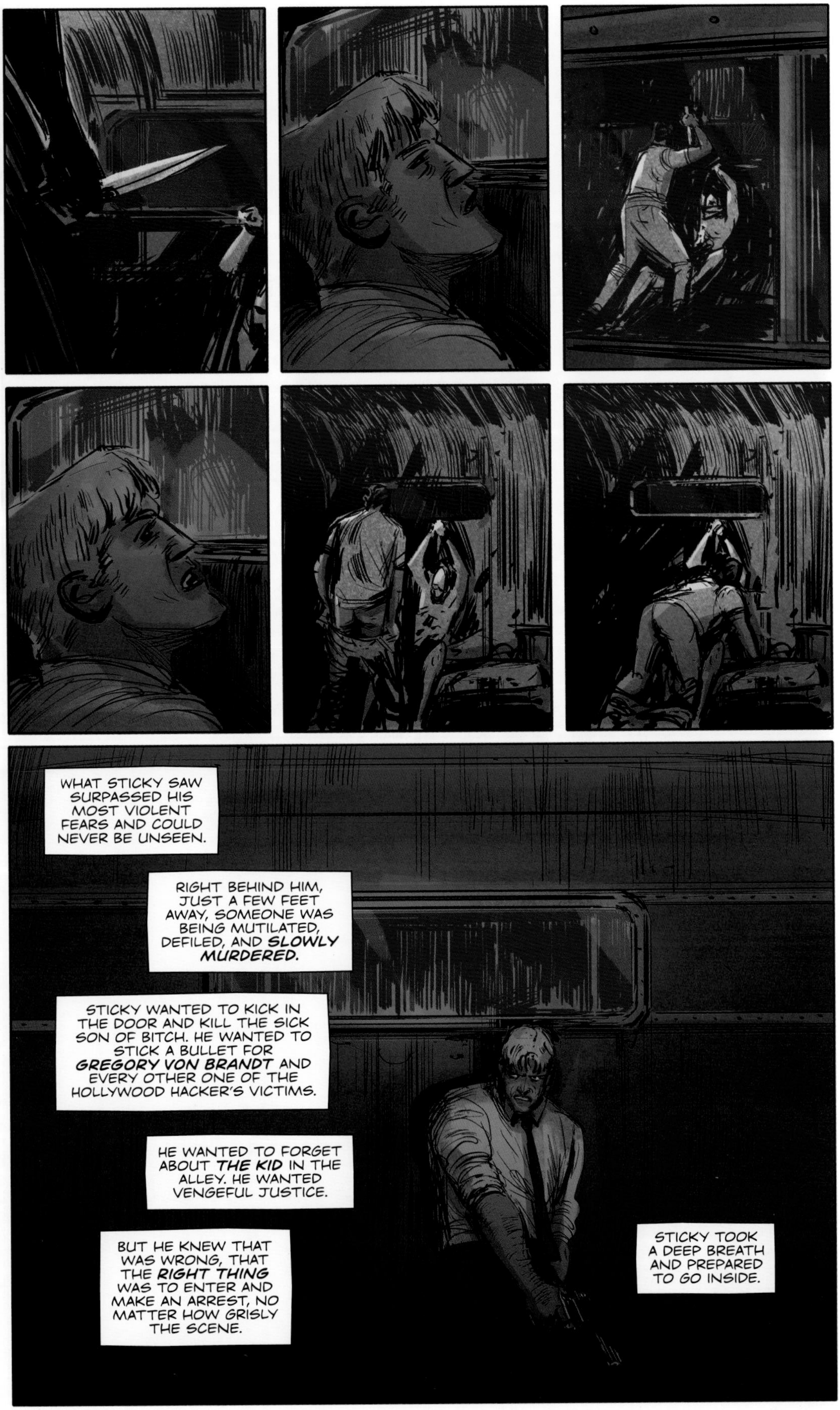
WHAT STICKY SAW SURPASSED HIS MOST VIOLENT FEARS AND COULD NEVER BE UNSEEN.
RIGHT BEHIND HIM, JUST A FEW FEET AWAY, SOMEONE WAS BEING MUTILATED, DEFILED, AND SLOWLY MURDERED.
STICKY WANTED TO KICK IN THE DOOR AND KILL THE SICK SON OF BITCH. HE WANTED TO STICK A BULLET FOR GREGORY VON BRANDT AND EVERY OTHER ONE OF THE HOLLYWOOD HACKER'S VICTIMS.
HE WANTED TO FORGET ABOUT THE KID IN THE ALLEY. HE WANTED VENGEFUL JUSTICE.
BUT HE KNEW THAT WAS WRONG, THAT THE RIGHT THING WAS TO ENTER AND MAKE AN ARREST, NO MATTER HOW GRISLY THE SCENE.
STICKY TOOK A DEEP BREATH AND PREPARED TO GO INSIDE.

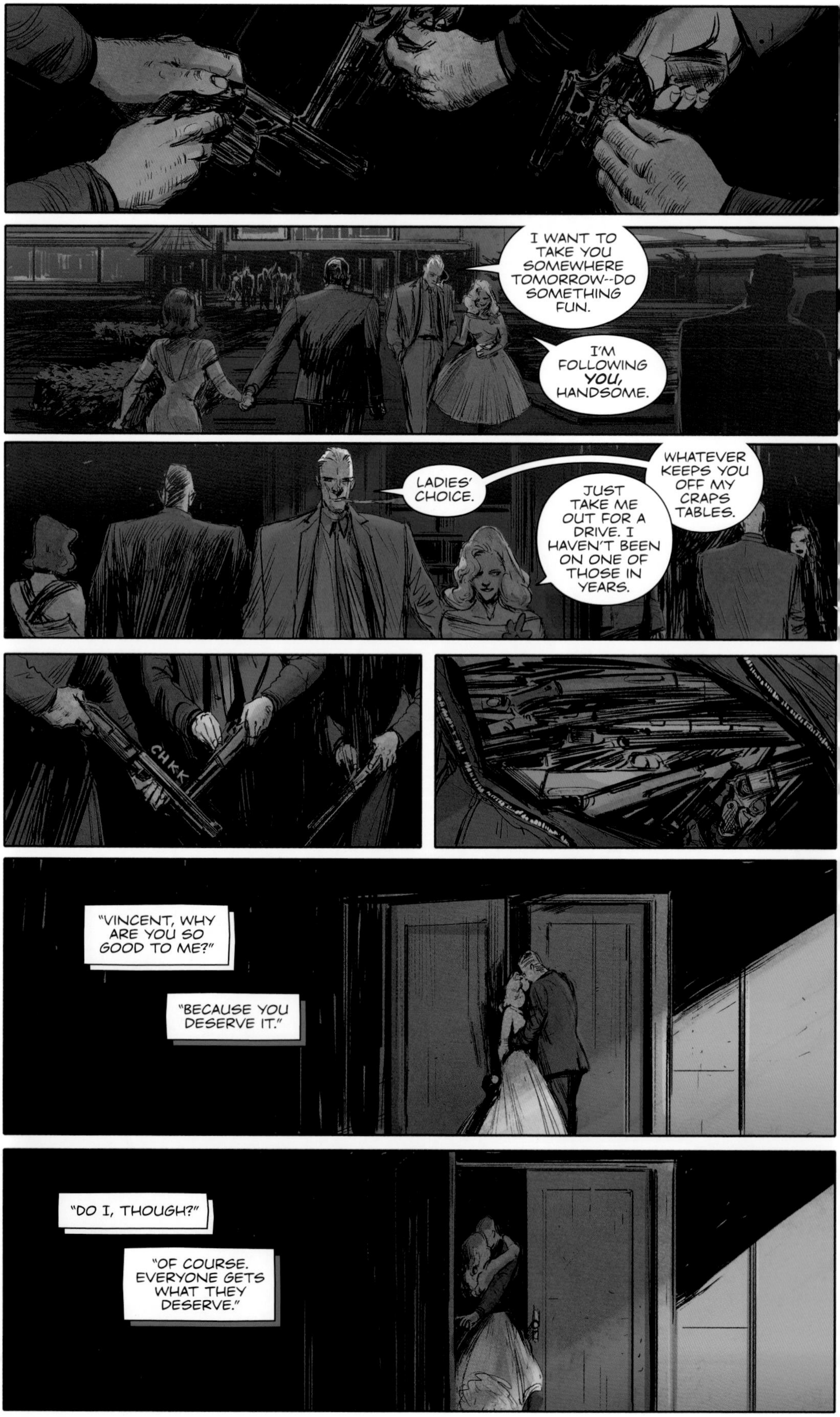

I WANT TO TAKE YOU SOMEWHERE TOMORROW--DO SOMETHING FUN.
I'M FOLLOWING *YOU,* HANDSOME.
LADIES' CHOICE.
WHATEVER KEEPS YOU OFF MY CRAPS TABLES.
JUST TAKE ME OUT FOR A DRIVE. I HAVEN'T BEEN ON ONE OF THOSE IN YEARS.
CHKK
"VINCENT, WHY ARE YOU SO GOOD TO ME?"
"BECAUSE YOU DESERVE IT."
"DO I, THOUGH?"
"OF COURSE. EVERYONE GETS WHAT THEY DESERVE."

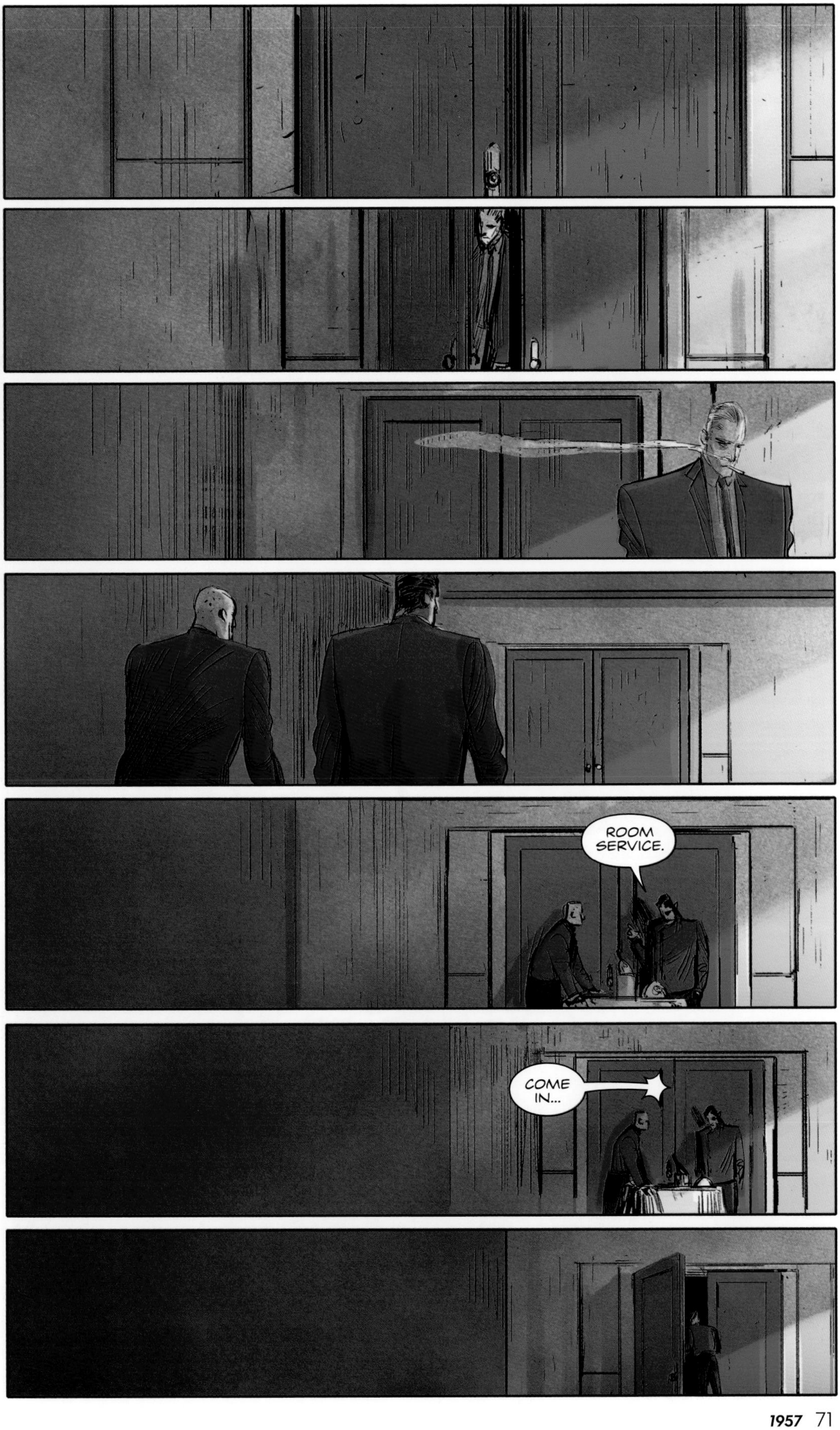
ROOM SERVICE.
COME IN...

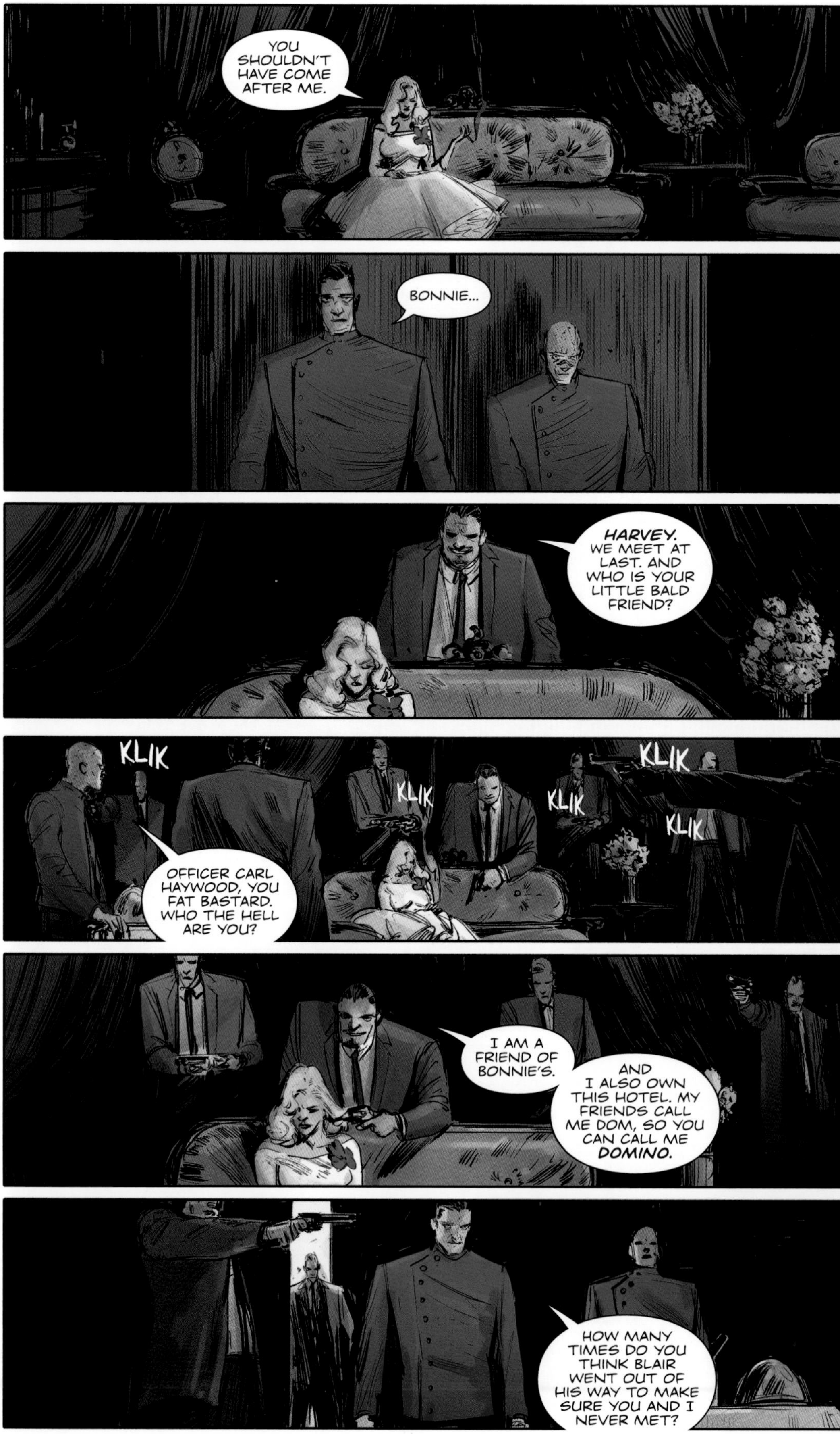
YOU SHOULDN'T HAVE COME AFTER ME.
BONNIE...
***HARVEY.*** WE MEET AT LAST. AND WHO IS YOUR LITTLE BALD FRIEND?
KLIK
KLIK
KLIK
KLIK
KLIK
OFFICER CARL HAYWOOD, YOU FAT BASTARD. WHO THE HELL ARE YOU?
I AM A FRIEND OF BONNIE'S.
AND I ALSO OWN THIS HOTEL. MY FRIENDS CALL ME DOM, SO YOU CAN CALL ME ***DOMINO.***
HOW MANY TIMES DO YOU THINK BLAIR WENT OUT OF HIS WAY TO MAKE SURE YOU AND I NEVER MET?

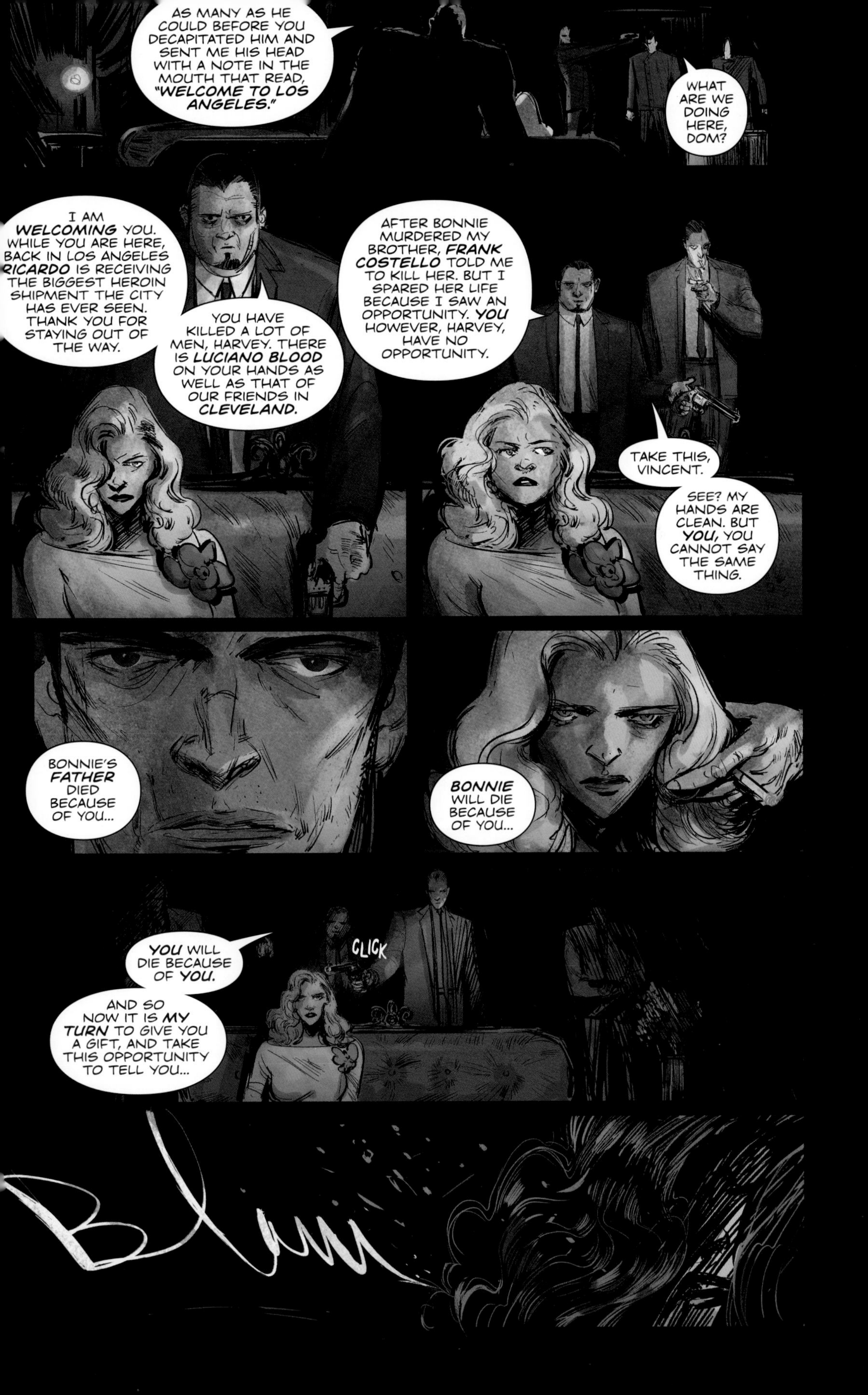
AS MANY AS HE COULD BEFORE YOU DECAPITATED HIM AND SENT ME HIS HEAD WITH A NOTE IN THE MOUTH THAT READ, "WELCOME TO LOS ANGELES."
WHAT ARE WE DOING HERE, DOM?
I AM WELCOMING YOU. WHILE YOU ARE HERE, BACK IN LOS ANGELES RICARDO IS RECEIVING THE BIGGEST HEROIN SHIPMENT THE CITY HAS EVER SEEN. THANK YOU FOR STAYING OUT OF THE WAY.
YOU HAVE KILLED A LOT OF MEN, HARVEY. THERE IS LUCIANO BLOOD ON YOUR HANDS AS WELL AS THAT OF OUR FRIENDS IN CLEVELAND.
AFTER BONNIE MURDERED MY BROTHER, FRANK COSTELLO TOLD ME TO KILL HER. BUT I SPARED HER LIFE BECAUSE I SAW AN OPPORTUNITY. YOU HOWEVER, HARVEY, HAVE NO OPPORTUNITY.
TAKE THIS, VINCENT.
SEE? MY HANDS ARE CLEAN. BUT YOU, YOU CANNOT SAY THE SAME THING.
BONNIE'S FATHER DIED BECAUSE OF YOU...
BONNIE WILL DIE BECAUSE OF YOU...
CLICK
YOU WILL DIE BECAUSE OF YOU.
AND SO NOW IT IS MY TURN TO GIVE YOU A GIFT, AND TAKE THIS OPPORTUNITY TO TELL YOU...
BLAM

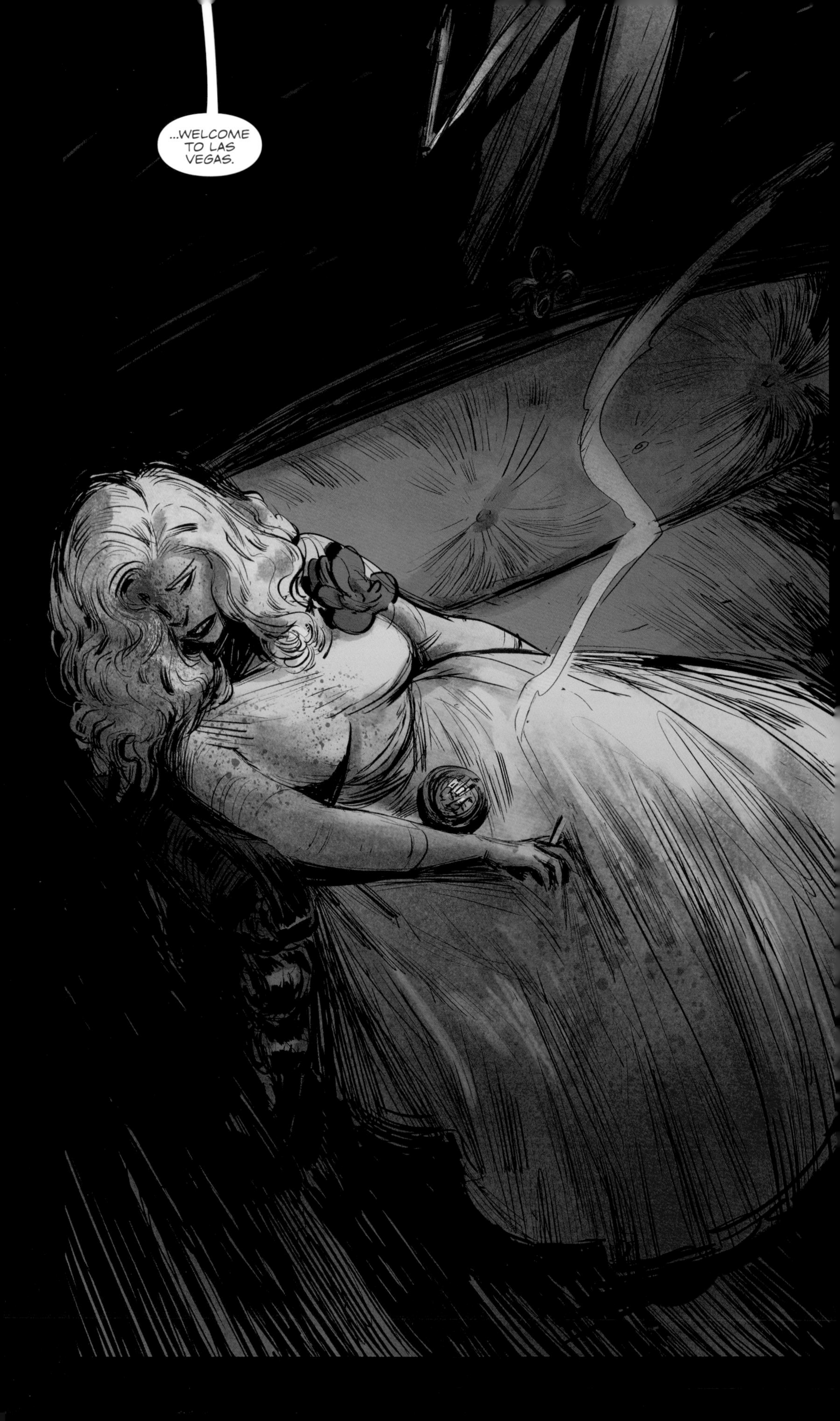
...WELCOME TO LAS VEGAS.

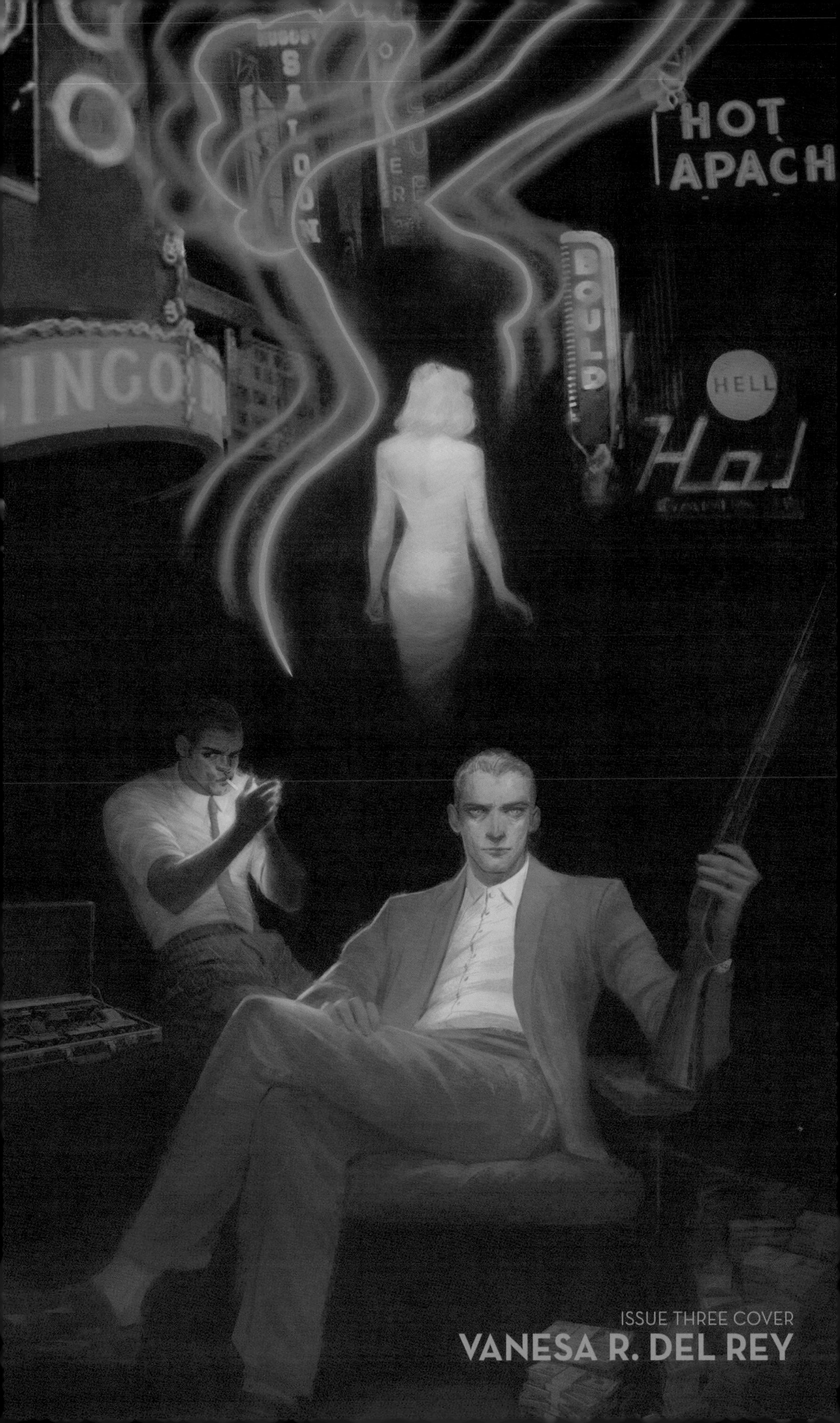
HOT
APACH
HELL

ISSUE THREE COVER
**VANESA R. DEL REY**

CHAPTER **FOUR**
# EXIT WOUNDS

THEY SAY
THE EYES ARE
THE WINDOW
TO THE SOUL.

BUT SOMETIMES,
EVEN WHEN YOU
CAN SEE INTO A
MAN'S SOUL...

...THERE'S STILL
NO TELLING WHAT
HE'S CAPABLE OF.

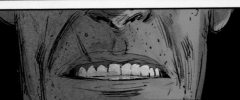

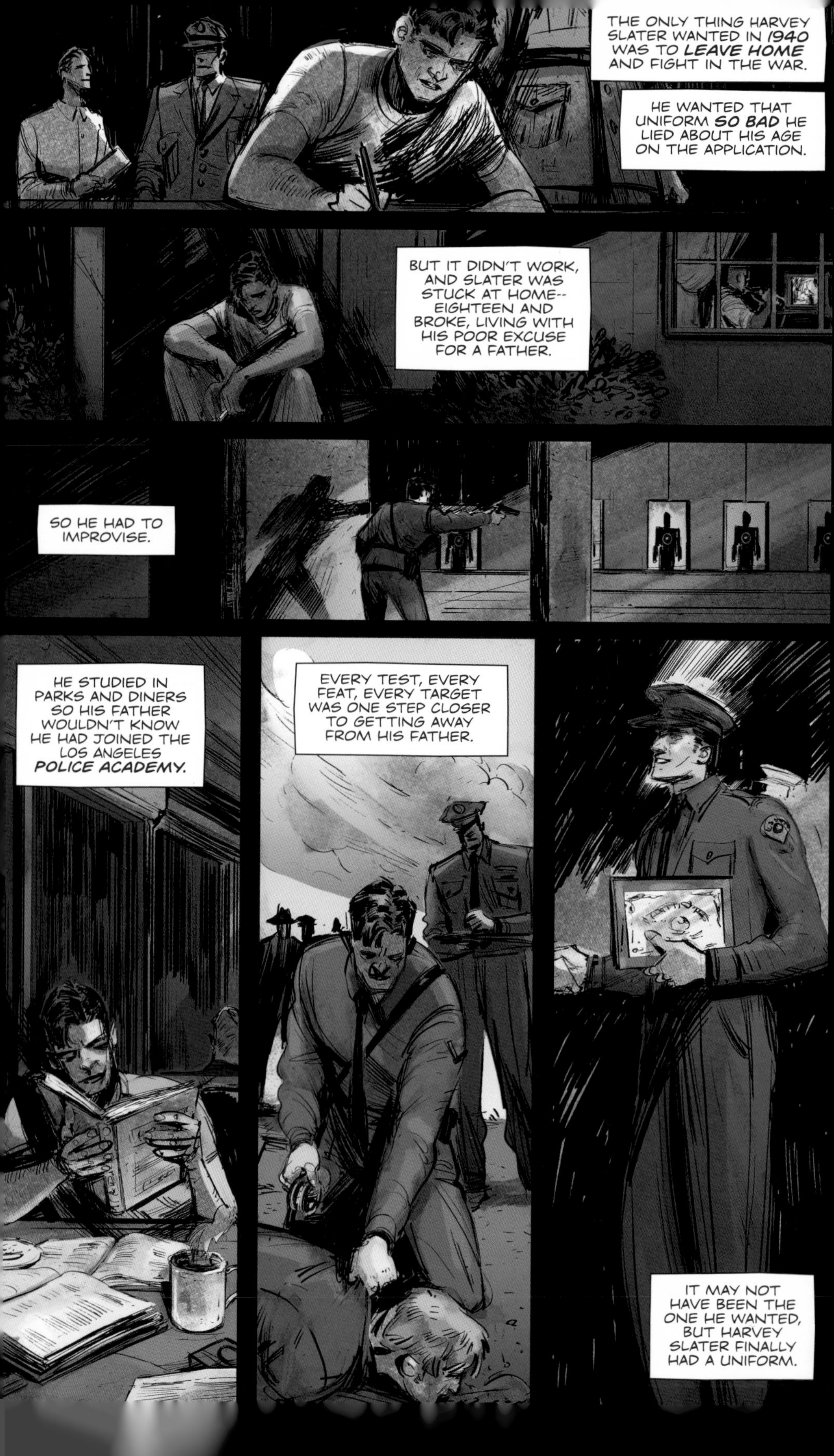
THE ONLY THING HARVEY SLATER WANTED IN *1940* WAS TO ***LEAVE HOME*** AND FIGHT IN THE WAR.
HE WANTED THAT UNIFORM ***SO BAD*** HE LIED ABOUT HIS AGE ON THE APPLICATION.
BUT IT DIDN'T WORK, AND SLATER WAS STUCK AT HOME--EIGHTEEN AND BROKE, LIVING WITH HIS POOR EXCUSE FOR A FATHER.
SO HE HAD TO IMPROVISE.
HE STUDIED IN PARKS AND DINERS SO HIS FATHER WOULDN'T KNOW HE HAD JOINED THE LOS ANGELES ***POLICE ACADEMY.***
EVERY TEST, EVERY FEAT, EVERY TARGET WAS ONE STEP CLOSER TO GETTING AWAY FROM HIS FATHER.
IT MAY NOT HAVE BEEN THE ONE HE WANTED, BUT HARVEY SLATER FINALLY HAD A UNIFORM.

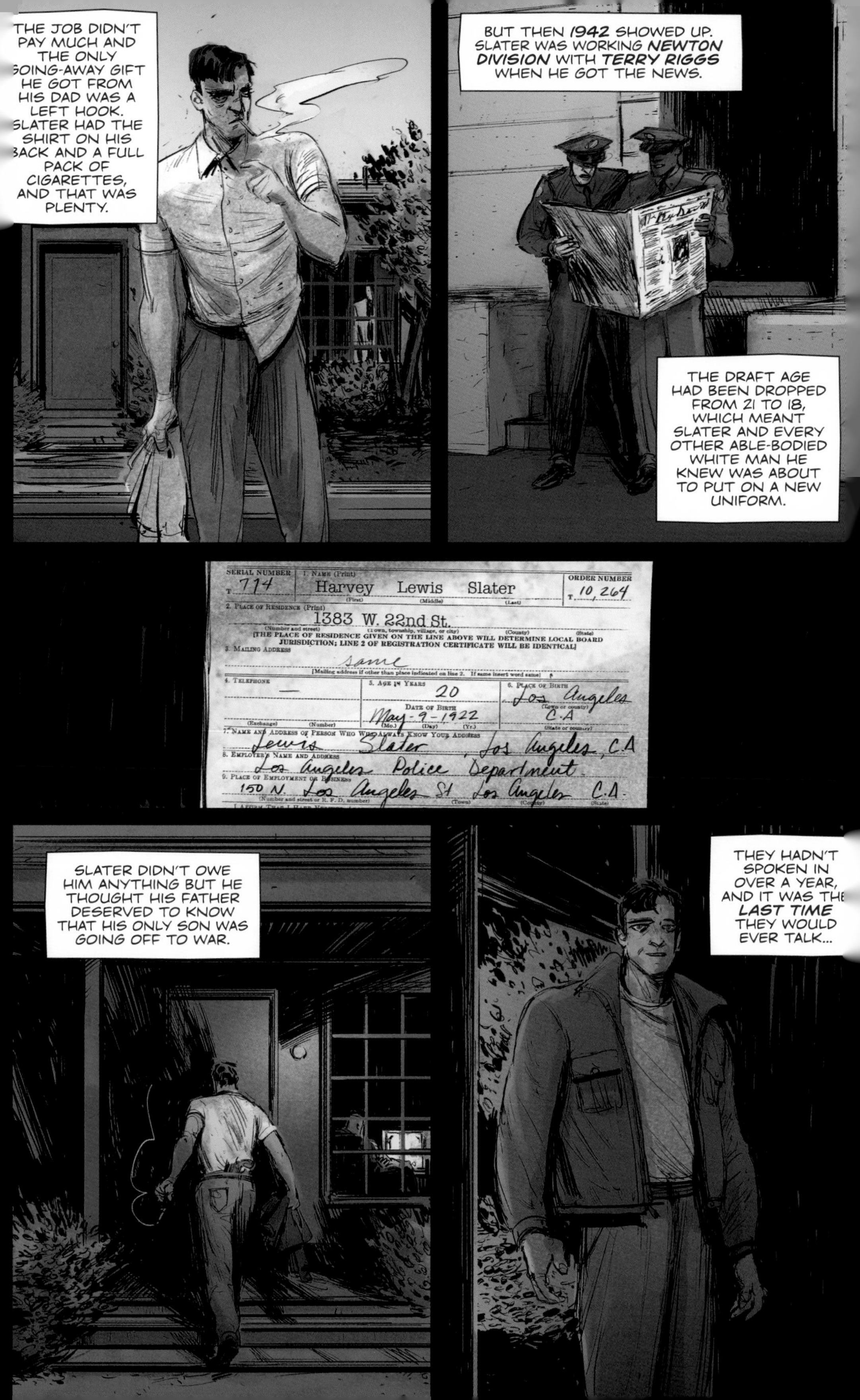
THE JOB DIDN'T PAY MUCH AND THE ONLY GOING-AWAY GIFT HE GOT FROM HIS DAD WAS A LEFT HOOK. SLATER HAD THE SHIRT ON HIS BACK AND A FULL PACK OF CIGARETTES, AND THAT WAS PLENTY.
BUT THEN **1942** SHOWED UP. SLATER WAS WORKING ***NEWTON DIVISION*** WITH ***TERRY RIGGS*** WHEN HE GOT THE NEWS.
THE DRAFT AGE HAD BEEN DROPPED FROM 21 TO 18, WHICH MEANT SLATER AND EVERY OTHER ABLE-BODIED WHITE MAN HE KNEW WAS ABOUT TO PUT ON A NEW UNIFORM.
SERIAL NUMBER T 714
1. NAME (Print) Harvey Lewis Slater
(First) (Middle) (Last)
ORDER NUMBER T 10,264
2. PLACE OF RESIDENCE (Print)
1383 W. 22nd St.
(Number and street) (Town, township, village, or city) (County) (State)
[THE PLACE OF RESIDENCE GIVEN ON THE LINE ABOVE WILL DETERMINE LOCAL BOARD JURISDICTION; LINE 2 OF REGISTRATION CERTIFICATE WILL BE IDENTICAL]
3. MAILING ADDRESS
same
[Mailing address if other than place indicated on line 2. If same insert word same]
4. TELEPHONE —
(Exchange) (Number)
5. AGE IN YEARS 20
DATE OF BIRTH May-9-1922
(Mo.) (Day) (Yr.)
6. PLACE OF BIRTH Los Angeles
(Town or county)
C.A
(State or country)
7. NAME AND ADDRESS OF PERSON WHO WILL ALWAYS KNOW YOUR ADDRESS
Lewis Slater, Los Angeles, C.A
8. EMPLOYER'S NAME AND ADDRESS
Los Angeles Police Department
9. PLACE OF EMPLOYMENT OR BUSINESS
150 N. Los Angeles St Los Angeles C.A
(Number and street or R. F. D. number) (Town) (County) (State)
SLATER DIDN'T OWE HIM ANYTHING BUT HE THOUGHT HIS FATHER DESERVED TO KNOW THAT HIS ONLY SON WAS GOING OFF TO WAR.
THEY HADN'T SPOKEN IN OVER A YEAR, AND IT WAS THE ***LAST TIME*** THEY WOULD EVER TALK...

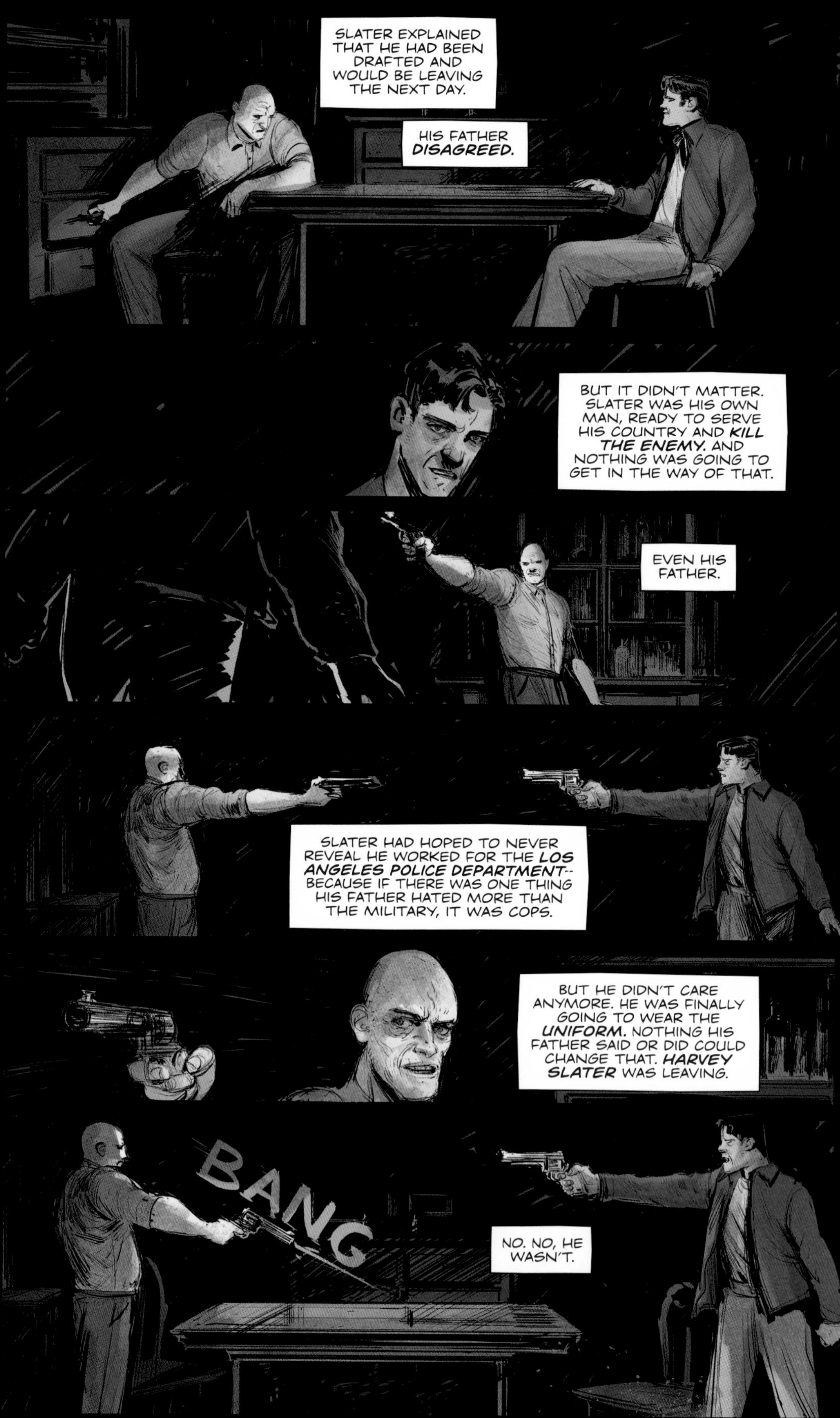
SLATER EXPLAINED THAT HE HAD BEEN DRAFTED AND WOULD BE LEAVING THE NEXT DAY.
HIS FATHER **DISAGREED.**
BUT IT DIDN'T MATTER. SLATER WAS HIS OWN MAN, READY TO SERVE HIS COUNTRY AND **KILL THE ENEMY.** AND NOTHING WAS GOING TO GET IN THE WAY OF THAT.
EVEN HIS FATHER.
SLATER HAD HOPED TO NEVER REVEAL HE WORKED FOR THE **LOS ANGELES POLICE DEPARTMENT**-- BECAUSE IF THERE WAS ONE THING HIS FATHER HATED MORE THAN THE MILITARY, IT WAS COPS.
BUT HE DIDN'T CARE ANYMORE. HE WAS FINALLY GOING TO WEAR THE **UNIFORM.** NOTHING HIS FATHER SAID OR DID COULD CHANGE THAT. **HARVEY SLATER** WAS LEAVING.
BANG
NO. NO, HE WASN'T.

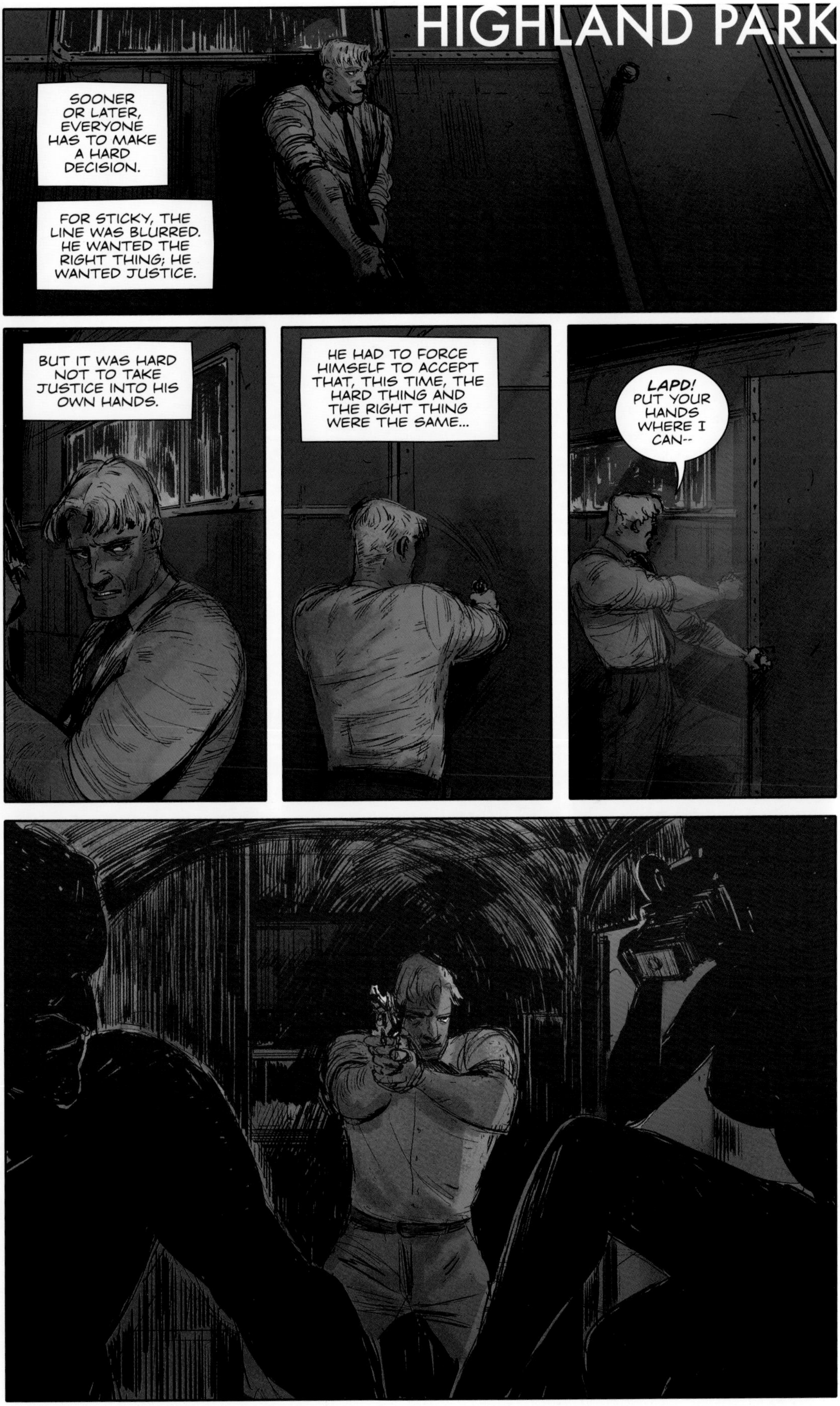
HIGHLAND PARK
SOONER OR LATER, EVERYONE HAS TO MAKE A HARD DECISION.
FOR STICKY, THE LINE WAS BLURRED. HE WANTED THE RIGHT THING; HE WANTED JUSTICE.
BUT IT WAS HARD NOT TO TAKE JUSTICE INTO HIS OWN HANDS.
HE HAD TO FORCE HIMSELF TO ACCEPT THAT, THIS TIME, THE HARD THING AND THE RIGHT THING WERE THE SAME...
LAPD! PUT YOUR HANDS WHERE I CAN--

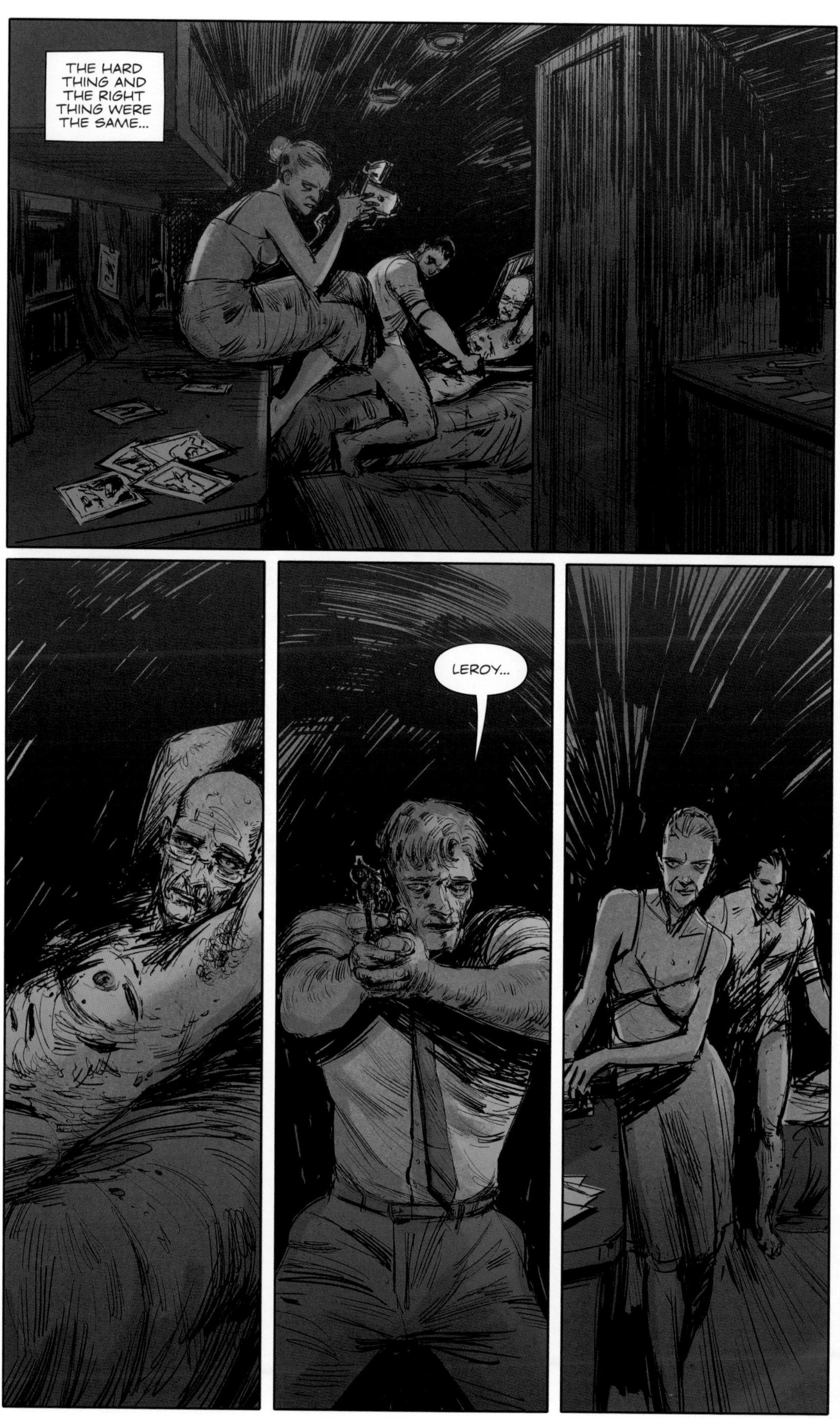
THE HARD THING AND THE RIGHT THING WERE THE SAME...
LEROY...

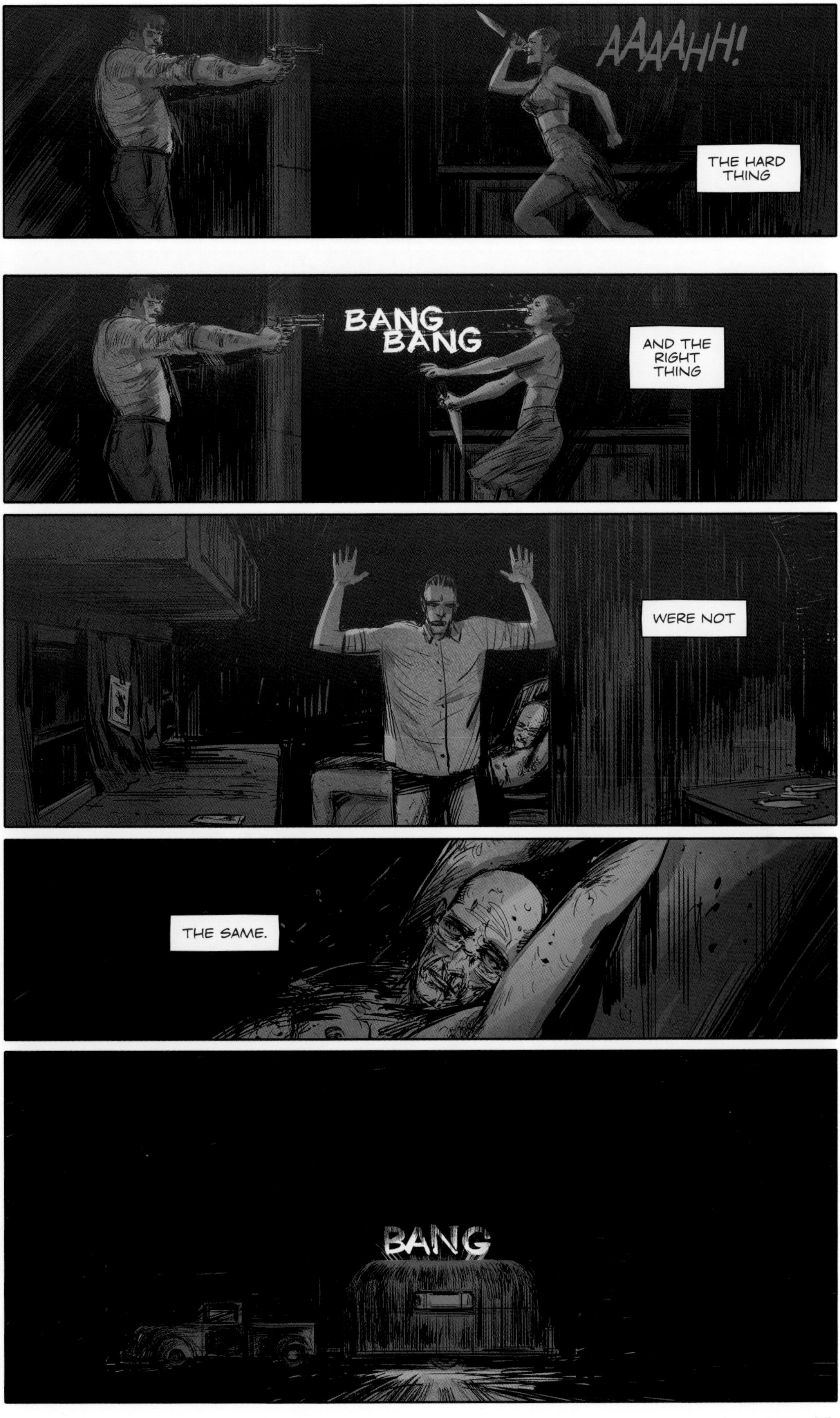
AAAAHH!
THE HARD THING
BANG BANG
AND THE RIGHT THING
WERE NOT
THE SAME.
BANG

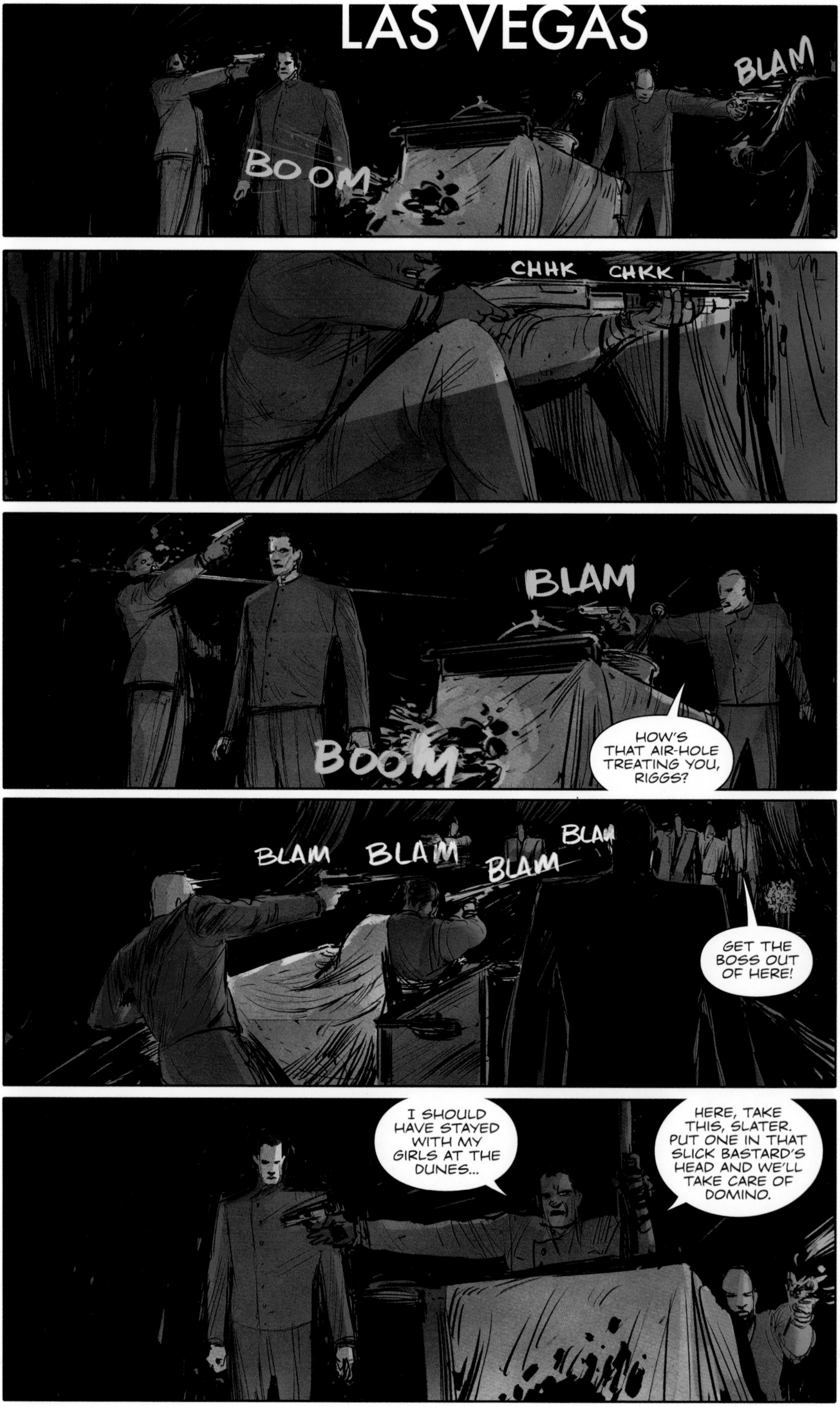
LAS VEGAS
BLAM
BOOM
CHHK CHKK
BLAM
BOOM
HOW'S THAT AIR-HOLE TREATING YOU, RIGGS?
BLAM BLAM BLAM BLAM
GET THE BOSS OUT OF HERE!
I SHOULD HAVE STAYED WITH MY GIRLS AT THE DUNES...
HERE, TAKE THIS, SLATER. PUT ONE IN THAT SLICK BASTARD'S HEAD AND WE'LL TAKE CARE OF DOMINO.

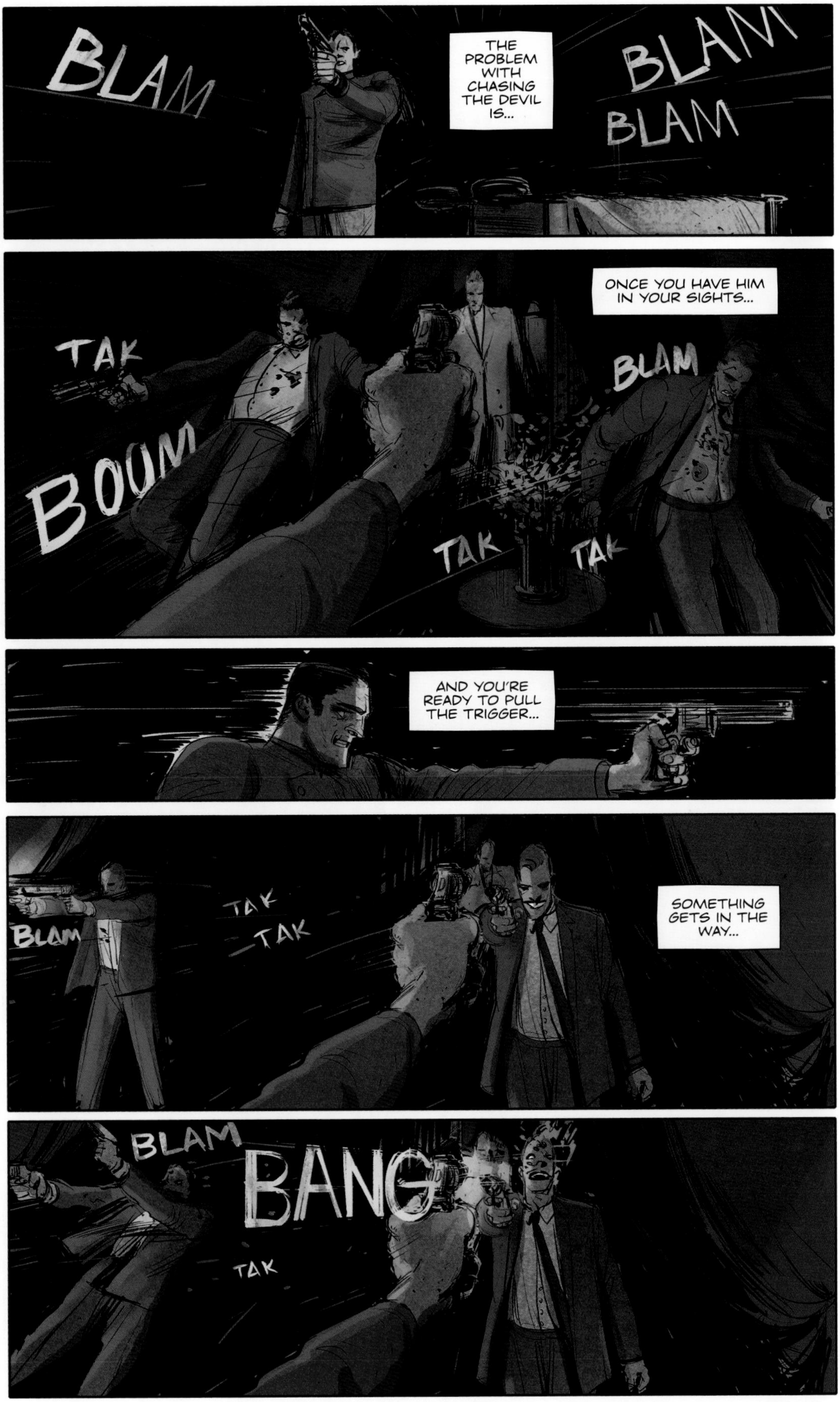
BLAM
THE PROBLEM WITH CHASING THE DEVIL IS...
BLAM
BLAM
ONCE YOU HAVE HIM IN YOUR SIGHTS...
TAK
BLAM
BOOM
TAK
TAK
AND YOU'RE READY TO PULL THE TRIGGER...
TAK
TAK
BLAM
SOMETHING GETS IN THE WAY...
BLAM
BANG
TAK

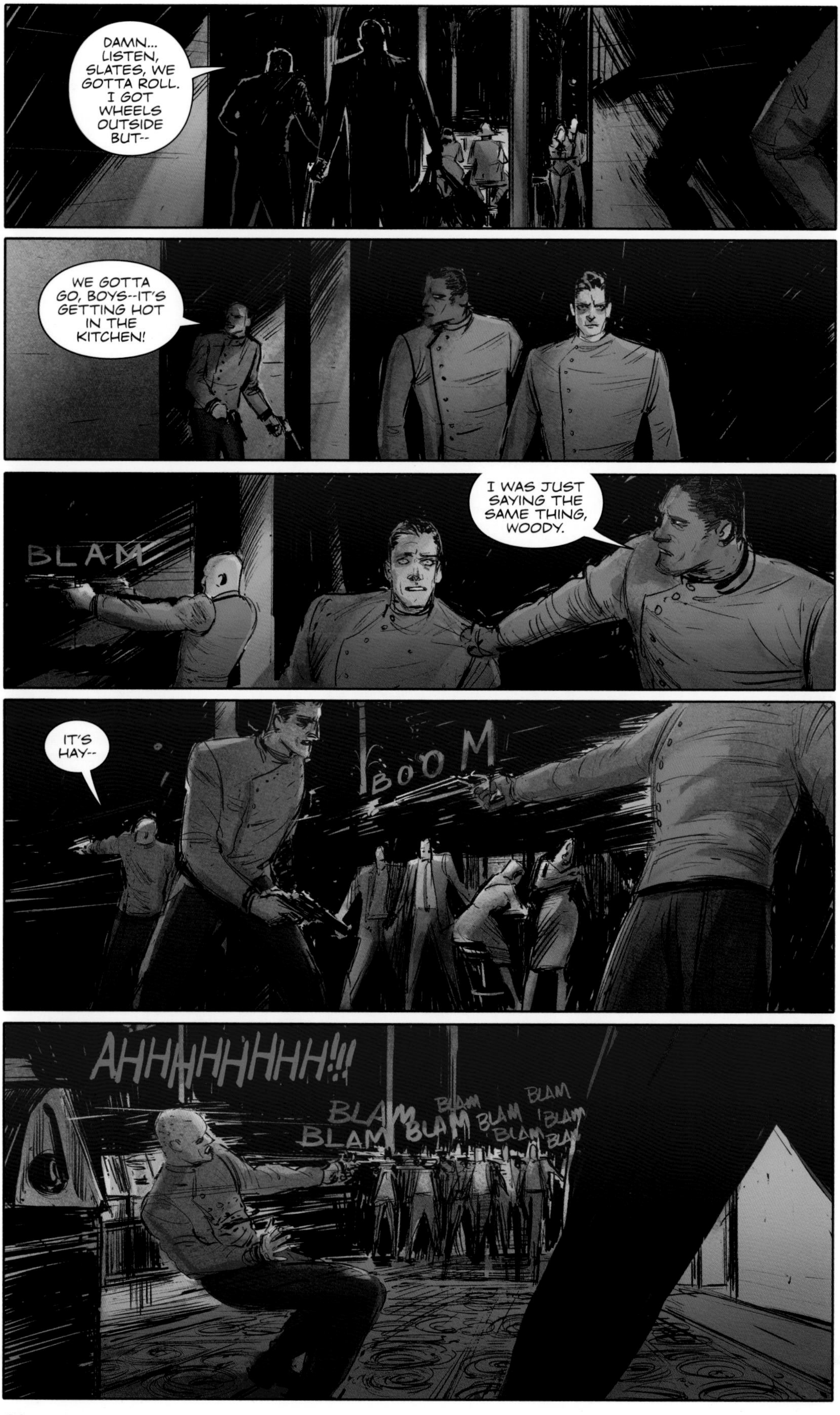
DAMN... LISTEN, SLATES, WE GOTTA ROLL. I GOT WHEELS OUTSIDE BUT--
WE GOTTA GO, BOYS--IT'S GETTING HOT IN THE KITCHEN!
BLAM
I WAS JUST SAYING THE SAME THING, WOODY.
IT'S HAY--
BOOM
AHHHHHHHHH!!!
BLAM BLAM BLAM BLAM BLAM BLAM BLAM BLAM BLAM BLAM

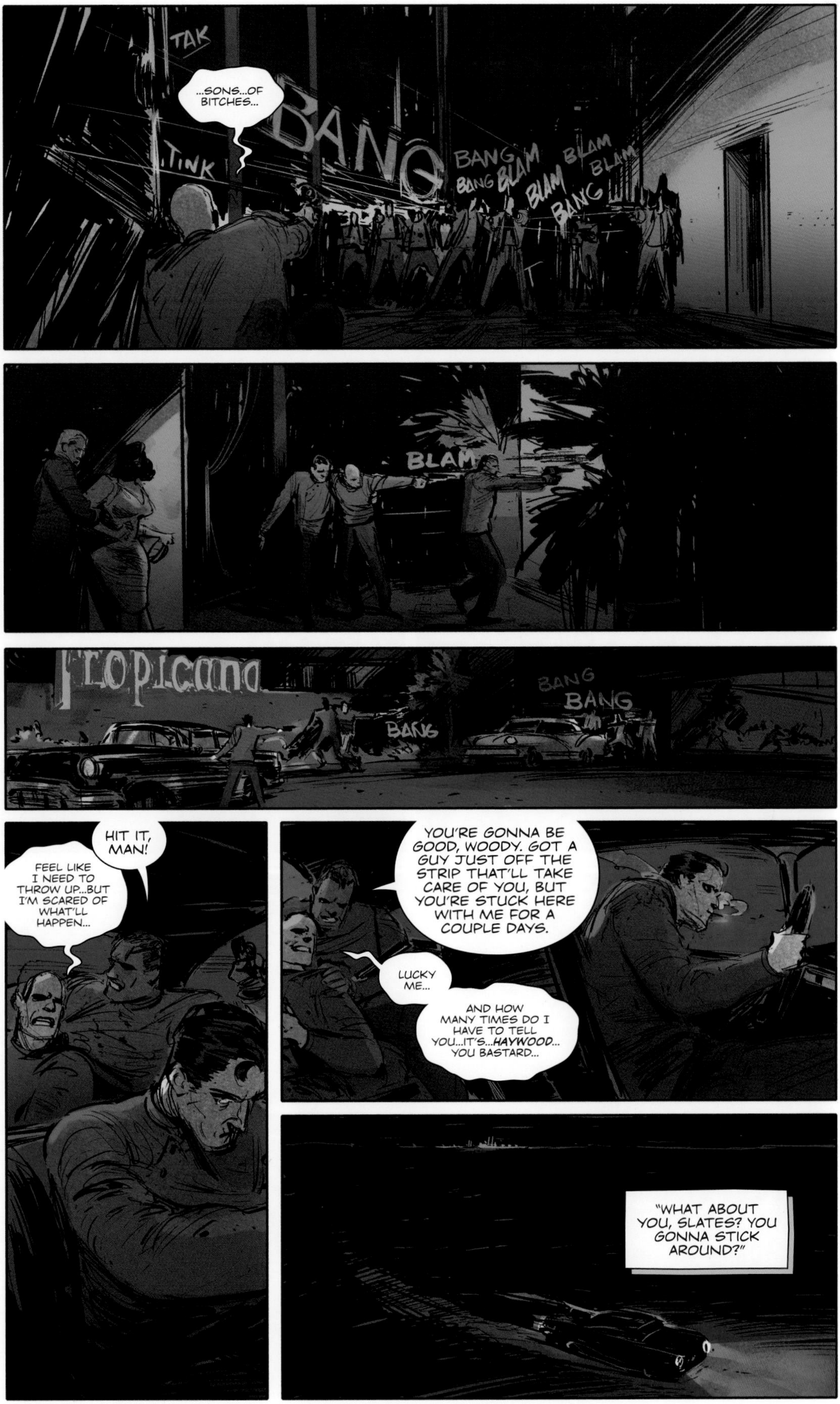
TAK
...SONS...OF BITCHES...
BANG
TINK
BANG BANG BLAM BLAM BLAM BLAM BLAM BANG
BLAM
Tropicana
BANG
BANG
BANG
HIT IT, MAN!
FEEL LIKE I NEED TO THROW UP...BUT I'M SCARED OF WHAT'LL HAPPEN...
YOU'RE GONNA BE GOOD, WOODY. GOT A GUY JUST OFF THE STRIP THAT'LL TAKE CARE OF YOU, BUT YOU'RE STUCK HERE WITH ME FOR A COUPLE DAYS.
LUCKY ME...
AND HOW MANY TIMES DO I HAVE TO TELL YOU...IT'S...HAYWOOD... YOU BASTARD...
"WHAT ABOUT YOU, SLATES? YOU GONNA STICK AROUND?"

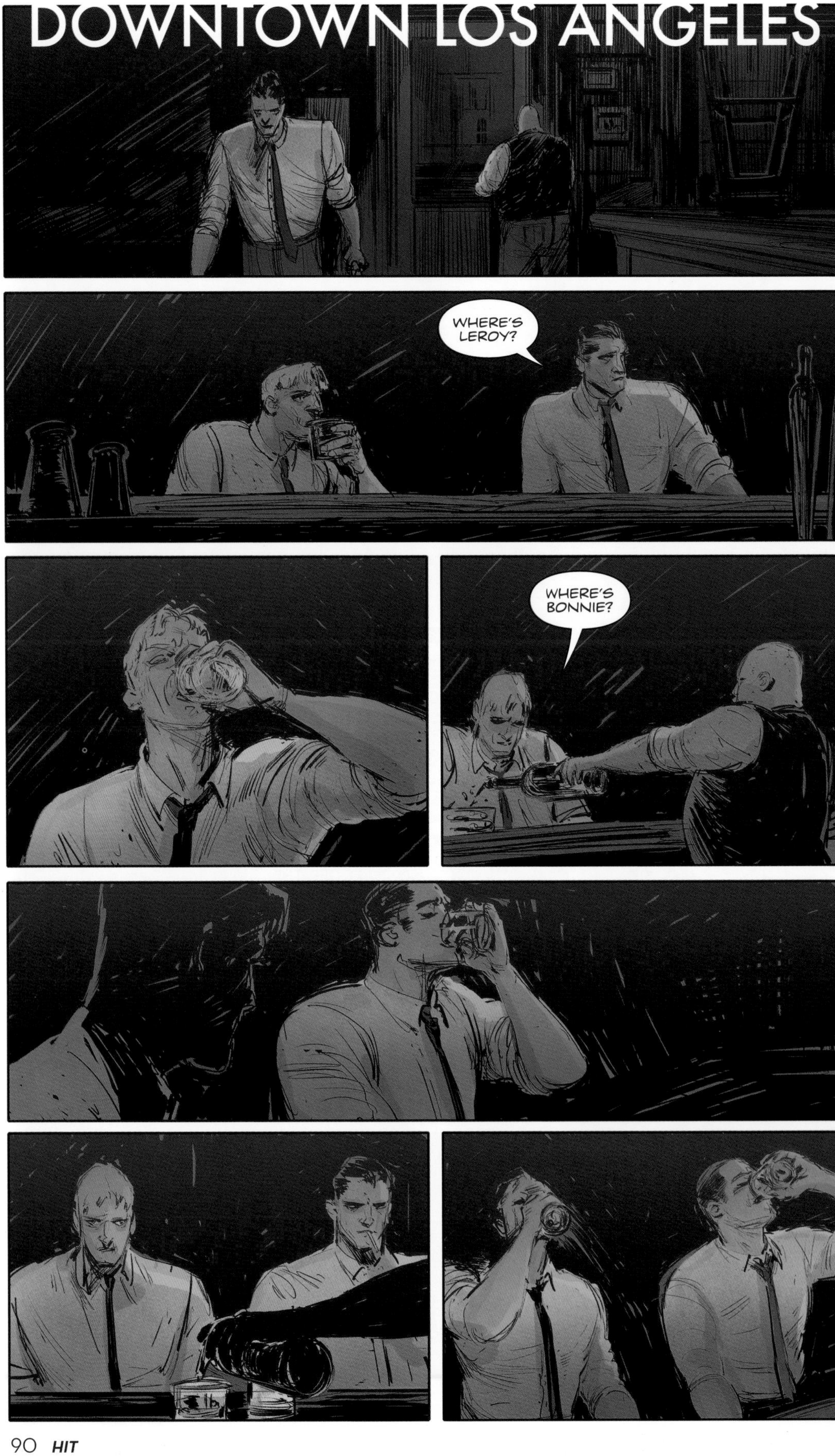
DOWNTOWN LOS ANGELES
WHERE'S LEROY?
WHERE'S BONNIE?

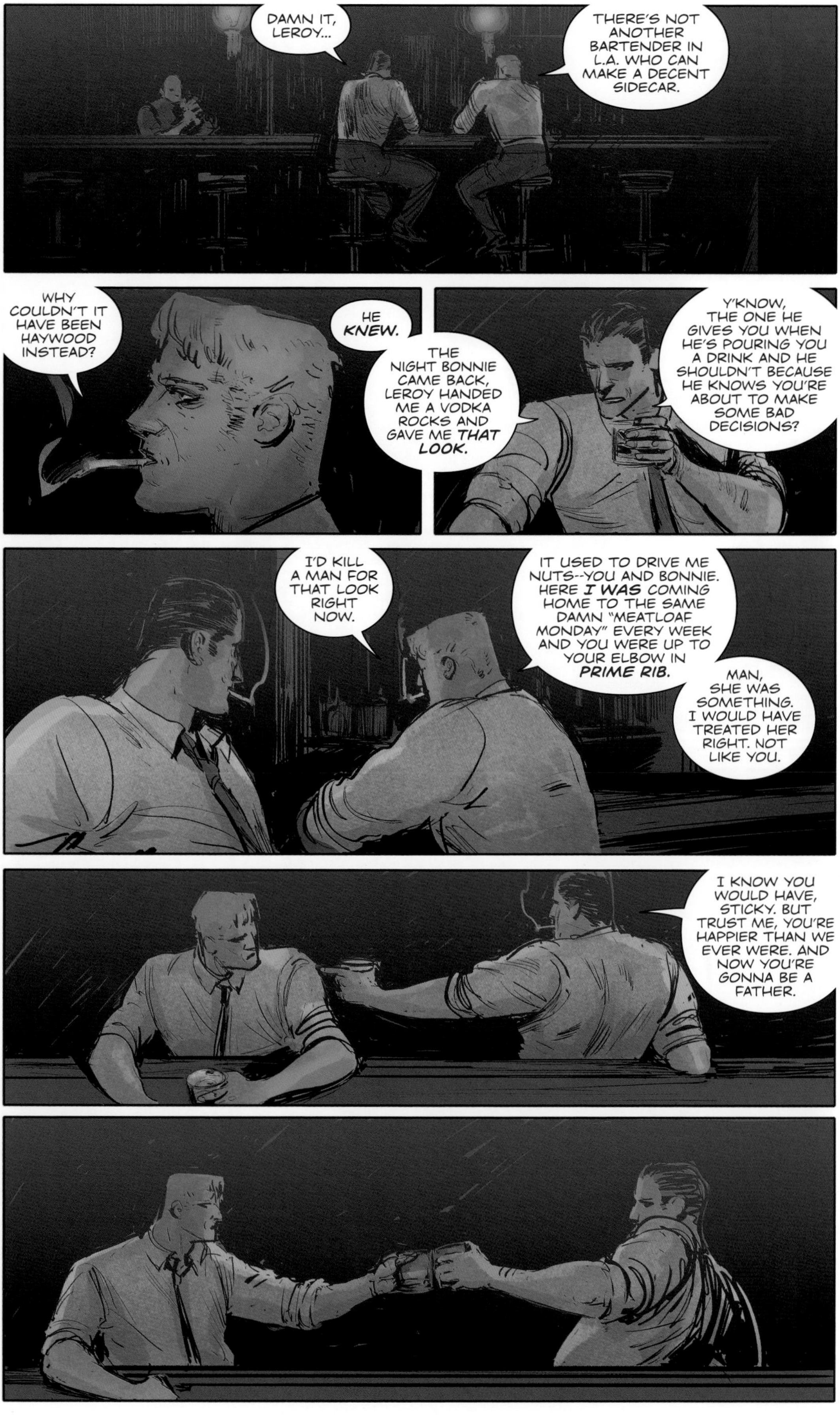
DAMN IT, LEROY...
THERE'S NOT ANOTHER BARTENDER IN L.A. WHO CAN MAKE A DECENT SIDECAR.
WHY COULDN'T IT HAVE BEEN HAYWOOD INSTEAD?
HE *KNEW.*
THE NIGHT BONNIE CAME BACK, LEROY HANDED ME A VODKA ROCKS AND GAVE ME *THAT LOOK.*
Y'KNOW, THE ONE HE GIVES YOU WHEN HE'S POURING YOU A DRINK AND HE SHOULDN'T BECAUSE HE KNOWS YOU'RE ABOUT TO MAKE SOME BAD DECISIONS?
I'D KILL A MAN FOR THAT LOOK RIGHT NOW.
IT USED TO DRIVE ME NUTS--YOU AND BONNIE. HERE *I WAS* COMING HOME TO THE SAME DAMN "MEATLOAF MONDAY" EVERY WEEK AND YOU WERE UP TO YOUR ELBOW IN *PRIME RIB.*
MAN, SHE WAS SOMETHING. I WOULD HAVE TREATED HER RIGHT. NOT LIKE YOU.
I KNOW YOU WOULD HAVE, STICKY. BUT TRUST ME, YOU'RE HAPPIER THAN WE EVER WERE. AND NOW YOU'RE GONNA BE A FATHER.

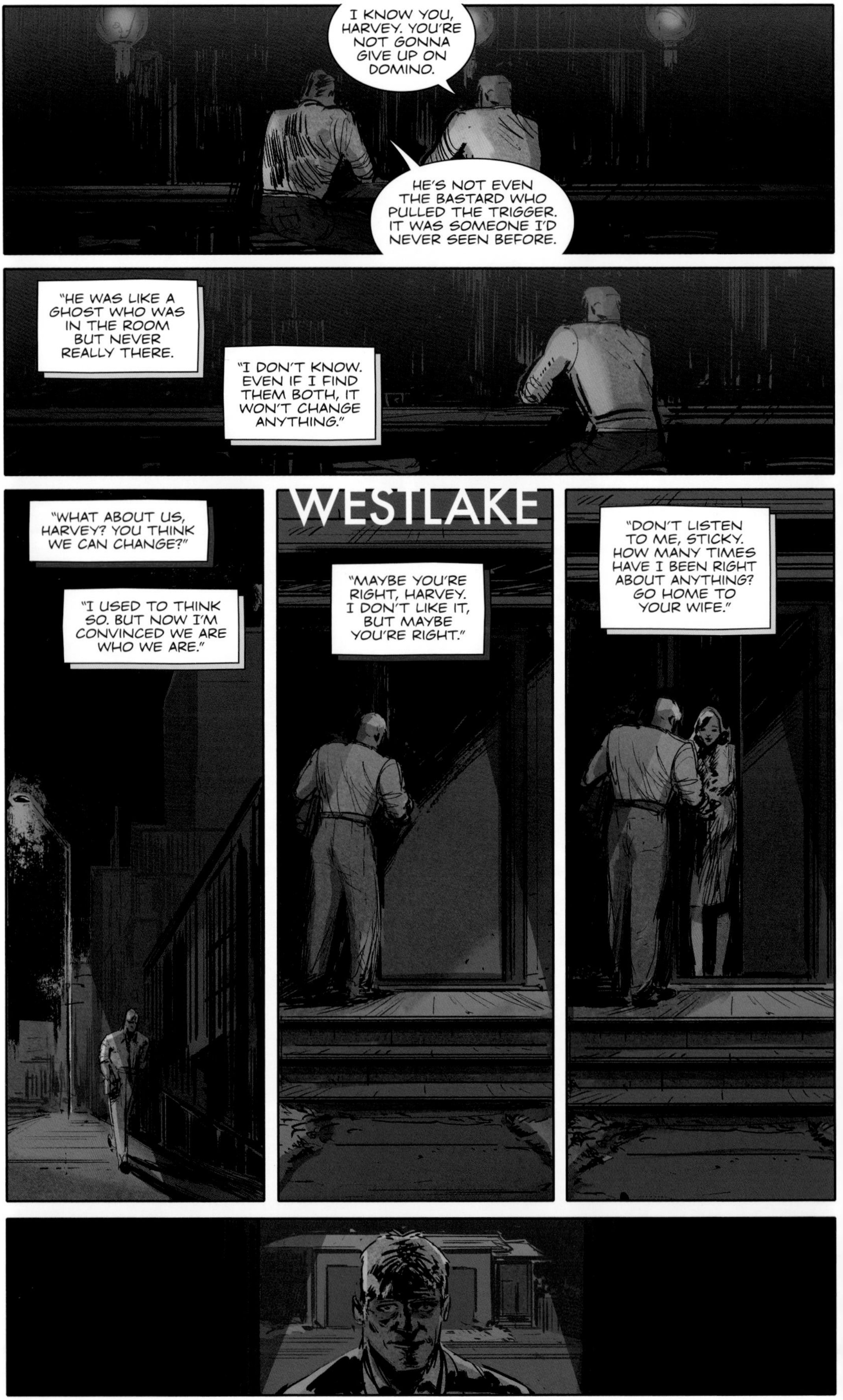
I KNOW YOU, HARVEY. YOU'RE NOT GONNA GIVE UP ON DOMINO.
HE'S NOT EVEN THE BASTARD WHO PULLED THE TRIGGER. IT WAS SOMEONE I'D NEVER SEEN BEFORE.
"HE WAS LIKE A GHOST WHO WAS IN THE ROOM BUT NEVER REALLY THERE.
"I DON'T KNOW. EVEN IF I FIND THEM BOTH, IT WON'T CHANGE ANYTHING."
"WHAT ABOUT US, HARVEY? YOU THINK WE CAN CHANGE?"
"I USED TO THINK SO. BUT NOW I'M CONVINCED WE ARE WHO WE ARE."
WESTLAKE
"MAYBE YOU'RE RIGHT, HARVEY. I DON'T LIKE IT, BUT MAYBE YOU'RE RIGHT."
"DON'T LISTEN TO ME, STICKY. HOW MANY TIMES HAVE I BEEN RIGHT ABOUT ANYTHING? GO HOME TO YOUR WIFE."

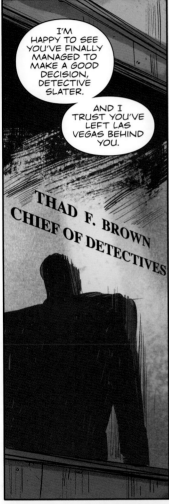

I'M HAPPY TO SEE YOU'VE FINALLY MANAGED TO MAKE A GOOD DECISION, DETECTIVE SLATER.

AND I TRUST YOU'VE LEFT LAS VEGAS BEHIND YOU.

THAD F. BROWN
CHIEF OF DETECTIVES

I'VE LEFT A LOT OF THINGS BEHIND ME.

I WAS SORRY TO HEAR ABOUT *MS. BLAIR.* HER FATHER WAS A VERY DEAR FRIEND, GOD REST HIS SOUL. IN FACT, HE'S PART OF THE REASON YOU'RE HERE.

WHEN CAPTAIN BLAIR CAME TO ME REQUESTING PERMISSION TO PUT TOGETHER A SPECIAL TASK FORCE, I POINTED AT THE *GANGSTER SQUAD.*

BUT HE HAD GRANDER IDEAS. BLAIR WANTED A MORE PERMANENT SOLUTION SO I LET HIM TRY IT OUT, AND IT WAS WORKING...UNTIL HIS DAUGHTER PUT HIM IN A PRECARIOUS SITUATION. HE WAS A *GOOD MAN,* ALBEIT CORRUPTIBLE.

YOU HOWEVER, DETECTIVE SLATER, ARE *NOT* A GOOD MAN. THAT'S WHY I GAVE *BLAIR* PERMISSION TO OPERATE A *HIT SQUAD.* NOT YOU. AND EVEN THOUGH BLAIR WAS GONE, THE JOB WAS NOT YOURS TO TAKE.

BUT THAT DOESN'T MEAN YOU'RE NOT GOOD AT WHAT YOU DO. YOU MOST CERTAINLY ARE, AND YOU WOULDN'T BE HERE IF YOU WEREN'T.

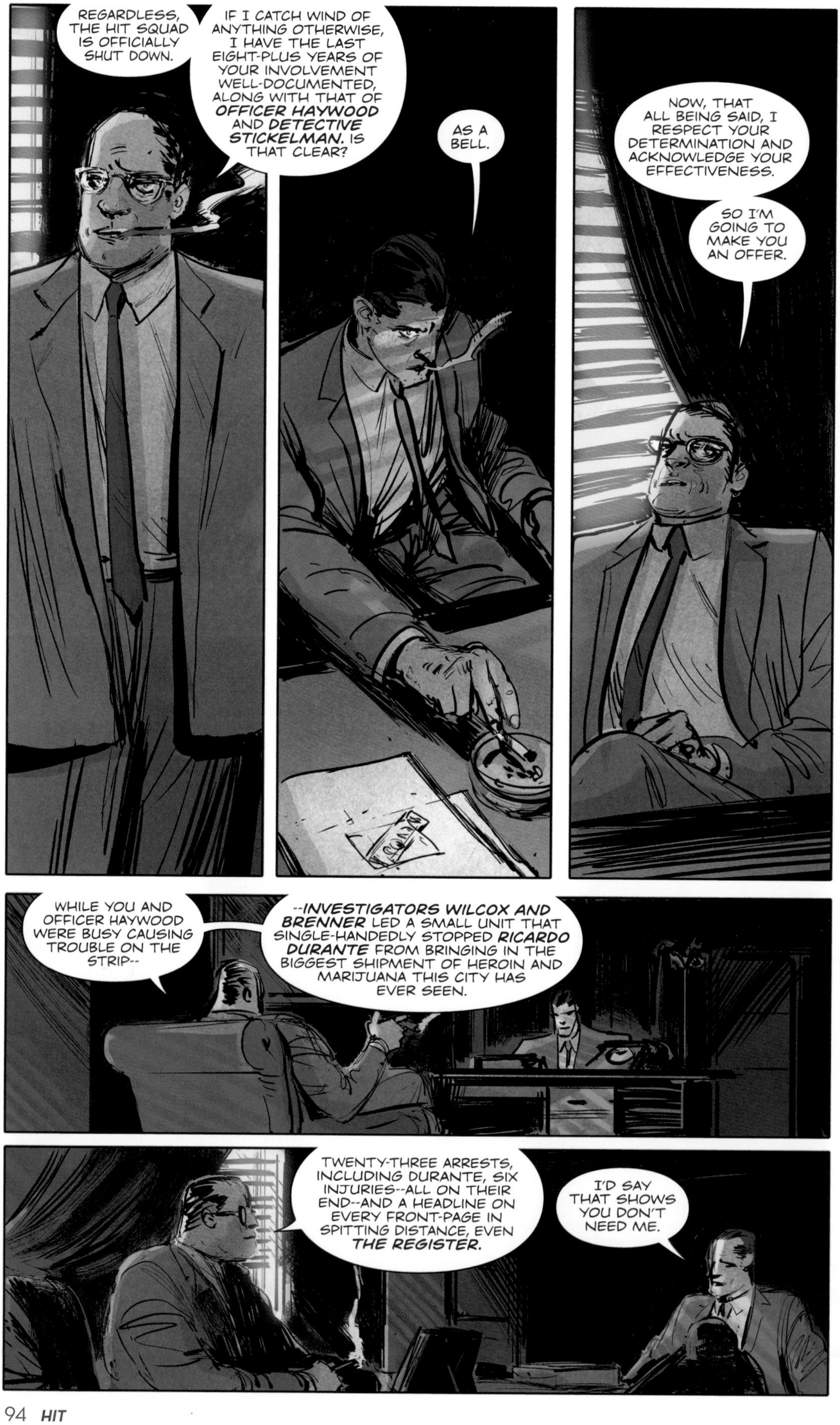
REGARDLESS, THE HIT SQUAD IS OFFICIALLY SHUT DOWN.
IF I CATCH WIND OF ANYTHING OTHERWISE, I HAVE THE LAST EIGHT-PLUS YEARS OF YOUR INVOLVEMENT WELL-DOCUMENTED, ALONG WITH THAT OF OFFICER HAYWOOD AND DETECTIVE STICKELMAN. IS THAT CLEAR?
AS A BELL.
NOW, THAT ALL BEING SAID, I RESPECT YOUR DETERMINATION AND ACKNOWLEDGE YOUR EFFECTIVENESS.
SO I'M GOING TO MAKE YOU AN OFFER.
WHILE YOU AND OFFICER HAYWOOD WERE BUSY CAUSING TROUBLE ON THE STRIP--
--INVESTIGATORS WILCOX AND BRENNER LED A SMALL UNIT THAT SINGLE-HANDEDLY STOPPED RICARDO DURANTE FROM BRINGING IN THE BIGGEST SHIPMENT OF HEROIN AND MARIJUANA THIS CITY HAS EVER SEEN.
TWENTY-THREE ARRESTS, INCLUDING DURANTE, SIX INJURIES--ALL ON THEIR END--AND A HEADLINE ON EVERY FRONT-PAGE IN SPITTING DISTANCE, EVEN THE REGISTER.
I'D SAY THAT SHOWS YOU DON'T NEED ME.

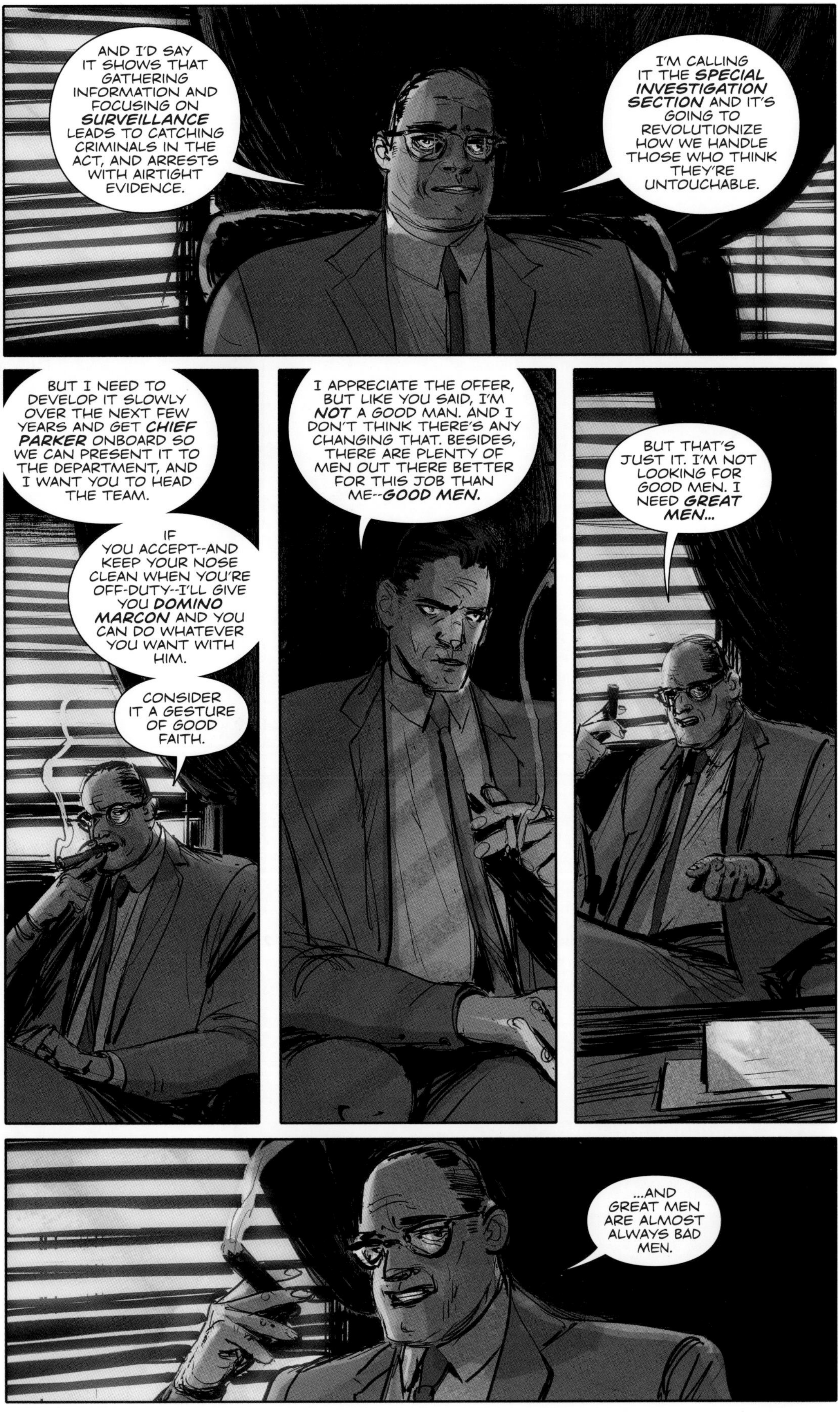
AND I'D SAY IT SHOWS THAT GATHERING INFORMATION AND FOCUSING ON SURVEILLANCE LEADS TO CATCHING CRIMINALS IN THE ACT, AND ARRESTS WITH AIRTIGHT EVIDENCE.
I'M CALLING IT THE SPECIAL INVESTIGATION SECTION AND IT'S GOING TO REVOLUTIONIZE HOW WE HANDLE THOSE WHO THINK THEY'RE UNTOUCHABLE.
BUT I NEED TO DEVELOP IT SLOWLY OVER THE NEXT FEW YEARS AND GET CHIEF PARKER ONBOARD SO WE CAN PRESENT IT TO THE DEPARTMENT, AND I WANT YOU TO HEAD THE TEAM.
IF YOU ACCEPT--AND KEEP YOUR NOSE CLEAN WHEN YOU'RE OFF-DUTY--I'LL GIVE YOU DOMINO MARCON AND YOU CAN DO WHATEVER YOU WANT WITH HIM.
CONSIDER IT A GESTURE OF GOOD FAITH.
I APPRECIATE THE OFFER, BUT LIKE YOU SAID, I'M NOT A GOOD MAN. AND I DON'T THINK THERE'S ANY CHANGING THAT. BESIDES, THERE ARE PLENTY OF MEN OUT THERE BETTER FOR THIS JOB THAN ME--GOOD MEN.
BUT THAT'S JUST IT. I'M NOT LOOKING FOR GOOD MEN. I NEED GREAT MEN...
...AND GREAT MEN ARE ALMOST ALWAYS BAD MEN.

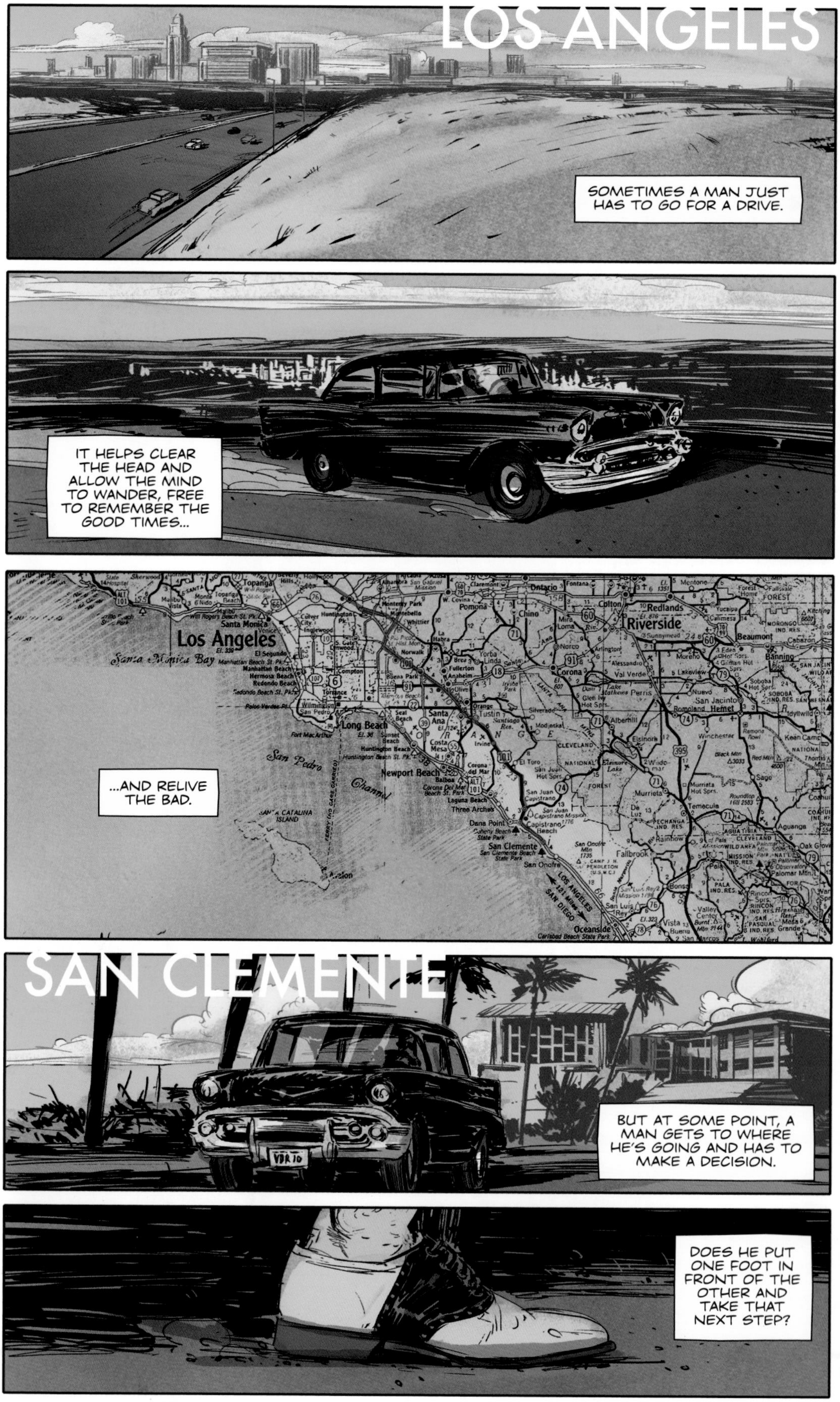
LOS ANGELES
SOMETIMES A MAN JUST HAS TO GO FOR A DRIVE.
IT HELPS CLEAR THE HEAD AND ALLOW THE MIND TO WANDER, FREE TO REMEMBER THE GOOD TIMES...
...AND RELIVE THE BAD.
Los Angeles
Santa Monica Bay
Santa Monica
Long Beach
Newport Beach
Riverside
Redlands
Corona
Pomona
Ontario
Santa Ana
San Clemente
Oceanside
San Pedro Channel
SANTA CATALINA ISLAND
LOS ANGELES
SAN DIEGO
SAN CLEMENTE
VBR 10
BUT AT SOME POINT, A MAN GETS TO WHERE HE'S GOING AND HAS TO MAKE A DECISION.
DOES HE PUT ONE FOOT IN FRONT OF THE OTHER AND TAKE THAT NEXT STEP?

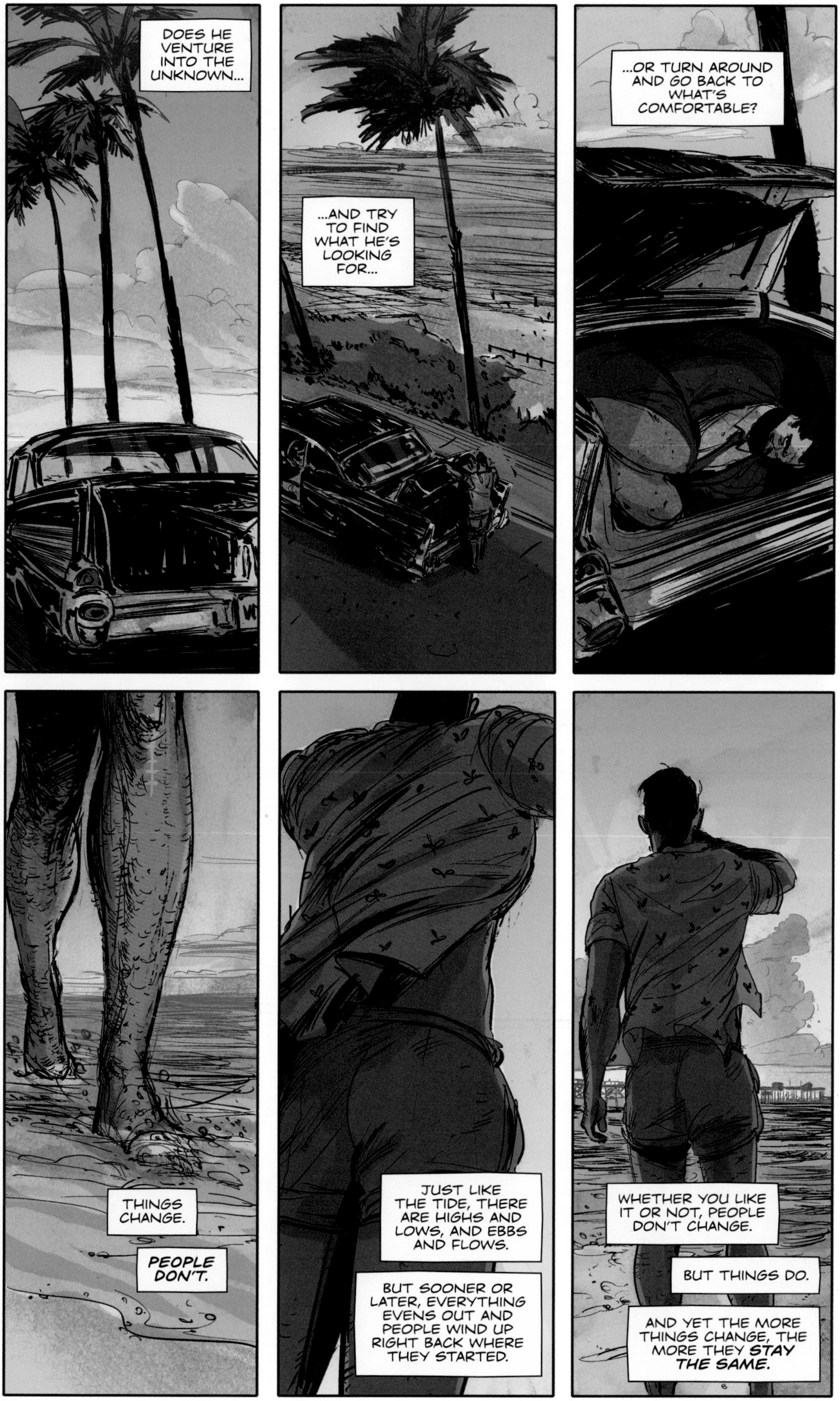
DOES HE VENTURE INTO THE UNKNOWN...
...AND TRY TO FIND WHAT HE'S LOOKING FOR...
...OR TURN AROUND AND GO BACK TO WHAT'S COMFORTABLE?
THINGS CHANGE.
PEOPLE DON'T.
JUST LIKE THE TIDE, THERE ARE HIGHS AND LOWS, AND EBBS AND FLOWS.
BUT SOONER OR LATER, EVERYTHING EVENS OUT AND PEOPLE WIND UP RIGHT BACK WHERE THEY STARTED.
WHETHER YOU LIKE IT OR NOT, PEOPLE DON'T CHANGE.
BUT THINGS DO.
AND YET THE MORE THINGS CHANGE, THE MORE THEY STAY THE SAME.

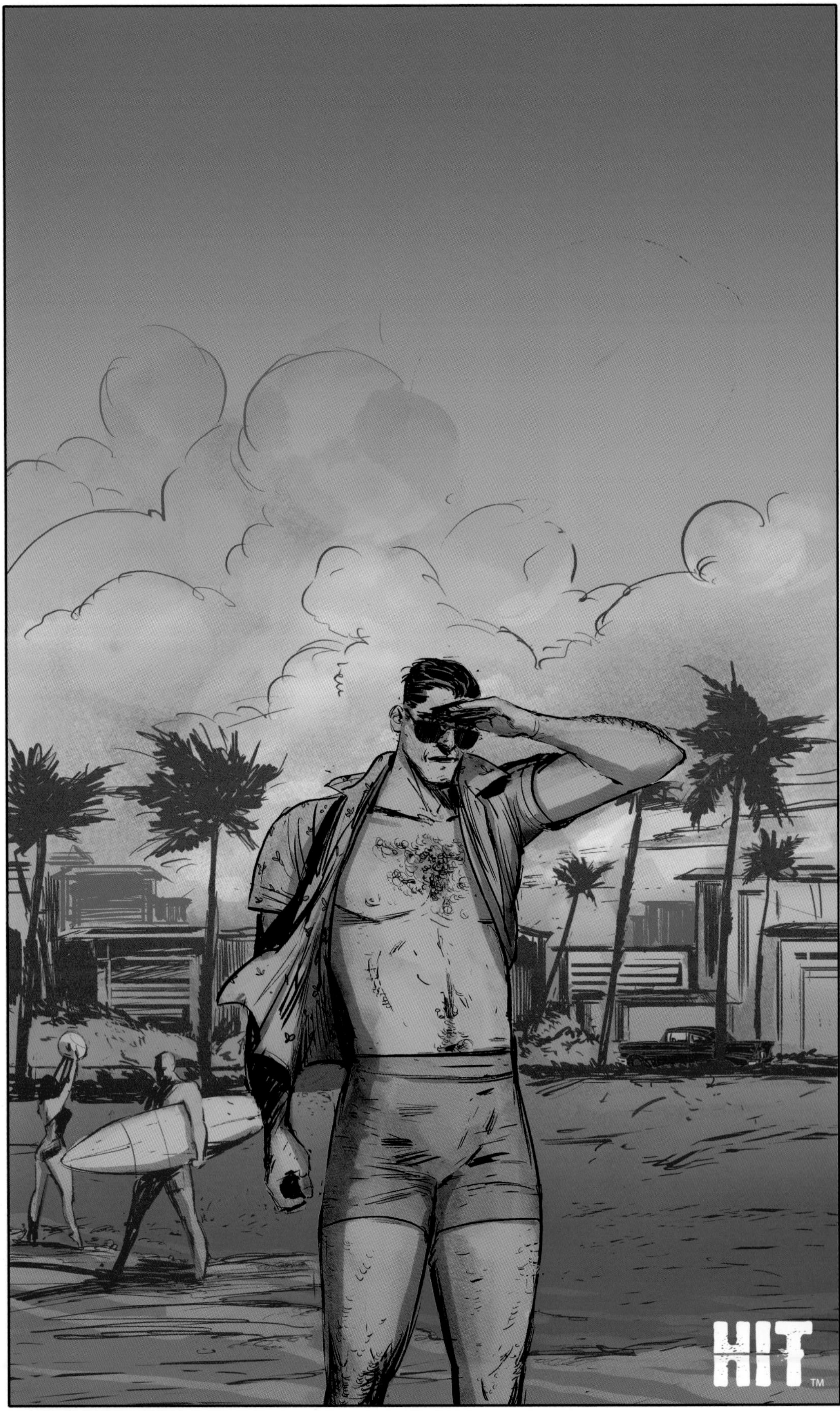
HIT™

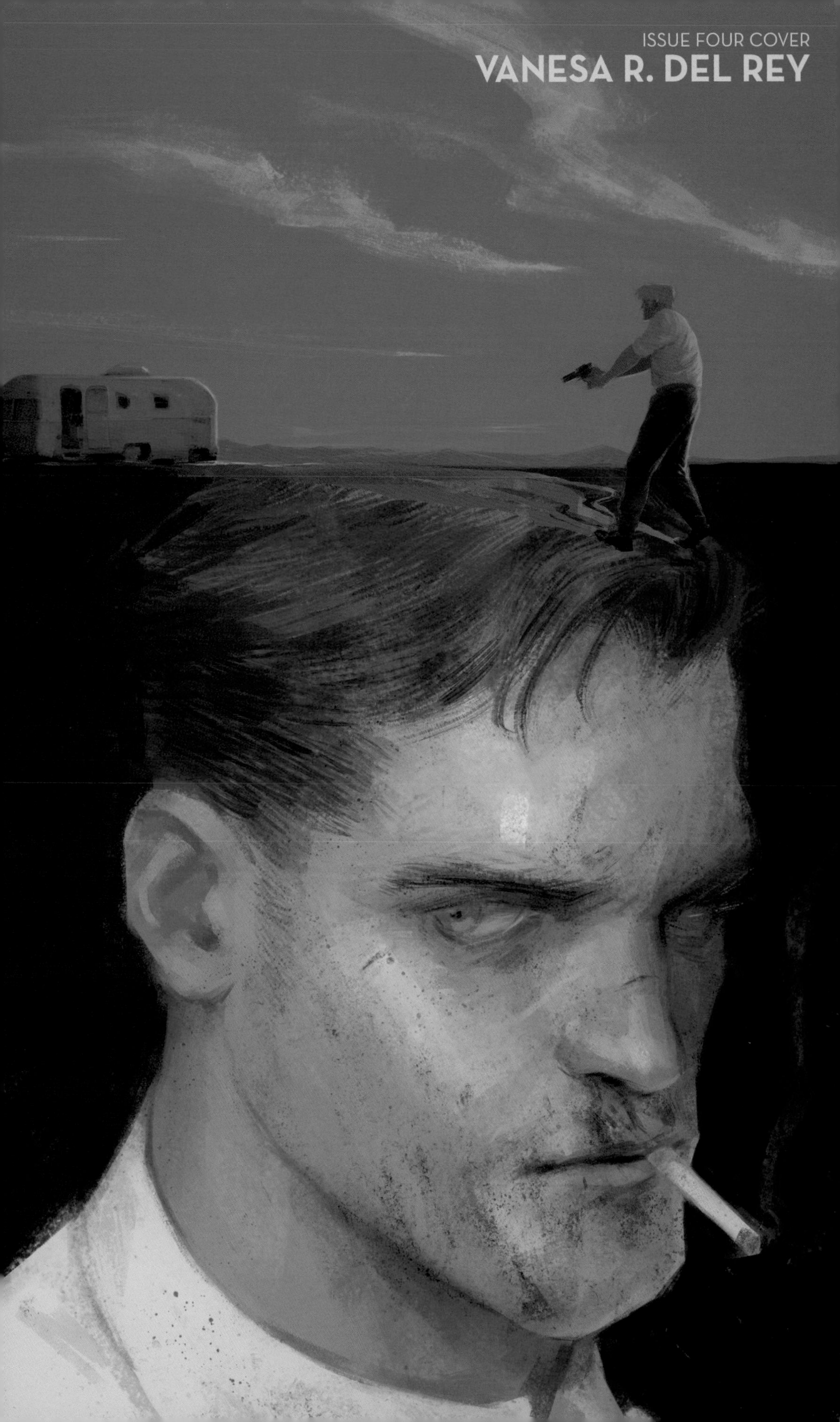

ISSUE FOUR COVER
**VANESA R. DEL REY**

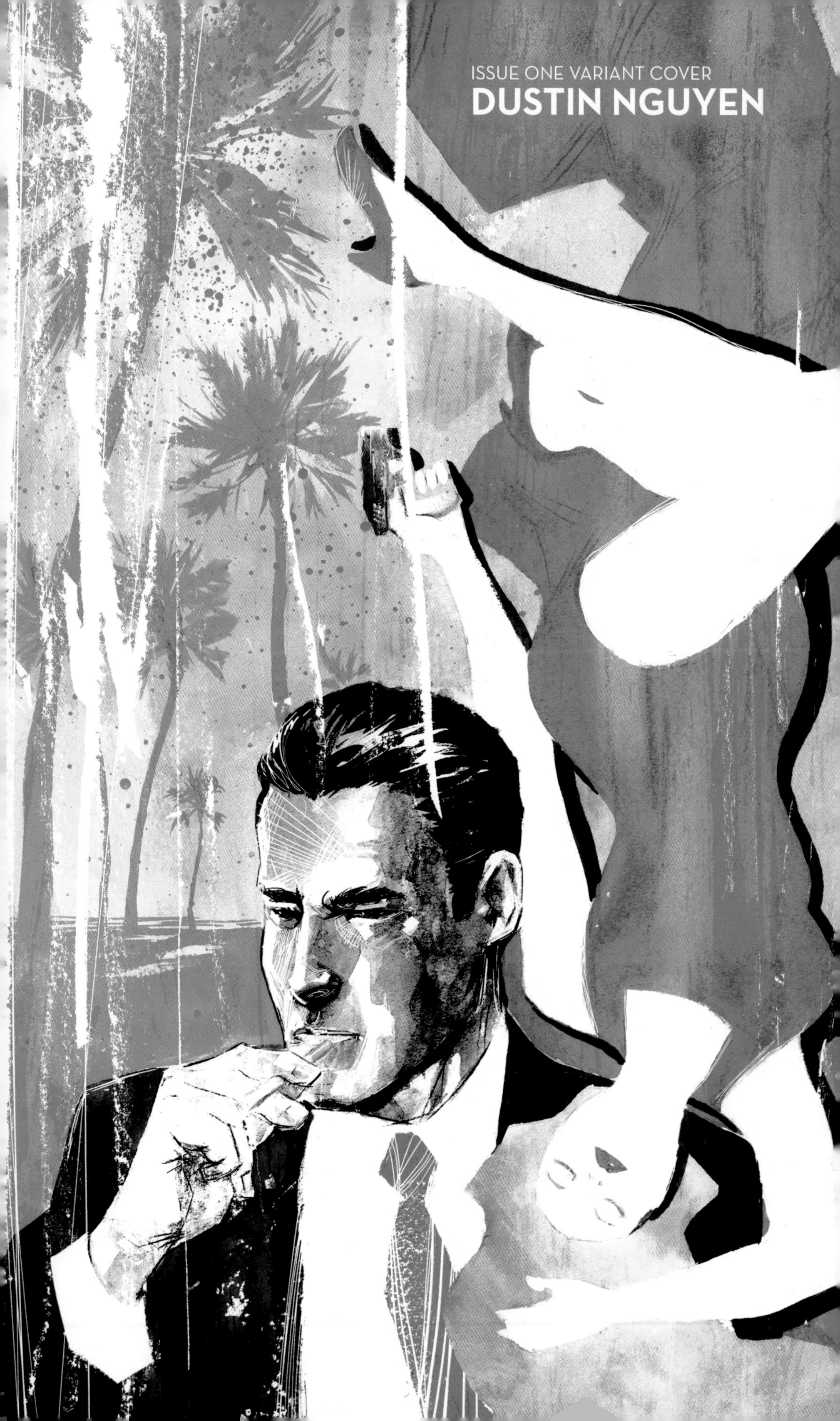

ISSUE ONE VARIANT COVER
**DUSTIN NGUYEN**

ISSUE ONE UNLOCKED RETAILER
VARIANT COVER
**TERRY DODSON**

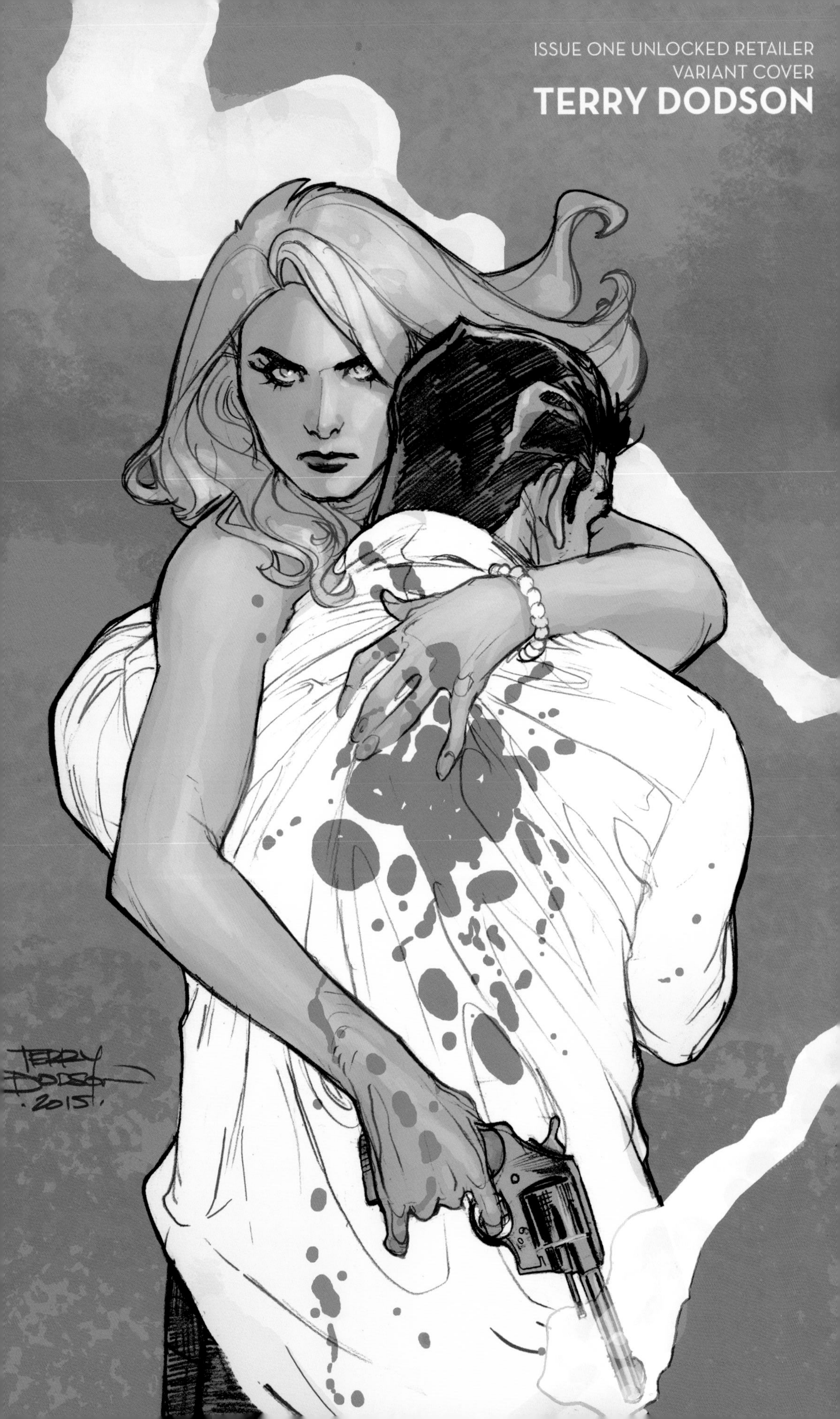
TERRY DODSON
.2015.

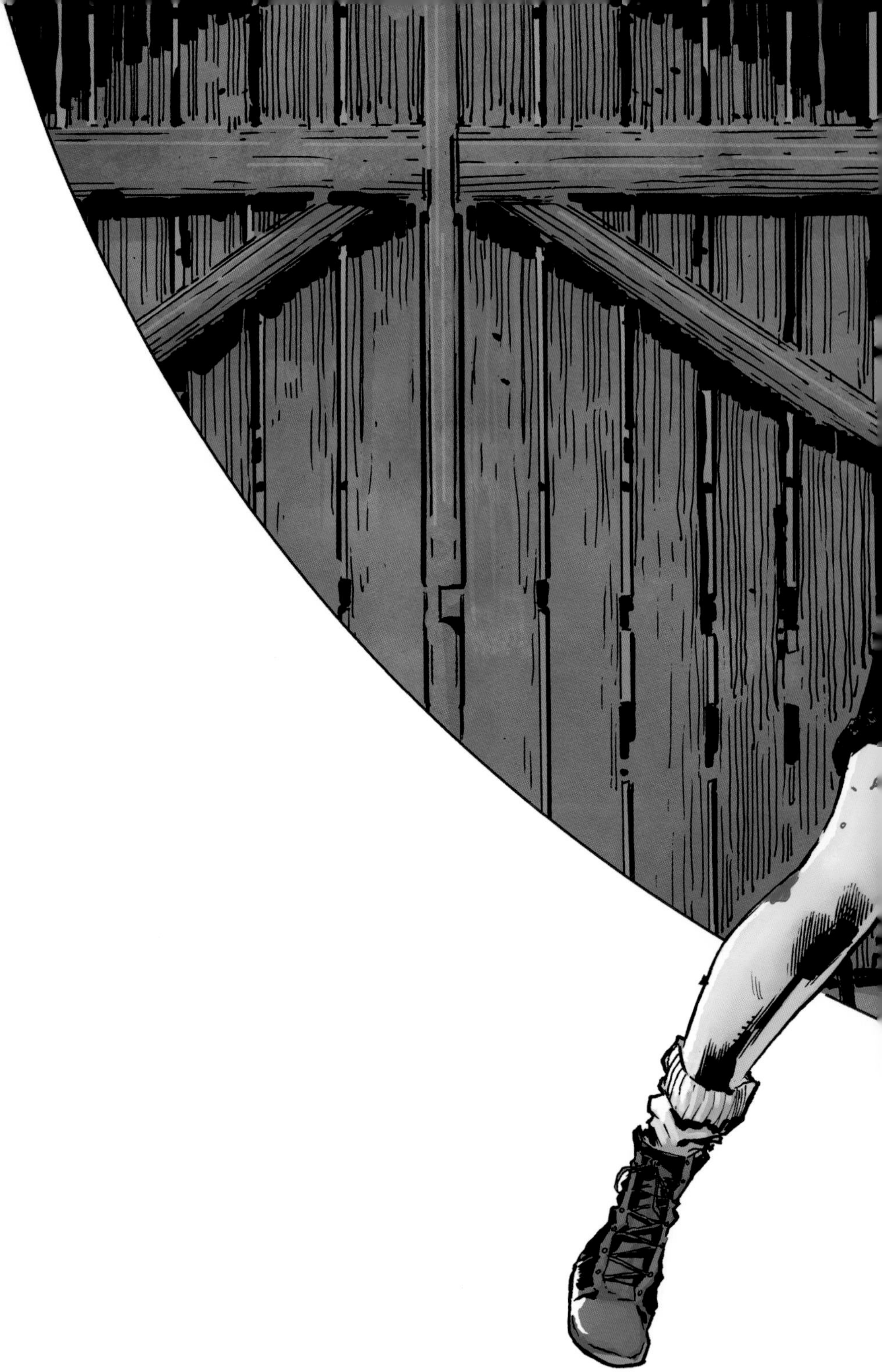

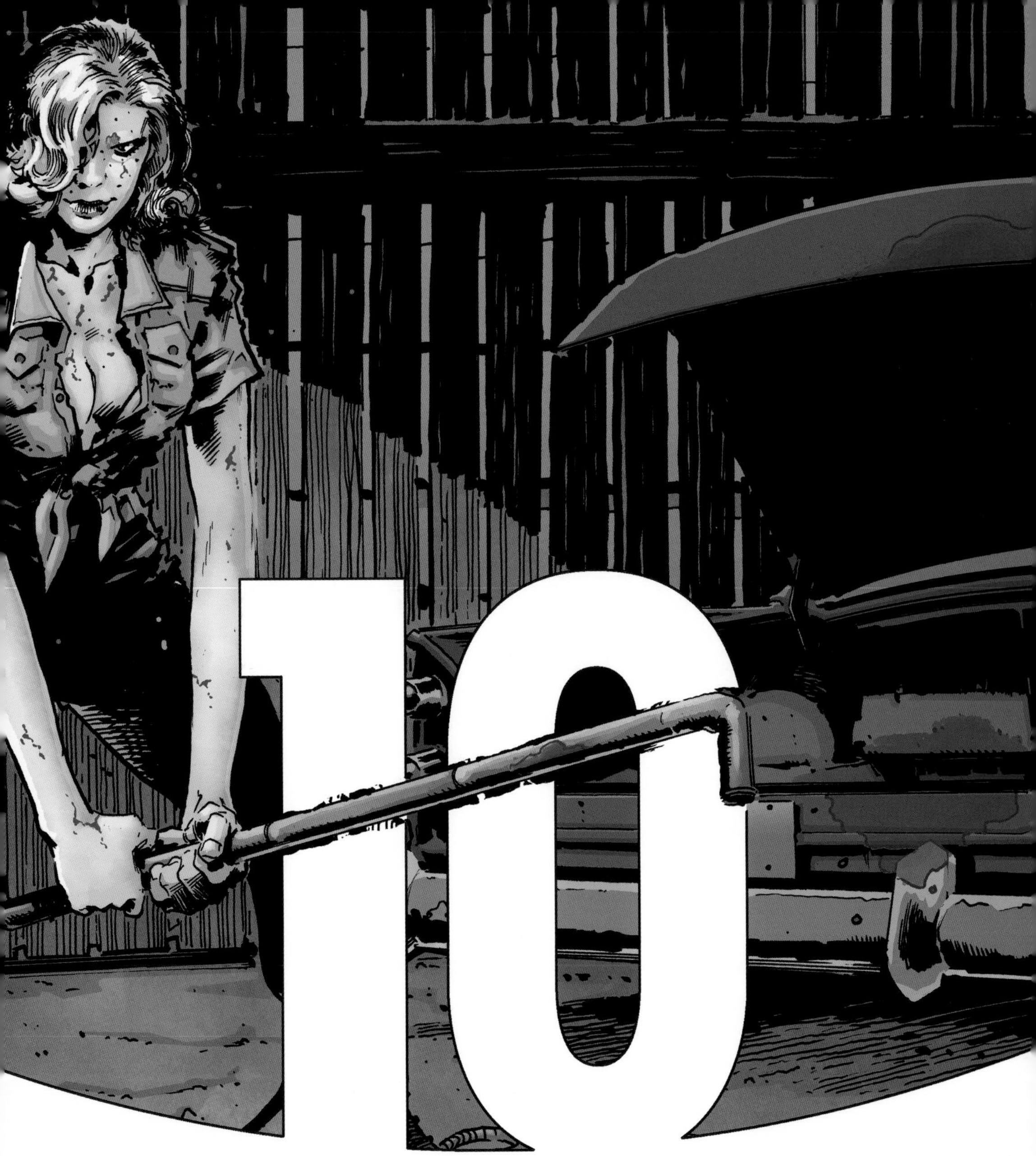
10

BOOM! 10 YEARS ISSUE ONE VARIANT COVER
**TREVOR HAIRSINE**
COLORS BY **JORDAN BOYD**

# Terry

## Bryce Carlson

Nickel-sized drops of blood blossomed into silver dollar spiders as they hit the fresh cut grass. The red on green reminded Terry Riggs of Christmas, and how the holidays he'd spent in Las Vegas had been the best he'd ever had.

But it was April, and it was warm. And Carl Haywood was losing a lot of blood.

Riggs had driven his new friend to the Glen Heather Estates, off the Strip above San Francisco Avenue. It was a nice neighborhood. White. Money. Safe. Three things that made it *dangerous* for a black man in a bellhop getup carrying a bloody, white cop up someone else's front lawn.

Haywood coughed up a couple tablespoons of dark blood and bile, and collapsed, landing hard on his side. The jolt of dead weight spun Riggs around and sat him down. He took a moment, staring back at the black Oldsmobile with whitewall tires by the curb—its rear passenger side door ajar and smeared with blood. Those thirty feet had felt like an eternity. The front door was only another fifteen, but they weren't going for the front door.

"C'mon, Woody. No sense dying *now*," Riggs grunted, pulling Haywood back to his feet.

Haywood gurgled obscenities behind closed eyes as he somehow managed to move his feet. Riggs had to give it to him. He may have been a bald, stubborn bastard with a belly full of gunshots wounds, but Haywood was one tough son of a bitch.

■

Even though he called Los Angeles home, Riggs was a Las Vegas man through and through. In the seven years he'd been there, he'd fallen in love—or lust—with Sin City and all it had to offer. The girls, the money, the glamour, the desert, the girls. Everything had its unique charm that spoke to Riggs in a way that was different and real. He was going to miss it.

Fifteen more minutes dragged on before they finally made it to the back door. Riggs slumped Haywood against the exterior brick wall of the house and knocked on the door window twice. He waited ten seconds and knocked twice again.

"What are you…a pussycat that got…locked out? Bang on the…*urgh*…damn door…" Haywood hiccupped some blood, coughed, and passed out.

Two more knocks and the deadbolt slammed back. An angry mustache protruded into the darkness as the door cracked open.

"*Terry?* What in God's good name are you doing here?" the mustache whispered.

"Evening, Monty," Riggs said with a smile, still catching his breath.

The mustache puffed as the nostrils above it flared, "I don't know if you're drunk or delusional but I'm going to refrain from calling the police and pretend this never happened. It's late. My wife's taking her face off, for Pete's sake. I'll talk to you tomorrow."

"We can't wait until tomorrow."

"*We?*"

Riggs reached his hand in and pulled out the man attached to the mustache—Dr. Chandler Montgomery—forcing him to look at the oozing mess that was Haywood bleeding on the side of his home.

"Good gravy, Terry… What the hell happened?" Montgomery exclaimed.

Looking at Haywood and then back at the doctor, Riggs calmly said, "I'm calling in a favor."

■ ■

Montgomery's barrel-chest nearly popped the suspenders off his white undershirt as he led the way, carrying Haywood's feet and breathing heavily through the stringy black hair strewn across his big, sweaty nose. His mustache looked even angrier than before.

"What'd you tell the wife?" Riggs had his hands nestled deep in what were now Haywood's blood-soaked armpits. He could feel ribs but not breathing.

"The same thing I tell her when I usually see you, Terry." Montgomery strained opening the garage door. "Only this time there's not a naked woman waiting for me after I lie directly to my wife's face."

Montgomery banged his elbow into a switch and two ceiling barn lights double-clicked on, revealing a tidy garage housing a flawless 1956 Chevrolet Bel Air in gorgeous two-tone: India Ivory and Pinecrest Green. Riggs recognized the car from the Dunes and wondered how his girls at the club were holding up.

"Up here," Montgomery barked.

They hoisted the bloody body onto an empty wooden workbench that was too clean and had never been used until then.

Haywood moaned as they situated him on his back. Montgomery huffed and ripped open Haywood's soggy, red bellhop shirt. Three buttons popped off and bounced away.

Riggs didn't realize Montgomery had walked to the '56 Chevy until the trunk popped. He was fixed on Haywood's mess of an abdomen.

Sticky craters pulsed blood with every weak breath and each staccato heartbeat. There was more blood than skin—thick, almost syrupy, and seemingly unstoppable, like an ooze. Thin strings reaching up to the tips of the curly golden hairs above the navel made little blood harps while broken skin around the entrance wounds poked out of the red sea like shark fins—a fantasyland of slow, hypnotic death.

Montgomery pushed through and thumped a slick black leather medicine bag on the workbench. Riggs stared at the thick, bubbling bog in Haywood's belly button and the maroon tears streaming down his ribs. It reminded him of the first person he ever watched die.

Back in 1942, the Thursday before the Fourth of July, Riggs and Harvey Slater were patrolling Newton Division and it was hot as hell out. Reported gunshots had brought them to Hope Street, a couple blocks away from Exposition Park, where Beverly Coble was wheezing and bleeding in the middle of her living room. The left side of her face was caved in—the cheekbone shattered and nonexistent while her swollen left eye spilled out of its crushed socket. Her dislocated jaw barely hung on and showed off a motor oil mouth of cracked teeth dangling below a cauliflower ear leaking black cherry blood that dripped down pieces of exposed skull that had torn through the skin. Riggs called it in and then he and Slater watched until the wheezing stopped.

"When you're done with that thousand yard stare, go to the utility sink and get a wet rag to put on his head," said Montgomery as he tied an apron around his waist.

"Whatever you say, Doc." Riggs did as he was told—something he wasn't accustomed to—and thought about how it would have been easier if Haywood just died.

Cold water from the cloth trickled down Haywood's face, which was getting paler, as Montgomery poured a bottle of antiseptic straight onto the gunshot wounds. The blood thinned, ran off the torso, and exposed three clean bullet holes—one on the right side and two in the upper abdomen. There were two more in the lower abdomen that were so close together the skin between them had ripped, making one big oval exposing muscle and a small bit of intestines.

Eyes closed, Haywood murmured through his teeth, "…Bastard…"

"You said it, Woody," Riggs quipped, lighting a cigarette.

Montgomery was not amused and cleaned the stomach holes with a grimace.

Riggs blew out a cloud of smoke. "You're world class, man, you know that? World class. Next time you come see me at the Dunes…it's on the house."

A smile crept across Montgomery's lips. The doctor may have been able to lie straight into his wife's face, but he couldn't hide his craving for playing tricks with house money.

"One more thing, though. I need dish soap and some rags your wife won't miss."

■ ■ ■

Pink towels soaked up small pools of blood on the floor behind the passenger seat while Riggs blotted the tan leather backseat with terry cloth dipped in water and dish soap. He went through this routine a handful of times and then did the old rinse and repeat with a clean cloth and water. One more pass with a dry towel and it was damn near impossible to tell that a gunshot victim had almost died in the backseat a couple hours prior.

Montgomery's street was dead quiet except for the echo up and down the block of Riggs long snapping bloody soak rags onto the lawn. It reminded him of the late nights he and Slater spent patrolling Newton Division with the windows down. A bottle would shatter on Main Street and they could hear it on Broadway. Sometimes they'd hit the siren just to see how long it would echo. He didn't miss Los Angeles, but he missed those nights.

Freshly lit cigarette in lip, Riggs sat on the curb with a sigh. He straightened out his arms behind him—his palms on the cold sidewalk. It felt good on his dry, cracking hands. Riggs looked at the moon and followed it down to the rooftops, then to the street sign with big white letters. He laughed.

### BONNIE BRAE AVENUE

No matter what he did, he couldn't escape Bonnie. The girl that had weaseled her way into his life time and time again was slumped on a couch in the Tropicana with the back of her head hanging out of her skull, and yet, there she was, watching Riggs clean up another mess.

His relationship with the devilish blonde had been complicated. They first met in the fall of 1948 when Slater transferred to Hollywood Division and started seeing Bonnie even though he was still involved with Riggs's sister, Rhonda. As she usually did, Bonnie came out on top. And once he wiped away his sister's tears and had a long talk and a couple drinks with his former partner, Riggs—like everyone—couldn't help but kind of fall in love with "The Captain's Daughter." She was a beautiful mess that could take care of herself but always needed something, and her father being the Captain of Hollywood Division made the forbidden fruit that much sweeter. But in 1950, everything changed. Bonnie owed money and couldn't go to Slater so she went to Riggs, who had no problem smuggling a brick of heroin out of the evidence room to help a friend. He had done plenty worse during his time in the uniform, but that was the thing that finally bit him. Bonnie's arrest sent Captain Blair on a rampage. After Slater's Hollywood partner, Ken Collins, got demoted and kicked down to Wilshire Patrol, Blair found out where the heroin came from. Riggs was on the street inside of a week with nowhere to turn. A former corrupt cop wasn't worth a damn to anyone in Los Angeles so he fled somewhere he could start over where nobody knew him. Bonnie had done the same thing and somehow they both wound up at the Dunes. When she told him about her time in Cleveland and changing her name from Bonnie Blair to "Bonnie Brae," Riggs laughed. In true Bonnie fashion, she had renamed herself after a little house in Echo Park that had been the birthplace of Pentecostalism, where masses had flocked decades before to writhe in the spirit and speak in tongues. But Riggs knew that Bonnie couldn't have been further from the Pentecostal truth, even though she was very talented with her tongue. Had he known that was the last conversation they'd ever have, Riggs would have churched it up some.

Most people didn't like feeling guilt or carrying a burden, but Riggs took solace knowing whether it was an avenue, a street, or a ghost in the sky, Bonnie Brae would always hang over his head.

■ ■ ■ ■

Haywood was out and being carried across the front lawn.

"Damn, Monty, what'd you stuff him with, gauze or bricks?" Riggs said, readjusting his grip. "How did he get heavier after losing that much blood? I know you had to leave most of the bullets in, but son of a bitch."

"Keep your voice down. I still have neighbors," said Montgomery, his left eye twitching as he exhaustedly worked to pull his own weight.

"What, they don't know you stitch up white boys with bullet holes in your backyard?"

"No, they don't, because it's not something I do."

"You just did." Riggs winked.

"I don't care if it is on the house, no woman is worth having to listen to you right now."

"Well, then, I guess I'll just have to give you two at once…"

Montgomery's creepy smile reappeared and it was obvious his mind was reeling with years of pent-up teenage thoughts. His feet swished through the blood-splattered grass and neither shadow nor dark of night could hide his adolescent glee.

They slid Haywood into the back seat. His belly was bandaged up with a few small dimes of red bleeding through. Riggs slammed the door, lit a cigarette, and threw out his hand, smiling at Montgomery, "You're an ace in the hole, Monty. I mean that. Can't thank you enough."

"Don't thank me yet. He won't be out of the woods for another couple days," Montgomery said, shaking Riggs's hand with a firm grip. "He's going to need constant care and monitoring."

"Don't worry, Doc. I got just the girl for that."

"I bet you do. Here." Montgomery pulled a piece of paper and a pen out of his pocket and wrote down "Bernard Bowen," a phone number, and a prescription. "Call him first thing. Pharmacy opens at 8:00 AM but he always gets there early. You tell him I sent you and you need this off the books. Give him ten dollars when you show up and you won't get any trouble."

"I think I can handle that," Riggs said.

"Good, because your friend in there won't make it to Tax Day without this medicine."

Riggs got into the car. "Understood. Thanks again, Monty. Now I owe you one."

"You owe me two," Montgomery smiled.

"Ha! Come by the Dunes. I'll get you taken care of." Riggs started the car.

"Good, Terry. Very good. When?"

Riggs popped it into gear and rolled forward. "Any time."

■ ■ ■ □

Most people thought Las Vegas was a sight to be seen at night but Riggs always found it to be at its best first thing in the morning. As he drove past the railroad station into West Las Vegas, the first bits of early sun popped over the eastern hills and lit up the valley. The peaceful desert calm was almost enough to make him forget about everything that had happened in the last twelve hours. Almost.

Her name was Claire and she lived on Monroe Avenue, walking distance from the Moulin Rouge. She had been Riggs's favorite cocktail waitress while he was there and in the years since it closed and went through the regime change, Riggs had peppered her with steady work—everything from dancing for private group parties to entertaining white sojourners who could afford to fulfill their taboo desire to take a dip in Sin City's ebony pool. Claire was a pro, and a friend.

After he dropped Haywood on the couch and grabbed a shower and a change of clothes, he pulled cash out of a safe he had hidden in Claire's garage. Then he slid two hundred dollars into Claire's silk robe pocket and kissed her neck. Before he lost her scent, Riggs was at the pharmacy, slipping Bowen twenty dollars instead of ten, and then back at Claire's making sure Haywood was properly medicated. Then he really got down to business.

Coffee. Old-fashioned donut. Cigarette. Claire with her legs wrapped around him. Another cigarette. Another shower. With Claire. Cigarette. Oldsmobile at the junkyard. Sand Dune White Plymouth Fury at the dealership. Paid in cash. Not bad for a Saturday morning.

Riggs spent the afternoon on the phone setting more things up—calling in favors, arranging meets, cashing in on old debts, and settling scores. By Monday night, he'd be flush and back in Los Angeles with Haywood, and Vegas will had already forgotten about the infamous Terry Riggs.

So he was going to make the most of his last Saturday night in town.

There was no doubt that Domino Marcon and Vincent Christianos had a casino-sized price on Riggs' head and people would be looking for him. The Dunes would be the first place they looked but that was *his* place and nothing was going to stop him from seeing it one last time and taking what was his.

It was the busiest night of the week and no one was going to be looking to make a big scene after the

Tropicana shootout the night before so Riggs walked right in the front door of the Dunes wearing a sharp charcoal suit that Claire had pressed for him and a crisp black hat. The air inside reeked of smoke and debauchery. He smiled and breathed it in.

Down the long, empty hallway backstage, a big Italian goon as wide as a slot machine stood outside the changing room door that led to Riggs's office while the music of the final dance number on stage swelled through the walls. Riggs walked casually with his hands in his pockets. He could tell the goon was sizing him up and still watching him as he disappeared into the shadows down the hall.

Five minutes later, a flock of half-naked dancers flooded the hallway and trotted by the overwhelmed goon holding the door. He smiled like an idiot as he watched the last girl step inside, and kept watching her.

Riggs had stabbed the goon five times in the ribs before he turned around and realized he had been played. When he finally saw Riggs, a knife plunged deep into that special fleshy spot below the Adam's apple and above the collarbone. Riggs left the knife in to minimize the mess as the gasping goon crumbled to his knees. He dragged his new friend into one of the empty rooms across the hall, pulled the knife, and left a fountain of a blood squirting wildly behind him as he exited stage right.

The girls were happy to see Riggs. They always were. He played it cool like it was just another day at the office. There was no sense burdening his beauties with good-byes. Instead, he gave them all a kiss—like he always did—and retreated to the back.

His office was upside down. Papers everywhere, furniture knocked over, phone unplugged, bottles broken. The desk was eviscerated and the safe was cracked. Both were empty. Riggs lit a cigarette as he leaned against the wall and used his right leg to slide the heavy oak desk out a bit.

Underneath where the left side of the desk had been, Riggs used his goon-slaying blade to pry up two loose floorboards. It wasn't as good of a score as what he had in the safe but it would do. He stuffed his suit and pants pockets with ten thousand dollars in cash, two boxes of shotgun shells, a pouch of gold, and a pearl necklace that had belonged to his late grandmother. Then he slipped the sawed-off shotgun he had stolen from Newton Division into his pants and covered the butt with his jacket.

Riggs left his office and his girls and the action, and walked out of the Dunes for the last time.

■ ■ □ □

Sunday was full of meets. While Claire took care of Haywood on the couch, Riggs bounced around a handful of neutral, public spots off the Strip. It wasn't for him—he could take care of himself. It was for the safety of the friends and associates he had spent the last seven years doing business with. Riggs knew everyone and everyone knew Riggs, and he didn't want the Syndicate target on his back to catch anyone in the crosshairs. It meant sitting down in places that weren't all that sexy but it was best for all involved.

The game was simple.

First person showed up with a briefcase and sat across the table. While the waiter fetched drinks, Riggs took the briefcase to the restroom and counted the money. It was all there. A coffee, some laughs, a handshake, and Riggs was off to the next one.

Sitting in his Plymouth Fury, Riggs pulled a stack of cash out of the briefcase and popped it into an envelope. He walked up to a different coffee shop, sat down across from someone else, and guided the envelope across the table. A coffee, some laughs, a handshake.

Coffee turned into cocktails and the *Great Exchange* was in full swing. Mostly cash, but Riggs was an equal opportunist and happily accepted jewels precious metals, and firearms. Everyone was happy.

By the time the sun started to set, a quarter million dollars of cash and assets had changed hands. Riggs was up a hundred thousand dollars in cash and fifty thousand dollars in valuables and artillery, leaving him in a position to do something most people seldom could and blow Vegas with more than what he came with. And even more rare, all debts were paid.

Except for one. Simeon Charles.

Simeon was a low-level pimp caught up in the drug game—a game he was always losing, especially when he went to the race track. Back in '53, Riggs had *invested* in a rather large heroin buy that Simeon had put together with the promise of tripling that investment in four weeks. Four years and Riggs hadn't seen a dime.

It was an easy conversation. Simeon had been one of the phone calls on Saturday and the money was due Monday. Not the promised profit, just the initial investment. Simeon swore he'd have it.

At a quarter to midnight, Riggs pulled up outside of a modest single family home in West Las Vegas. The lights were on inside and he saw Simeon walking around, alone.

Riggs went to his trunk, grabbed a duffle bag, and knocked on Simeon's front door at the stroke of midnight. Simeon peeked out from behind the curtains and apprehensively opened the door. Riggs didn't need to say anything. It was obvious Simeon was high. He did all the talking—mostly to himself. He repeated over and over again that he was good for the money and would have it Monday like he promised. Riggs pointed at the clock sitting on the Danish bar in the corner and Simeon realized Monday had come right on time.

If Simeon didn't have the money then, he wouldn't have it later. So Riggs pulled the Newton sawed-off shotgun out of the duffle bag and put it in the pimp's dried out mouth. It was a long time coming, a debt that was owed. And unlike the bastard begging on his knees, Riggs made sure to pay back on time.

Simeon's useless brains splattered across the glass coffee table and wood floor like a watermelon dropped from a bridge. The way the body slumped over reminded Riggs of how he found Beverly Coble in her living room. And the hole in the back of Simeon's head looked like the one in Bonnie's back at the Trop. That made Riggs smile a little bit. He zipped up his duffle bag and walked out.

They crossed San Francisco Avenue, heading south on the Los Angeles Highway. It was late Monday afternoon. Haywood, fully conscious for the first time in days, watched Riggs turn his eyes out his window at the Las Vegas Race Track in the distance. Riggs kept staring at it in his side mirror as he drove deeper into the Strip.

The Dunes drew his gaze the opposite direction, out the passenger side window. Riggs lit a cigarette.

They both turned their heads as the Tropicana came up on the left. It seemed to stare back at them. Riggs knew there were at least two men in that hotel that wanted him dead—the only two men, along with the inadvertent help of Harvey Slater and the late Bonnie Brae, who had finally found a way to run everyone's favorite Las Vegas *ladies' man* out of town.

Haywood smirked and Riggs blew a stream of smoke out his nostrils as they glared at the luxurious oasis glistening in the middle of a barren desert, surrounded by dirt and sand and rock and nothingness.

"Good thing all those bastard wops in there are lousy shots." Haywood said slowly, still in pain.

Riggs raised an eyebrow and smiled, "Yeah, good thing."

Las Vegas was in the rearview mirror and nearly three hundred miles of desert sat between the Plymouth Fury and Los Angeles. Riggs had two duffle bags in the trunk. One with a hundred thousand dollars in cash wrapped in clothes, and one busting at the seams with assorted artillery.

He had given the bag of jewelry and other valuables to Claire as a thank you for taking care of Haywood. Except for his grandmother's pearls. He kept those.

"I'll be happy to be out of this damn desert. Godforsaken wasteland…" Haywood grumbled, looking out at the rocky hills as the sun headed for the horizon.

"You would have dug it if you were sitting with my girls instead of getting shot," said Riggs.

"I doubt that."

"Trust me, man. I spent most my life in Los Angeles. You've never seen girls like these."

"That's great," Haywood shot back.

"No, Woody, you don't understand," Riggs chuckled. "It's like the difference between beef stew and prime rib."

"I get it."

"The quality of tail and amount of money flowing through that town—"

"I said I get it," Haywood snapped.

Riggs smiled as he took a long drag off his cigarette. "A lot of good looking boys, too."

Haywood shifted in his seat and sniffed.

"I can get you whatever you want, Woody—"

"I want you to shut up and focus on driving so I can get home and not be anywhere near the sound of your voice," Haywood said, looking out the window.

"Whatever you want…"

"You're still talking."

"Damn, man." Riggs said. "I thought you *guys* were supposed to be sweet." He clicked on the radio.

Haywood stared straight ahead, listening to the promise of music being swallowed by static—one more reason to hate the desert. Riggs cycled through the dial and then cut it, leaving them with a therapeutic engine hum on the empty highway.

The sun sunk lower and the silence got louder. Riggs took long, methodical drags off his cigarette and thought about his return to Los Angeles, wondering what it would be like to step foot back in Watts.

They were an hour outside of Vegas when a series of wet, gurgled coughs shattered the silence. Riggs looked over and saw blood down the front of Haywood's shirt, and some still dripping from his mouth.

"Son of a bitch…" Haywood mumbled through red teeth.

Riggs put his cigarette out in the ash tray, "Ah, God, Woody."

"…I'm okay…"

More blood came out.

Riggs pulled over onto the dirt and went to the trunk. He grabbed some clothes from the money bag and got Haywood cleaned up and in a fresh shirt that was two sizes too big for him.

The sun started to set as Riggs cruised back onto the highway and left a pile of bloody clothes on the side of the road.

Twenty more miles. The sun was behind the hills and the Plymouth Fury's headlights were caught in the desert's twilight.

Riggs turned and said, "You still here, Woody?"

Haywood gurgled obscenities behind closed eyes.

Ten more miles and it quickly turned to night. Riggs looked over at Haywood again and noticed blood on his shirt. He hadn't heard any coughing, which meant the blood was seeping from the stomach.

"Hey," said Riggs.

Haywood didn't move.

"Hey!" he said louder.

Nothing.

The Plymouth Fury screeched to a stop on the side of the highway, kicking up a tower of dust that slowly wrapped around the car and wafted through the headlights. Other than the idling engine, there wasn't a sound for miles.

A few minutes passed and the car kicked into gear. But instead of pulling back onto the highway, it spun a hard right in the dirt and headed off road, straight into the black heart of the desert.

□ □ □ □

An hour later, the Plymouth Fury pulled back onto the highway and headed toward Los Angeles. Riggs lit a cigarette, looked over at the empty passenger seat, and then stared out at the dark stretch of road ahead. The headlights hit a sign:

LOS ANGELES   200

Riggs had been in the desert long enough. He knew the rules.

The house always won.

Didn't matter if you had a hot hand, knew the right people, or came in with a bankroll—no one beat the desert. Big or small, sooner or later, you lost. And after seven good years and a hell of a run, Terry Riggs' luck finally ran out.

The house won and sent him home.

# PUBLICATION DENIAL NOTIFICATION

TITLE OF PUBLICATION: _____ Hit: 1957 06/15 N3 _____

The above listed publication has been reviewed and denied in accordance with Board Policy-03.91 Uniform Offender Correspondence Rules for the reason(s) checked below:

- ☐ (a) Publication contains contraband.

- ☐ (b) Publication contains information regarding the manufacture of explosives, weapons or drugs.

- ☐ (c) Publications contains material that a reasonable person would construe as written solely for the purpose of communicating information designed to achieve a breakdown of prisons through offender disruption such as strikes or riots.

- ☐ (d) A specific factual determination has been made that the publication is detrimental to prisoner's rehabilitation because it would encourage deviate criminal sexual behavior.

- ☐ (e) Publication contains material on the setting up and operation of criminal schemes or how to avoid detection of criminal schemes by lawful authorities charged with the responsibility for detecting such illegal activity.

- ☒ (f) Publication contains sexually explicit images.

REMARKS: _____ Reason F. Page 5 contains sexually explicit images. _____

_____

_____

_____

If there is a desire to appeal the rejection of the aforementioned publication, this may be accomplished by writing to the Director's Review Committee, P. O. Box 99, Huntsville, Texas 77342-0099. The appeal must be mailed so as to arrive at the Texas Department of Criminal Justice – Institutional Division **WITHIN TWO (2) WEEKS** of the date shown below.

Mail System Coordinators Panel
Department/Unit

July 14, 2015
Date

_____
Publication

Boom Entertainment, Inc.
Publishers/Sender

5670 Wilshire Blvd., Suite 450
Address

Los Angeles, CA  90036-5679
City/State/Zip Code

EDITOR'S NOTE: Following the release of Issue Three in the summer of 2015, we received an indiscriminate envelope from the Texas Department of Criminal Justice which contained the following letter—a fitting tombstone for our beloved Bonnie. Maybe some of our other incarcerated readers were able to smuggle a copy or two into the system…